The Politics of Health Policy Reform in the UK

Calum Paton

The Politics of Health Policy Reform in the UK

England's Permanent Revolution

palgrave
macmillan

Calum Paton
Keele University
United Kingdom

ISBN 978-1-137-47342-4   ISBN 978-1-137-47343-1   (eBook)
DOI 10.1057/978-1-137-47343-1

Library of Congress Control Number: 2016950007

Printed on acid-free paper

This Palgrave Macmillan imprint is published by Springer Nature
The registered company is Macmillan Publishers Ltd. London

*'Dedicated to my wife Tracey, my daughter Leah,
my son Josh - and also to my mother and late father who gave
me a start (and much more) in life'*

Foreword

This book is in many ways the culmination of my research and work of over thirty years on the politics and substance of the so-called NHS reforms and of evolving health policy in general (primarily 'market reforms', pursued at first in the UK and subsequently in England alone since devolution). Resultingly, among the references are quite a few to some of my earlier works on particular, earlier reforms. The reader should interpret this as a short-cut to more detailed work and more references on individual reforms rather than as evidence of an over-sized ego on my part. Another word about references: some statements in the book, and references to people (politicians, NHS leaders and others), are based on confidential interviews and conversations either with these people or about these people. Rather than clutter, the text with notes which simply say, 'Confidential interview' or 'Conversation with the author', I have simply let them stand. Where there is an unattributed or unreferenced statement by or about a key actor or event, it falls into this category.

The book both tells the story of reform and seeks to explain it in terms of political science. I have attempted to create a narrative which does not make the distinction between story-telling and explanation too stark, that is, to minimise jargon in the latter and structure the former in terms of key political and policy episodes. This means that, in some cases, the political explanation comes at the end of a chapter (as with Chap. 1, dealing with the original Thatcher reforms) and, in other cases where there is a need for it, the political explanation comes in chapters of its own (e.g. Chaps. 3, 7 and 8.) In general, the book follows a chronology (from the origins of the 'internal market' policy to the present day) but within and between chapters, some issues are treated outside this strict chronology in order to aid the analysis. To give just one example, foundation trusts are treated later than a strict chronology would imply, so that the continuity between New Labour and subsequent Coalition policy can be explored.

ACKNOWLEDGEMENTS

I am pleased to acknowledge two sources upon which I have drawn respectively in two chapters of this book. In Chap. 8, I have adapted my article for Social Policy and Administration and incorporated it into the chapter: 'Garbage-Can Policy Meets Neo-liberal Ideology: 25 years of redundant reform of the English NHS', Social Policy and Administration, 48, 3; 2014 (June), pp. 319–342. I would like to thank the editor of SPA, Professor Ian Greener, for permission. In Chap. 9, I have adapted and incorporated my paper published in 2014 by the Centre for Health and the Public Interest (CHPI), 'At what cost? Paying the price for the market in the English NHS', published in February 2014 (www.chpi.org.uk). I would like to thank Sally Ruane on behalf of CHPI for permission.

The original version of the book front matter was revised: An acknowledgement has been added. The Erratum to the book front matter is available at DOI 10.1057/978-1-137-47343-1_11

INTRODUCTION

This book aims to explain why and how health policy has changed, and the NHS has been 'reformed', over the last 30 years. In terms of what is understood by policy, the most attention—and certainly international attention—has been focused on the UK and English 'market reforms' which were initiated in the UK in the late 1980s and continued in England after devolution in 1998, unlike in the rest of the UK. The primary aim of this book is to explain the causes and the course of these reforms, which have rightly come to be identified with England rather than with the whole UK. Thus by policy reform, I refer to the national set of reforms which have repeatedly restructured the NHS—not to all possible meanings of the term 'policy' at all levels within the system. Of course the type of policy reform which I investigate affects other types of policy, not least through diverting attention from other policy priorities, and attention is drawn to this in various places below.

Much has been written about the objectives of 'the reforms', especially as proclaimed by their progenitors, about whether or not these objectives have been achieved (Le Grand et al. 1998; Mays et al. 2011), and about whether or not there have been other outcomes, especially of the perverse sort (Paton et al. 1998; Paton 2006). And the politics of 'the reforms' have been discussed whenever the UK (subsequently England) has embarked on yet another round of reorganisation in pursuit of reform. Yet these political explanations have not been adequately reconciled and synthesised. And more importantly, there has not been an adequate political explanation of the ongoing course of reform over time which is theoretically robust yet sensitive enough to embrace the often-tortuous complexity of the reform saga.

This book aims to do this. As a result, it takes the UK (to 1998) and England (from then to the present day) as the benchmark. It is in England that 'market reform' has taken on a life of its own and become orthodoxy—reversing the situation right up to the mid-1980s when seeking to reform a major public service by incorporating the market was seen as eccentric even in the heart of the Conservative Party. Variations in the rest of the UK, especially in Scotland and Wales, are rightly seen as a reaction 'against' England—both in terms of policy objectives per se and in terms of their political motivation. Even where the English 'reforms' are seen as irrational or arational, the reason for the rest of the UK eschewing them (in the case of the later reforms) or abandoning them (in the case of the 1990s reforms) has been primarily political, and this even where such abandonment is in effect a partial return to the status-quo ante. By this, I mean that the devolved parliaments and assemblies have been eager to appear distinct from England for its own sake as well as to reject 'the market' in public health services. And they did have to reject the market—rather than simply never adopt it—as the Thatcher 'internal market' reforms which were implemented in the 1990s were UK-wide.

Thus the book tells the English story—and it is a story, albeit one structured here in terms of political explanation and punctuated with the reasons for each succeeding 'reform'. The story moreover tells how each such reason relates to what has gone before—both in terms of new (or repeated) policy objectives and in the less-advertised terms of more covert requirements to make (or keep) the system manageable. In the language of political science, it analyses how policy does or does not follow a path and also how this evolution is or is not related to the requirements of policy implementation in a pragmatic manner. Developments in the rest of the UK are presented briefly, where relevant, as different variants of the 'counter-factual' by reference to England. The emphasis upon England is reinforced by a more straightforward fact: England's population is more than 80% of the UK total. Thus the English story is the story of most of the UK, and I say so as a Scotsman, albeit one who has lived primarily outside Scotland since 1974.

REFERENCE

Le Grand, J., Mays, N., & Mulligan, J. (1998). *Learning from the NHS internal market.* London: King's Fund.

Mays N., Dixon A., Jones, L. (2011). Understanding New Labour's Market Reforms of the English NHS, London: King's Fund.

Paton, C. (2006). *New Labour's state of health: Political economy, public policy and the NHS.* Ashgate: Avebury.

Paton, C., et al. (1998). *Competition and planning in the NHS: The consequences of the reforms* (2nd ed.). Cheltenham: Stanley Thornes.

Contents

CHAPTER 1

The Politics Behind the Conservative 'Internal Market' in the 1990s

THE BACKGROUND: OF 'REFORM' AND 'THE MARKET'

It is important to define these two terms, which are much-bandied about both by supporters and opponents of 'market reform' in health services. For convenience, the word 'reform' will be used from now on without inverted commas. But, as in the Introduction above, it should have such a characterisation, or alternatively be written with a hyphen, that is, re-form. That is because much reform is not improvement. Yet the prescriptive use of the word is deliberately played upon by reforming politicians to imply that those who oppose their reforms are dinosaurs or at least, in Tony Blair's infamous but effective phrase, 'the forces of conservatism' (Blair 1998),that is, Old Labour, in Blair's New Labour eyes.

This is—as one suspects Tony Blair considers history, following Henry Ford—bunk. To oppose particular reforms does not imply a Panglossian belief that all is currently for the best in the best of all possible words. But it does imply an open mind, and a healthy scepticism when confronted with politicians of a messianic bent peddling 'solutions' which are the political equivalent of the 'solutions' and reforms marketed by management gurus, with those who oppose or beg pause dismissed as 'laggards'. Additionally, the prescriptive component which the word reform has come to incorporate has led some, indeed many, commentators to develop a reform fetish: even when they oppose particular reforms, their bias is to assume that an alternative 'grand reform' or systemic change is required.

© The Author(s) 2016
C. Paton, *The Politics of Health Policy Reform in the UK*,
DOI 10.1057/978-1-137-47343-1_1

None if this is to deny that reform is sometimes necessary and indeed desirable. It is simply to point to an incontrovertible fact—that the *direction* which reform has taken as regards England's health policy concerning the NHS over the last 30 years, and its legitimacy, is now seen as an orthodoxy. This is an assumption unjustified by the evidence, as I will show.

That direction is towards 'more market'. So let us now examine what we mean by market reform. There have always been markets in supply to the NHS, as with drugs and equipment. There have also been varying arrangements through which particular services and professions have been organised and 'contracted' as with GP services since the NHS's foundation in 1948. The latter can only be called markets if the aim is to mislead in order to proselytise for markets more widely.

What market reform means however is organising the supply of core clinical and managerial services through competitive markets rather than through public service. The latter is sometimes called 'planning', although in the neo-liberal age that word has come to have prescriptive connotations of the negative sort—a 'boo' word just as reform has become a 'hurrah' word. Planning in this general sense does not necessarily mean central planning, hierarchy (in the negative sense, through which the economist's neutral, technical term has been coopted by the marketeers), or 'command and control', where once again a technical term from the military has been applied pejoratively to the NHS.

One must further distinguish amongst the following terms—the market; the private market; and competition. The first phase of the NHS reforms (1991–1997) was overtly to create an 'internal market', that is, a market in which the suppliers were public, NHS bodies. Later this was extended to include tendering by private suppliers on a systematic basis, as opposed to ad hoc and occasional use of the private sector which had indeed been possible since 1948. Next, markets may or may not be competitive—either in design or (more likely) in outcome. Seeking to reap the benefits of competitive markets within the NHS, in line with neo-classical economic theory, has indeed resulted in more heartache and cost—than ever anticipated by reform enthusiasts.

Another important distinction is between neo-classical economic theory and neo-liberalism—and between both and the so-called new public management.

Neo-liberalism (Plewhe 2009) is the revival of classical economic liberalism in a modern context—the re-assertion of the doctrine that the state cannot do much, if anything, better than the market and/or private arrangements. This is one variant of individualism—and one which is many poles apart from (for example) the 'new liberalism' in the UK from the early twentieth century onwards, perhaps traceable to the older John Stuart Mill; equally, poles apart from modern US liberalism as the left-of-centre alternative to US conservatism (which contains within its contradictory cocktail elements of neo-liberalism in the sense of Hayek (1944) and the Friedmans (1980).

It is thus possible to subscribe to neo-classical economic theory as a description of what happens when certain conditions for the 'perfect market' are realised, and—as with health policy reformers such as Le Grand (Le Grand 2003) to seek to model and indeed realise in practice these conditions as far as possible in order to create or mimic public-sector markets. This does not make such 'neo-classicists' neo-liberals, although there is an overlap in values and indeed also beliefs in many instances.

Neo-classical perfect competition is a technical prescription (although, as I say, many of those who believe in its possibility also are suspicious of the state): it is theoretically possible to believe in its application in a context of public financing and public provision, as with the NHS. That is, the competition need not be private competition.

On the other hand, neo-liberalism is much more of a world-view, with both descriptive and overtly prescriptive elements (think of the title of the Friedmans' book, 'Choose Freedom' and Hayek's title, 'The Road to Serfdom'.) Nevertheless, it should also be remembered that, just as the power of an autonomous state may be required to realise the conditions for neo-classical competition, the state may be required to ensure the conditions of the 'neo-liberal' society or polity. For example, the democratic polity may have a tendency to result in an interventionist state which undermines neo-liberalism (the claim of public choice theorists)—and paradoxically therefore a different type of state action (to restrict democracy) may be necessary.

Yet overall one can be a neo-classicist without being a neo-liberal and indeed (perhaps less commonly) a neo-liberal without being a neo-classicist. Hayek himself was sceptical of the claims that 'justice' either economic or political could be guaranteed through neo-liberalism: he justified it on other grounds.

Turning to the 'new public management', it can merely be noted here that it refers to the use of business, and particularly private business, techniques, incentives, and management approaches and structures in public services generally and in the public sector specifically where provision of services is public, that is, the providers are publicly owned. It need involve neither neo-classical market competition as a technique or belief, let alone neo-liberalism.

Why does all this matter for health policy and NHS reform? In a nutshell, it matters because there has been a perceptible evolution, both chronological and psychological yet not in my view logical, from the 'new public management' to market competition to a wider distrust of the state, in England, in health policy. In the 1980s, we saw the 'new public management' (before it was called such) applied to the UK NHS, following the Griffiths Report (1983). In the 1990s, we saw the 'internal market' justified (if not necessarily created) on the basis of neo-classical market theory. And from the Noughties onwards, we have seen a wider penetration of the state through private interests, not least through the Private Finance Initiative (PFI) and the take-over of key management and 'commissioning' arrangements by private interests—whether or not on a competitive basis, and usually not.

THE INTERNAL MARKET: TECHNICAL FIX OR POLITICAL FIST?

The mechanism which soon was christened the 'internal market' by Alain Enthoven (1985) was first suggested as a technical solution to a practical problem in the NHS, not as an ideological alternative to public service. It was initially seen as a means by which 'money could follow the patient', by those who believed that this was not possible the pre-reform NHS. Thus it was about efficiency rather than ideology, although I think that it was and is a mistake to believe that market mechanisms within the NHS are likely to be efficient.

It is true that those economists who advocated it or supported the idea were mostly either 'free market' converts who were on a political trajectory to the Right, like Alain Enthoven, who had begun as a Democrat working for Robert McNamara in the Department of Defense in the Kennedy Administration but by now was closer to Republicans, or the small minority of die-hard neo-liberal stalwarts associated with the Institute of Economic Affairs who sensed that the tide of history which had beached them might be turning. Yet at this stage this ideological current was not embedded in either public service discourse in general or the culture of the NHS debate in particular.

It was indeed only much later, in an academic rewriting of history, that the Thatcher reforms to the NHS, which created the internal market, were interpreted as having been launched as a response to a social climate of anti-statism or, less controversially, 'consumerism'. But there was no 'comsumer tide' or demand for 'patient choice' from patients or the public on any meaningful scale. This is a post-hoc rationalisation for the 'inevitability' of reform, and history simply is not like that.

Just as the intellectual supporters of the idea had included those of neo-liberal bent, of course the politicians and advisers in the Thatcher administration who were enthusiastic about the idea included those who saw it in grander terms as part of the fight-back against the state and the public ethos. Thatcher's Health Secretary from 1987–88, John Moore, was for example associated with the neo-liberal Mont Pelerin Society. But those who came to support the Thatcher reforms, including the lady's old enemy Kenneth Clarke, the Health Secretary (1988–90) most associated with them, often did so for pragmatic reasons, or at least for managerial reasons rather than ideological ones.

Indeed the internal market was a Janus-faced policy. To some it was a half-way house to more thoroughgoing anti-statist reform to health-care. To others, it was a means of keeping the NHS flame warm in a cold political climate: that is to say, it preserved public provision while embracing reform enough to please the Thatcherites. Indeed John Moore had wanted more thoroughgoing privatisation, and a move to an insurance system for financing. It was his inability to come up with any practical or affordable scheme for such which finished him off politically after only one year in the job, along with the Chancellor Nigel Lawson's justified scepticism that such privatisation would allow financial control (Lawson 1992).

Margaret Thatcher eventually saw the idea as being in tune with her own personal anti-statism, admittedly, although it is interesting to remember that she had shunned the idea when it was presented by Enthoven at a private seminar in Downing Street in summer 1984 when he was working on his monograph. This seems to have been ironical: aware of his dubious status in NHS circles as the potential privatiser from California, Enthoven was at pains to present his 'market' idea as compatible with public sector health services, as a kind of 'market socialism'. Presenting it thus to Thatcher was however to treat with kid gloves the one part of Enthoven's audience where such protection was unnecessary. He was shown the door and it was left to Dr. David Owen, inter alia the former Labour Health Minister and by now leader of the Social Democratic Party, to adopt the idea as a public sector reform without overtones of privatisation, having procured Enthoven's report from the Nuffield Trust before its publication.

THE RED HERRING OF INTERNATIONAL REFORM

As reform took on momentum through the 1990s and later, international 'lessons' for the NHS were increasingly sought. This was more as a result of the self-aggrandising nature of the health reform industry—looking for ideas (or actual services) to sell—than out of any rational or carefully-structured search. For, as has recently been noted, there is no conclusive body of evidence—indeed no *body* of evidence at all, as opposed to fragmentary items which can be selected to prove the point either way—which tells us that NHS-style ('Beveridge' or 'state') healthcare, Continental ('Bismarckian') social insurance for healthcare, combinations thereof, or particular types thereof, offers the best model for equitable and high-quality health-care which is affordable (EHMA 2000).

The task for the UK has therefore been to improve upon its chosen system, the NHS. Yet the ahistorical and arational import of both ideas and 'lessons' from other systems has grown geometrically and has probably contributed to many falsehoods, often in the form of reassurance about certain worrying consequences of 'reform'. For example, worry about the growth of administrative-managerial costs in the English NHS has been dismissed as ignoring the fact that only now is England approaching the level of such costs in many other 'Western' systems, as in the USA, much of Continental Europe et al (House of Commons Select Committee 2010)—entirely missing the point that the comparative advantage of the NHS has lain inter alia in avoiding such costs.

Beyond the issue of costs, important as they are at a time of long-lasting so-called austerity in public services, the role and nature of reform in systems very different to the NHS is often advocated for the NHS even when the NHS's problems, such as they are, may be almost the opposite of those in the systems to be copied. For example, it may be rational to rationalise a bloated private, non-competitive system through the application of competitive pressures—as may be the case in Bismarckian systems such as in Germany, Switzerland and Belgium. But the NHS's problems may not be susceptible to such a 'solution', which—in a very different context—may create new costs rather than diminish those already existing (Paton 1996). Creating markets where they are not necessary is a prime example.

PLANNING AND MARKETS

This brings us back to the internal market at the end of the 1980s. What is the technical problem to which markets were alleged to provide the answer?

In the 1980s, the NHS was experimenting at regional level (in England) with different ways of funding hospitals and district services at sub-regional level. Simplifying somewhat, there were two main approaches: firstly, using a formula to allocate resources from the Region to District Health Authorities according to population need as measured by the formula; and secondly, developing regional plans for where to site major services (such as the larger hospitals) and then sending the money to match such developments (both the 'capital' moneys for developments and the 'revenue' money for recurrent costs.) The former approach can be termed 'resource-based planning' and the second approach 'plan-based resourcing' (Paton 1985; Mays and Bevan 1987).

One of the main reasons that it was difficult to allocate all or most funds to the more local Districts (of which there might be typically eight or ten in a Region) was because of patients flowing across the boundary from their District of residence to another District for treatment, if not out of the Region altogether. It was possible to fund the receiving District or Region directly for such so-called Cross-Boundary Flows—or at least to adjust the formula for allocating resources to take account of such flows. This seemed straightforward in principle even although there were numerous alternative options at the technical level as to how to do it. But there was a non-technical reason for the difficulty, or at least a reason which straddled the technical and the political—in the sense of raising the spectre of the overall adequacy of NHS funding, and therefore taking the debate from 'low administration' into 'high politics.'

In a nutshell, if patients crossing boundaries were costed at the actual or average cost for their specialty or diagnosis, then this became the tail which wagged the dog in terms of funding—for what was left over for the core residential population—the clear majority, in most cases—which did not cross the boundary was, per capita, significantly less per capita receiving treatment and/or per population need. This was because there was not enough money in the system—at prevailing costs, at least—to ensure that all 'needed' care could be reimbursed (i.e. hospitals and other providers paid.) The result was rationing, or more accurately unmet need, since it was not a systematic process which deserved the name of rationing.

In a system where Districts were responsible both for accounting for local need and for running their local services, there was no intrinsic reason to cost at the level of individual patient care—and it is a serious misconception that this is a desirable or necessary feature of any health-care system. One of the comparative advantages of the NHS used to be that it could account for salient costs without 'individual billing' (whether that billing is for commercial purposes or for 'internal' accounting or contracting purposes.) Yet where the lack of adequate resources—for the overt purposes of the system; this is not (only) a value judgement—was being fudged, it came to be seen as desirable that the discrepancy between the two types of patient (those treated locally and those flowing across boundaries) be tackled.

ENTHOVEN: A 'MAN FROM MARS'

On a parallel track in the mid-1980s, and without any ideological desire to promote markets (quite the reverse, if anything), the Nuffield Trust had invited Alain Enthoven, a health policy reform advocate from the USA, to comment on the management of the NHS—hence the title of his short 1985 monograph, 'Reflections on the Management of the NHS'. Enthoven, aware that he might be seen as an outsider out of sympathy with the NHS, had wanted to call it 'A Man from Mars Reflects on the NHS', but the Nuffield Trust's redoubtable Chairman Sir Edgar 'Bill' Williams had seen this title as intolerably vulgar.

Enthoven's main stimulus to describe what he called 'gridlock' in the NHS was his perception that the famous London teaching hospitals were being denied adequate resourcing for what they did by the fact that the 'money did not follow the patient.' He meant that such hospitals were not adequately paid for those patients who flowed into London for care, especially of the more specialist variety.

Yet Enthoven was wrong about this. The hospitals were reimbursed according to the formula for the average specialty costs of such patients, at least in terms of their Districts' target allocations. Now it can be fairly pointed out that it took a long time for target allocations to be realised in practice (as achieving this involved winners and losers, with the resulting political complexity) and indeed also that, even when the District received the money, that did not guarantee that it would reimburse such hospitals pro rata for what they had 'earned'. But these factors were less material than the fact that the hospitals were under-funded more because their host Districts (e.g. Lambeth District, with St. Thomas's and Guy's hospitals) were not getting enough money from the Regions and central NHS 'above' for their local residential populations.

It was pointed out at the time that these hospitals rightly considered it in their financial as well as clinical interests to receive the flows from outside the District. The argument for an 'internal market' was thus initially based on a false premise—that the existing system did not reimburse care for patients who 'chose' (or rather, had the choice made for them, in most cases, by the GP) to go outside the locality.

Now this does not alter the fact that there is an argument for costing all care overtly, even as a means of exposing the degree to which the NHS is underfunded at existing levels of available services and efficiency. But this is not on its own an argument for a market, and for contracting between 'purchasers' and 'providers'. Nor does it determine whether such an exercise should occur at the level of the specialty, the patient group (e.g. Diagnosis Related Group of Health Related Group) or the individual patient. It is 'horses for courses': it depends what one needs the information for. But the rewriting of history has extended to a conflation of market mechanisms and information requirements. And Enthoven's short commentary had produced a sound bite—the 'internal market'—which would prove useful when politicians had boxed themselves in in 1988–89.

THE THATCHER FACTOR

A third separate political track concerned the growing frustration of the Prime Minister personally with taking the flak for alleged NHS underfunding, during the winter of 1987–88, ironically just after another convincing general election victory in which health had hardly featured. It was this that led her to make attack the best form of defence, in launching what she called on BBC Panorama in January 1988 a 'fundamental review' of the NHS—unknown to her Health Secretary, the hapless John Moore. When Moore's stewardship of what soon became known as the Prime Minister's Review of the NHS, proved hopeless, Kenneth Clarke was brought in as Health Secretary in July 1988. Clarke was a managerialist rather than an ideologue, and—when Thatcher belatedly realised that the 'internal market' idea could suit her—he became the midwife for the policy. Clarke always saw it as a means of putting the metaphorical bomb under what he saw as NHS clinical and managerial complacency, rather than a means of implementing the economist's neo-classical dream or the political head-banger's neo-liberal utopia. Indeed Clarke was to make it clear in 1989 on BBC Panorama that it was not himself but his opponents who talk about markets. He also scoffed at the idea that 'contracts' between Health Authority and GP 'purchaser' and hospital and community 'providers' be legally enforceable as opposed to an internal managerial tool—as a lawyer, he joked, he knew how lawyers could rip off the NHS. (Shades of Nigel Farage, the UKIP leader, persuading his party to oppose the PFI in 2015 on the grounds that, as a City expert, he knew how the City was ripping off the NHS in providing private finance.)

Thus there were different tracks of political activity. One was 'low politics', or administration—the search for a solution to a mostly technical problem, albeit one embedded in the structural underfunding of the NHS. The second was the pragmatic search for an NHS reform which was elegant yet practical. The third was the ideological neo-liberal track—at first, confined to some advisers, think-tanks, and possibly to Thatcher herself, although she was a split political personality between traditionalist and pragmatist, on the one hand, and ideologue or fanatic, on the other.

The 1992 general election was the turning-point for health policy. The Labour leader at the time, Neil Kinnock, has said that, had Labour won, they would have retained the 'purchaser/provider split' in the NHS. This is in part owing to the lobbying of Kinnock by some left-of-centre medics and public-health doctors who supported this ostensibly market mechanism but not the market itself. Their view was that it would allow health authorities to make needs-based plans for public health and wider community services rather than just funding their own local hospitals. This view had also been reflected in the reaction to the reforms by some (at the time) left-of-centre pundits, such as Chris Ham, writing in *Marxism Today* (Ham 1989), a now-defunct journal which, despite its title, was proto-Blairite is arguing that the Labour Party had to represent consumerism and also acknowledge that the 'post-Fordist' economy now made electoral success based on a socialist appeal to a working-class impossible. Ham and some others, who had not proposed the market reforms but now seemed to see them as both inevitable and desirable, attempted to rebrand them as a means to achieving allegedly desirable health policy objectives such as moving from hospital care to community services where possible.

To me, this was a major misconception, although well-intentioned: effective planners and managers could more easily shape services they controlled rather than being bound in to finance 'self-governing' hospitals through contracts. Moreover, in order to run a market, purchasers and providers had to be local, whereas the task of rationalising the hospital sector (where necessary) could only be effectively carried out by planning authorities with authority beyond the local: the biggest hospitals which contained the specialist services had regional catchment populations. Thirdly, the implementation of the reforms bears out the misconception: the so-called market was actually used as a pawn of government diktat to enforce the priorities of the day—which, especially at the point of the electoral cycle before elections, usually lay in shortening waiting-times through pump-priming hospital funding and raiding non-hospital budgets more ruthlessly than the old District planning authorities had ever done.

Had Labour won in 1992, however, then the NHS—even if the purchaser/provider split had remained—would have retained the sensible 'Griffiths' reforms of the 1980s while eschewing the 'permanent revolution' which became the default position by the 1980s. That is, the 'purchaser-provider split' would have been more a management tool to allow a separation of planning and management (Labour Party 1992) than the harbinger of the permanent revolution which was to plague the NHS for (at least) the next 25 years.

In a pithy statement noting the move to the market from the more reasonable 'general management' reforms of the 1980s, Gordon McLachlan, the now-retired Secretary (CEO) of the Nuffield Trust, who had ironically commissioned Enthoven to look at the NHS in 1984 which then led to the suggestion of an 'internal market', wrote to me in July 1983, 'I hope you are busy critiquing these disastrous reforms, including this "purchaser-provider crap", which obscures the real problem.' Sir Roy Griffiths, who had proposed the general management reform of 1983, counselled privately that another ambitious reform would divert attention from the long-term bedding-in of his own reform, and moreover that effective general management did not require 'the market'. This was a practical expression of my own view that the 'new public management' is not the first step of a neo-liberal journey unless ideologues make it so.

But it was too late. Mrs. Thatcher had responded to complaints about NHS under-funding by making attack the best form of defence. This was indeed her most habitual way of getting her way—attacking when others put their heads above the parapet rather than forging a lonely ideological path. For, despite her subsequent reputation, she had been cautious in her earlier Prime Ministerial years about privatisation—both of key 'monopoly' industries and of key public services such as the NHS. The government had been badly burned by the leaking of the cack-handed Central Policy

Review Staff (CPRS) ('think tank') review of the welfare state carried out by the unworldly John Sparrow, which had proposed mass privatisation of key public services. Thatcher had disowned it, out of necessity and perhaps a little more: as with John Moore's subsequent inability to find a meaningful alternative to the NHS in 1988, she was impatient of ideology without substance. Yet when presented with an opportunity by the arguable naivety of her opponents, as perhaps with the miners' strike in 1984 (Moore 2015), she was quick to pounce. Thus it was that the NHS Review was born (Paton 1989) and 'the market' placed on the agenda—through a double whammy of chance (the turbulence of the 'NHS winter' of 1987–88 and then the availability of Enthoven's hitherto-obscure idea of the 'internal market.')

POLITICAL EXPLANATION

We may ask: what does this episode tell us about policy-making? How rational was it, and how much was it subservient to a particular way of doing politics?

Firstly, we must clear up some potential confusion. Comprehensiveness and rationality must be distinguished. The Thatcher reforms were an example of comprehensive rather than incremental policy: they took a systemic rather than piecemeal approach to reform. This did not mean that the end-result was comprehensive reform of the NHS, for the implementation process threw many spanners in the engine of reform and many roadblocks along the way. But the policy per se was radical in intent, at least in terms of the governance of the NHS.

Rationality, on the other hand, is another dimension: it refers to whether or not the policy was geared effectively to well-articulated ends. The ends themselves may be disputed, but—taking them as overtly defined or at least, if covert, well-divined—a rational policy would be one which marshalled evidence and judgement in pursuit of those ends. Rationality, in other words, is not a judgement about ends (as to whether they are right or wrong) but a judgement about the coherence of ends and means. It is a pragmatic approach. On this criterion, the Thatcher reforms were arational—not necessarily irrational, but less concerned with rationality in policy than with offering a political 'solution' to a 'problem' which was self-induced. The problem of funding which caused disquiet within the medical profession and the media was redefined as a problem of 'perverse incentive' (i.e. failure to ensure that hospitals' income reflected their workload in treating all patients irrespective of the latter's location). Ministers did not understand that this redefinition involved a sleight of hand, as discussed above. In any case, it suited them that the debate became one about efficiency. This allowed the market reforms to seem technically plausible while also furthering the ideological direction-of-travel of those Conservatives who were hostile to 'the state' and the possibility that the public sector could be successful.

A third dimension must be introduced: is policy unitarist, pluralist, or elitist? That is, is it agreed by all or most social interests (unitarism), contested on the basis of different social groupings having different stances which are capable of expression in the political process—pluralism, or dominated by an elite whether political or economic? (Elitism is a general term here, which may include the notion of class dominance or ruling interests.)

So far, I have suggested that the Thatcher reforms were comprehensive and arational. To this might be added the idea that they represented the interest of the ruling political elite rather than commanding general assent. For the reforms were bitterly opposed by the organised medical profession and by other employee groups. It is only in false hindsight that they seem to represent an emerging orthodoxy, with (most) history written by the winners.

As well as the opposition outside the government's not-so-big tent of 'insider' groups and networks, there was quite a variety of options proposed to the Thatcher Review over the course of 1988. But these were all within the tramlines of market reform, and indeed the 'internal market' was one of the few options most compatible with a public NHS. The other options tended to emphasise the privatisation of healthcare financing, as with the perennial suggestions from the Institute of Economic Affairs, now running a Health Unit directed by former Labour Councillor David Green, for whom, after his Damascene conversion, privatisation was the answer irrespective of the question. Green was to propose a private insurance alternative to the NHS for years to come, latterly trading with the newer think-tank incarnation Civitas. A similar phenomenon could be found at the Adam Smith Institute, then under its founding Director Madsen 'Mad' Pirie, and subsequently run by Eamonn Butler, described amusingly in Alan Bennett's diaries as a 'nylon-underpanted' right-winger who wished to dismantle the NHS.

Other think-tanks had a field day, especially the Centre for Policy Studies (CPS), set up in 1975 to provide an overt neo-liberal challenge to the then-Conservative mainstream by Thatcher's original mentor Sir Keith Joseph and former Marxist turned neo-liberal ideologue Alfred Sherman. As with Labour's reforms in the early 2000s, quite a few of the key players were former leftists who were applying their millenarian tendencies in the opposite direction having skipped the middleman of pragmatism. The CPS's leading light was former young No. 10 Policy Unit thruster (to which he had been recruited in 1983 by the hard-Right John Redwood), David Willetts. The latter later re-invented himself as the thinker of moderate Conservatism, post-Thatcher, acquiring the nickname 'Two Brains', but at this time he was a fully paid-up member of Maggie's militant neo-liberal tendency. Yet in the end, it was the more pragmatic Kenneth Clarke who sought to square the circle between a reform which was worthy of the name (by late 1988, the NHS Review was running into the sand and desperately seeking a solution) and yet which was capable at least in theory of implementation in the real world of the NHS.

Thus the 'internal market' became the chosen option. Pluralism in policy choice was severely restricted to options acceptable to the now-dominant Right in government (this was Thatcher's high noon, when MPs formed groups with hubristic names such as No Turning Back), and wholly excluded the wider policy and political community, including all the important professional interests in the NHS. At this stage, even the NHS management community was ignored, although in the future NHS reform was increasingly to coopt much of that community and seek ideas therein from those sympathetic to the direction of travel. The aim of the Thatcher government was to avoid 'fudge and mudge', or the dreaded compromise. But such unilateralism should not be mistaken for a wider unitarism or unanimity.

Such were the 'immediate' harbingers of NHS reform. Wider or 'underlying' causes have been claimed to include a rising tide of 'consumerism' (Tuohy 1999) or wider civic dissatisfaction with state medicine. This is convenient and 'politically correct' but actually politically wholly incorrect. The Thatcher reforms were an elite initiative which was not occasioned by wider social pressure other than that brought about by the medical profession and various pressure-groups seeking more NHS funding. It was later, when New Labour began its own market reform in 2001, that some ferment against professional elitism might be invoked. But as we shall see below, whatever the truth of this—even in 2001, such motivation was manufactured or given oxygen from the centre rather than representing a genuine social movement.

Wider considerations of political economy might also suggest that the reforms were tailored or at least intended either to extract more value more cheaply from the public sector NHS or to benefit a growing private healthcare sector (by no means the same thing.) That is: are such reforms functional for the private sector either economy-wide or health-sector specific? This issue will be discussed later in the book, once the trajectory of reform up to 2015 has been discussed.

THE CONSEQUENCES OF THE INTERNAL MARKET

This is familiar territory, and rather than a full summary of what is a large literature, only the relevant consequences for the argument of this book will be outlined here. Firstly, the internal market was a UK-wide policy, given its passage into law by the NHS and Community Care act of 1990, eight years before devolution, and therefore it was implemented throughout the UK. But it was only in England that the market was developed enthusiastically as a dynamic policy. In Scotland and Wales, the organisations to operate the purchaser/provider split were created, and to a lesser extent in Northern Ireland too. But in all these three countries, there was less market behaviour, in the context of much less of a market culture, and so when, post-devolution, the market was abolished in these countries, the task was much less difficult than it would have been in England (indeed than it was, in the brief interregnum from 1997 to 2000 when there was an attempt to 'abolish' the market culture without reversing the institutions of the purchaser/provider split other then GP Fundholding).

In England, by the mid-1990s, the market culture had significantly infused the NHS and enthused at least an elite tranche of NHS senior managers. Budget-holding by general practitioners (the so-called GP Fundholding) (Glennerster and Matsaganis 1994) not only 'took off' but also mutated into various experimental and developmental forms. These latter versions of GP purchasing, whereby groups of GPs rather than the traditional agency of the Health Authority made the contracts for services with NHS providers, indeed became the linchpin of the reforms after 1995 when they took on a different emphasis. This was a focus upon primary-care purchasing (later 'commissioning') (Mays et al. 2001) as a means of service innovation and indeed allegedly of meeting long-standing priorities, rather than the more generalised mechanics of a market.

This new emphasis was in part down to policy innovation from the 'bottom up', that is, as a result of initiatives from both GPs and local management, but more significantly it was a convenient means of keeping the reform agenda going when 'market competition' per se had begun to throw up at least conundrums for policy and management and arguably insuperable problems in the context of a public NHS.

In a nutshell: with both constrained resources and a policy objective of reducing hospital bed numbers, it made no sense—and was indeed impossible—to create the excess capacity required to provide market competition on the 'supply side'. One policy objective ('the market'), which was about process and structure rather than healthcare outcomes, was in conflict with another ('planning', albeit without using this word itself, which no longer dared speak its name in the ascendant neo-liberal era). Furthermore, if hospitals were to compete across-the-board, then how could they cooperate in offering complementary and specialised services? This came to a head, amongst other places, in Sheffield in 1995, where the local Health Authority found the aggressive competition between the two main hospitals (long since merged into one Trust) unhelpful to say the least. Ministers found themselves supporting both sides of the argument, and Health Minister Brian Mawhinney, deputy to Health Secretary Virginia Bottomley (both close to Prime Minister John Major, less of an ideologue than Thatcher) was eventually forced to prioritise long-standing clinical and bed-number objectives over the arcanities of the market (Paton et al. 1998).

This turning-point led (in an echo of the Thatcher Review itself) at the central political level to a rather desperate attempt for a new 'big idea' to disabuse any opponents of the reforms that they were labouring to produce a mouse—hence 'primary-care purchasing', or sometimes (not the same thing) 'local purchasing.' The momentum for a new direction was aided by the 'reform industry' in which so-called jobbing academics saw the reforms as a continuing (or permanent) process, for no compelling reason, and so kept coming up with ideas, and variants thereof, for new initiatives, for which Ministers (and especially Health Secretary Virginia Bottomley) were grateful. Such policy consultants could earn some corn, bring home the bacon, and save Ministers' bacon at the same time.

By 1997, when Labour won the general election with a manifesto which promised to 'abolish' the internal market, the market—such as it was—had produced equivocal benefits at high cost. Some micro-level benefits were ascribed to the GP Fundholding scheme, and some system-wide productivity increases slightly higher than the norm since 1948 of 2% per decade were noted. But the latter occurred as central targets for output and waiting-times were refined, as a harbinger of New Labour's target culture to come. But the main ambition of those non-Conservative proponents of the purchaser/provider split—to change priorities rather than simply produce more—was thwarted, as hospital waits became even more the political order of the day than before. Interestingly ex-junior Health Minister Edwina Currie had noted in her diary as the reforms were mooted in 1988–89 that what were blazoned as a major policy was in fact an unremarkable exercise in 'bean-counting.' This was quite prescient.

As reform took on its Maoist hue of permanent revolution over the succeeding years, the cumulative cost of all this became more of an issue than was ever acknowledged by mainstream politicians and even academics (whose evaluations of reforms tended to conclude glibly that costs were unknowable.) My own partial estimations of cost, made conservatively, will be noted in later chapters, Here, we may remark that, ironically, the most effective scourge of the 'administrative cost' of the internal market from 1992 to 1997 was backbench Labour MP Alan Milburn, elected for Darlington in 1992 replacing right-wing Conservative Michael Fallon. After Robin Cook, Labour's razor-sharp Shadow Health Secretary from 1987 to 1992 moved on to other briefs, Milburn's questions in Parliament were pithy and rather damning.

The irony however was substantial. Partly as a result of his effectiveness in opposition as a scourge of the wastefulness of the internal market, Milburn became, first, Minister of State at the Department of Health in 1997 and (after a short interregnum as Chief Secretary to the Treasury) later Health Secretary towards the end of 1999, when the unfairly maligned Frank Dobson left to become Labour's candidate for London Mayor. Yet as Health Secretary, Milburn oversaw Labour's own market reforms and indeed promulgated arguably the most expensive re-organisation in the NHS's history from 2001 onwards. That is, the most expensive at least prior to Conservative Health Secretary Andrew Lansley's car-crash after 2010, the White Paper, Equity and Excellence (Department of Health 2010), which led to the Health and Social Care Act of 2012.

References

Blair, T. (1998). Speech to Labour Party Annual Conference.

Department of Health. (1997). *The new NHS: modern, dependable*. London: DoH.

DHSS. (1983). *Letter to the Secretary of State, October 6 (the Griffiths report)*. London: DHSS.

DoH. (2010). *Equity and excellence*. London: DoH.

EHMA. (2000). *The impact of reform involving market forces upon European health systems*. Dublin: European Health Management Association.

Enthoven, A. (1985). *Reflections on the management of the NHS*. London: Nuffield Trust.

Friedman, M., & Friedman, R. (1980). *Free to choose*. New York: Harcourt.

Glennerster, H., & Matsaganis, M. (1994). *GP fundholding: Wild card or winning hand?* Buckingham: Open University Press.

Ham, C. (1989, March). Clarke's strong medicine. *Marxism Today*, pp. 38–41.

Hayek, F. (1944). *The road to serfdom*. Chicago: University of Chicago Press.

House of Commons. (2010). *Commissioning, fourth report of the Health Select Committee*. London: The Stationery Office (TSO).

Labour Party. (1992). *Your good health*. London: The Labour Party.

Lawson, N. (1992). *The view from no. 11: Memoirs of a Tory radical*. London: Bantam Press.

Le Grand, J. (2003). *Motivation, agency and public policy*. Oxford: Oxford University Press.

Mays, N., & Bevan, R. (1987). *Resource allocation in the National Health Service*. London: Bedford Square Press/NCVO.

Mays, N., et al. (2001). *The purchasing of health care by primary care organizations*. Buckingham: Open University Press.

Moore, C. (2015). *Margaret Thatcher: The authorised biography*. London: Penguin.

Paton, C. (1985). *The policy of resource allocation and its ramifications*. London: Nuffield Trust.

Paton, C. (1989). The White Paper, Working for Patients. *Social Policy Review, 1988–89*. Cambridge: Cambridge University Press.

Paton, C. (1996). *Health policy and management: The healthcare agenda in a British political context*. London: Chapman and Hall.

Paton, C., et al. (1998). *Competition and planning in the NHS: The consequences of the reforms* (2nd ed.). Cheltenham: Stanley Thornes.

Plewhe, D. (2009). *The road from Mont Pelerin: The making of the neo-liberal thought collective*. Cambridge, MA: Harvard University Press.

Tuohy, C. (1999). *Accidental logics*. Oxford: OUP.

CHAPTER 2

The Changing Politics of New Labour: From 'Reintegration Without Reorganisation' to Retreading the Market Road

SEARCHING FOR A NARRATIVE: THE THIRD WAY

New Labour at its zenith was both priggish and triumphalist, and did not 'do' irony. Yet irony aplenty was embedded in its approach, including and going beyond that noted in concluding the last chapter. Perhaps the most prominent is that emerging from Labour's 1997 general election sound-bite concerning its NHS policy—'Reintegration without Reorganisation'. By 2007, when Tony Blair left the Premiership, this could be rephrased as 'Reorganisation without Reintegration'. So what went wrong—or right?

Labour's political aim in the general election of 1997 was to persuade the public that there were only '100 days left to save the NHS' but also to persuade the NHS management community that not much was in fact going to change, or at least that change would be evolutionary, indeed incremental. Despite being out of office for 18 years, Labour's policy was minimalist, reflecting Robin Cook's pithy statement way back in 1990 that the best health policy for Labour was that 'we are not the Tories.' When long-time health management consultant Gordon Best began to advise Cook, the latter asked how Best thought he might help. Best replied that he would help develop policy. Cook silently scribbled something on a scrap of paper and passed it over to Best. 'Read that to me, please, Gordon.' 'More than 80% of the public trust Labour on the NHS.' 'Exactly—so we don't want to risk policy messing that up!'

There was moderate confusion in NHS senior management ranks as regards Labour's plans. Some of those who had become enthusiasts for

© The Author(s) 2016
C. Paton, *The Politics of Health Policy Reform in the UK*,
DOI 10.1057/978-1-137-47343-1_2

peddling the market (or was it for pleasing their masters) thought that Labour would reverse course, and were restive; others, more realistically, were ready to accept whatever fine-tuning was likely to result. A po-faced London-based NHS Regional Director was quoted as saying without irony or humour, when asked about what New Labour meant for the NHS, 'Apparently purchasing's out and commissioning's in, but we don't know what it is yet.' There was not however the inappropriate political intervention from the management community which had been epitomised in 1992 by Bob Naylor (later to re-emerge as Sir Robert, or 'Bob the Builder' as he oversaw the largest Private Finance Initiative-funded hospital reconstruction in the country as Chief Executive of University College London Hospital). He had attacked Labour's policy and said he would not be able to work with it—leading Labour's Shadow Health Secretary going into the 1992 election, Robin Cook, to clarify waspishly that he need not worry, as he would not be given the opportunity!

There was however an apocryphal truth in the London Director's recourse to the latest management jargon rather than healthcare reality. For Labour wanted to abolish the internal market yet not abolish it—as part of its Third Way 'triangulation' strategy more generally whereby it defined what it was against (two 'unpopular' things—Thatcherite 'deregulation' and 'Old Labour' statism) in order to spin an alternative to both. Blair had borrowed this approach through his transatlantic 'wonkathons' at which his policy wonks, including the young David Miliband (christened 'Brains' by Alastair Campbell, Blair's Director of Communications), cross-fertilised with President Clinton's. In this context, the word, 'commissioning' was ideal. It was Janus-faced: on the one hand, replacing 'purchasing' (and therefore pleasing opponents of the market) and on the other hand, allowing the 'split' between the commissioner and provider to remain, pleasing supporters of the market.

The Third Way (in Labour policy generally, never mind healthcare) in its slightly more intellectually respectable version, was allegedly an alternative to the 'levellers' of post-war socialism/social-democracy yet also an alternative to the free-market obsessions associated rightly or wrongly with Margaret Thatcher (Commission for Social Justice 1994). Applied to the NHS, and dumbing down the concept, it came to mean neither state hierarchy nor the market. This meant—by elimination, rather than positive construction—'collaboration'. Academics added in the concept of 'networks' as an alternative to the economist's 'hierarchies' and 'markets'.

Yet, to see such approaches, or governance systems and mechanisms, as alternatives is naive. Networks are a virtually content-free concept, referring to webs of relationships, which may be organised using different incentives (if any) for different reasons, in different theories and practical situations. Equally, 'hierarchy' (for which read Labour's target regime) and markets may or may not be alternatives as opposed to complements, however tense the companionship.

Furthermore, performance management based on performance indication (and monitoring of such indicators) may or may not be a part of central hierarchy, and may or may not be an alternative to trust. Perhaps thinking at the behest of academics peddling tidy, mutually exclusive governance systems, New Labour embarked on a canter through different governance systems (the inherited purchaser/provider split, 1997 onwards; collaboration, 1997–99; targets, 2000 onwards; the 'new market', 2001–2 onwards, reinvigorated 2005–2007) and accumulated new systems without removing the old as it went along, causing great confusion. It might have been slightly better if they had acknowledged that different approaches to governance could co-exist, if not too many, and sought to analyse the compatibility or otherwise of different approaches. But that is not how politics usually works. What happened was one 'initiative' after another, with the new structures and organisations of each added to those of the previous one rather than any rational 'tidying' or rendering compatible of the different structures. What is more, these initiatives occurred in an increasingly 'pro-market' environment, and therefore direction,which assumed that trust and collaboration were out-of-date as reasonable ways to govern public services—yet with much of the NHS's business reliant upon these much-maligned concepts to join things up, square circles, and make things work.

GOVERNANCE AND THE 'PURCHASER/PROVIDER SPLIT'

But before the continual process of reorganisation got into full swing under New Labour, seemingly accelerating a process begun in the 1980s by the Conservatives, the first challenge in 1997 was how to govern the NHS in pursuit of key objectives. Rightly, Labour had identified quality of care as a priority, with some research evidence later on regarding the consequences of the internal market justifying this retrospectively if such justification were needed. It was probably not necessary, for there had been some high-profile scandals, especially concerning the Bristol paediatric cardiac service, and more generally concern about quality in certain respects despite the NHS's justifiable reputation as offering a good clinical service by international standards.

Labour's new Secretary of State for Health in 1997 was Frank Dobson, who had been a key member of Neil Kinnock's new-look Labour team in the 1980s but could by no means be described as a Blairite. He was enthusiastic about the policy of abolishing the internal market, although realistic enough to joke that (quoting an anti-hero, the right-wing economist Milton Friedman) 'you need a candidate to beat a candidate'—one of Friedman's more acceptable if deliberately obvious statements. In other words, what was to replace the market?

This question had bedevilled Labour in the mid-1990s, and the national party office's attempts to think it through had been no more insightful than the then-Conservative government's Efficiency Unit's attempts in the mid-1990s to economise on the costs of the market. This unit was located in the office of the Deputy Prime Minister Michael Heseltine, and was known irreverently as 'Heseltine's bumf-busters.' Both failed to grasp the nature of the pre-market and post-market NHS in terms of the linchpin issue of contracting. Both sought to diminish the effect, which was high administrative costs based on market contracting ('transactions costs'), without tackling the cause, which was market contracting.

In Chap. 1, I pointed out that the market was initially seen as eccentric and an aberration from the NHS's way of doing business. It might therefore seem odd that replacing the market should seem so problematic. But New Labour was paranoid about seeming to 'turn the clock back'. There was a kernel of sense here: the challenge was not simply to return to the pre-market structures but to find an effective means of planning needed services and ensuring that money followed workload. This would inter alia involve more effective coordination between hospitals and community-based services. But, afraid of sounding 'statist' or, in the jokey sloganeering, 'Stalinist', New Labour decided to keep the purchaser/provider split. Given this fait-accompli, the challenge for the likes of Dobson was how to change the NHS culture without a structural catalyst so to do.

Preserving the split meant that some form of contracting would remain: yet the aim was to remove the 'transactions costs' of the market, the main source of which was contracting, and in particular the individual patient care episodes necessitated by 'extra contractual referrals' (ECRs)—the bugbear of both Labour's policy team in opposition and also the government bumf-busters. Both asked what had occurred pre-market, not realising that without contracts there was no such thing as an ECR!

BUDGET-HOLDING BY GPS

What is more, another source of friction was GP Fund-holding (GPFH), also expensive, especially if one includes the opportunity cost of doctors' time. A major criticism of the market had in fact been a criticism of one aspect of the market as it had been created and then evolved in the NHS, rather than the market per se—that aspect being GPFH. It had been argued that patients registered with GPFH practices had an advantage over patients of traditional, non-GPFH practices, in that their doctors could make referrals to hospital with money directly attached, and therefore could get quicker treatment for their patients—which had of course been the very point of the policy. A dual system was inequitable, but Labour decided to abolish GPFH rather than give all GPs budgets (which it did indirectly and half-heartedly after 2005, and which the 2012 Act did—on paper at least—more directly.)

In other words, to be fair, duality was not an argument against GPFH, so much as an argument against the duality of some GPs holding budgets and others not. If GPFH was a transitional stage to all GPs becoming purchasers, then the objection might fall. This is a crucial point, as later reforms (under both New Labour then the Coalition government from 2010) sought to generalise alleged GPFH advantages across the whole English NHS.

Initially Labour abolished GPFH—indeed, by a sleight of hand, defined the market *as* GPFH and therefore claimed that the latter's abolition by April 1st 1999 represented the abolition of 'the market.' This of course left the wider market structures intact, although (from 1997 to 2001 in practice) damped down in operational significance. Yet GPFH was the target. But, since the reason for the target was inequity, then the door was left open to reinvent the scheme in other ways, with all GPs (nominally) involved. This was in fact what happened, in 2001; again in 2005; and even more in 2010–2012 under Conservative-Liberal Democrat Coalition government.

Yet if GPFH had other flaws, then to ape the idea might represent a fundamentally wrong-turning rather than a repair to the road being taken. And it did. It was trivially true that hospitals had to please GPFH: they had a guaranteed budget from the District Health Authority and had to make up the shortfall from the gadflies in the system, the GPs with budgets. The NHS was so tightly funded that breaking even required that every last penny be squeezed from purchasers by providers such as hospitals. To conclude from this that faster treatment for GPFHs' patients meant some sort of systemic efficiency on the part of GPFH was absurd. Yet that was exactly the conclusion drawn. Moreover, it was not even the case that all GPFH did achieve quicker treatment (Ambler 1995)—nationally, it was a mixed picture. The advantage achieved by GPFH for their patients, if and when they did achieve it, was likely to dissipate when GPFH was the norm, as GPFH would no longer be 'gadflies' whose advantage lay in the hospital pleasing them against the District with its hands tied.

A main argument against GPFH was in fact the costly nature of the scheme, including the opportunity cost of GPs' time. A leading GP budget holder and Department of Health adviser David Colin-Thome later described himself humorously but with insight as a 'reform junkie': that small minority of GPs who were either 'reform junkies' or, more likely, entrepreneurially minded, could handle the cost to their time. Most GPs however had no desire so to do. The same story has applied to all the successor schemes (see below): the 'Professional Executive Committees' (mostly GPs) of the later PCGs (from 1998) and PCTs (from 1998 and especially from 2001); the 'Practice-Based Commissioners' after 2005; and the Clinical Commissioning Groups from 2012. All these bodies were and are GP-dominated, but without reference to doctors in their titles so as not to offend the minority of other clinical professionals (mostly nurses) who might from time to time be on the various committees.

But an even bigger disadvantage of 'local GP commissioning', as it had become by 2001, was that strategic commissioning (i.e. service planning) required larger authorities or agencies than local GPs could furnish. GPs could be represented on such authorities. The rub was: a scheme local enough to involve all or most GPs would be too parochial to plan the system, and handle regional as opposed to local choices such as the siting, expansion, or contraction of many hospital and other specialist services.

Deepening Confusion

We may note here another disadvantage of the 'purchaser (or "commissioner")/provider split' as it evolved under New Labour. In order to give a boost to the now-statutory Primary Care Trusts (PCTs) in 2001, the government gave them responsibility for a variety of community services and for particular care-groups such as the elderly. This was partly to continue what Primary Care Groups (PCGs), their non-statutory predecessor (or, pre-2001, alternative), had been doing: the idea embodied in the December 1997 White Paper, The New NHS: Modern, Dependable

(Department of Health 1997) had been that primary/community-care based organisations would hold the budget plus the responsibility for non-acute care, contracting with hospitals (only) when necessary.

But a more pragmatic reason, born in 'low politics' (i.e. a political reason but not at the level of national political controversy), was that the new PCTs had to be given something substantial to do other than sign contracts to providers. The 2001 reform should not be confused with the 2002 market reform heralded in the Department of Health paper, The NHS Plan: Next Steps for Investment, Next Steps for Reform (Department of Health 2001). The 2001 reform was more about 'devolution'—supposedly about (indeed subtitled) 'devolving to the frontline', which meant local GPs in commissioning and hospital doctors in their directorate (and mental health specialists in the community) in provision. 'Devolution' did not mean a strict market-based purchaser/provider separation in which it was seen as a conflict-of-interest for commissioners/purchasers also to provide services.

So PCTs were in fact given services to manage which had previously been in community 'Self-Governing Trusts' in the 1990s as a result of the internal market, and also some less acute hospital services which were hitherto part of acute hospital Trusts, for example, peripheral hospitals in conurbations which provided rheumatology and rehabilitation services. But a problem of this approach was that tying in PCTs to local service concerns gave them a parochial mentality—and kept/made them small as regards population coverage.

Another problem was: since the market culture *was* back in the ascendancy, indeed formally so after 2002, and since the never-abolished purchaser/provider split created a 'them and us' mentality between PCTs and hospitals, PCTs as a result favoured their own providers over the separate hospital providers. They tried to be tough on hospitals in terms of performance expectations through contracts, but often oversaw low performance levels in their own providers.

Now this was neither fish nor fowl. If the market culture was ascendant and/or if PCTs were being parochial (i.e. favouring their own providers), then it *was* necessary to iron out a conflict-of-interest by removing their responsibilities for provision. But if there was not a market or market culture, then this would not be necessary: organisations would be expected to cooperate for wider reasons, as long as they were not prevented from so doing by the incentives within the prevailing performance management regime.

Furthermore, commissioners needed to be large enough to plan for real-life catchment populations for acute hospital services, and therefore pretending that commissioning should be done by 'local clinicians' was and is the mistake that has bedevilled English NHS reform since GPFH captured imaginations Right, centre, and (some) Left. It is in advising on community provision that GPs can best contribute. But if GPs are also to be the commissioners, this forces commissioning into too local a structure.

Better to give up on the purchaser/provider split and create larger strategic authorities which have GP advice organised parsimoniously and community units for provision. Or, if there is a market, remove the conflict-of-interest—but not as in 2010/12 by keeping GPs as the commissioners (see below), which makes removing the conflict more onerous than the problem.

Permanent Revolution: Blairite Restlessness

Another problem with all this jiggery-pokery from 1997 through to 2005 was that it necessitated almost continual reorganisation. The internal market had forced the creation of 'Self-Governing Trusts' to run hospitals, and also—as Ministers later realised 'on the hoof' to be necessary—mostly non-acute services such as mental health, elderly care, and community services generally. In 2001, these were taken over by PCTs in a big reorganisation of service provision as well as of service purchasing, the latter now called 'commissioning' but with little change in practice. Commissioning, if it meant anything, was supposed to mean assessment of the local population's needs then securing the services to meet those needs, but in practice 'commissioning' meant a scramble to get as much care as possible for as little money as possible, that is, buck-passing to providers, just as purchasing had been under the Conservatives' internal market.

The NHS business model (if we may dignify it by such a name) under the regime of the 'purchaser/provider split' resembled a shopper in a supermarket bypassing the till, pushing the trolley out of the door, and making a dash for the car park, throwing what money he had out of his pocket as he went. End-of-year financial haggle was the name of the game, and 'contracts' were not worth the paper they were written on (until Foundation Trusts came on the scene—see below.)

In 2005, the policy of removing PCTs' 'provider' services from PCT ownership (to avoid the apparent conflict of interest and allow the PCTs to focus on commissioning) was announced, although it was only accomplished from 2008 onwards in fact. But this meant recreating the 1990s 'community Trusts' only with a variety of weird and wonderful names to disguise the fact that history was repeating itself. After 2008, the newly refloated community organisations were to be designated 'third sector', that is, taken over by social businesses and charities, in a rather desperate premonition of David Cameron's short-lived 'Big Society' after 2010. But this simply never happened, which anyone outside the central government bubble would have predicted.

Oh what a tangled web we weave, when we practice to reform. But before continuing to explicate the ever-more-tangled strands of 'reform' under New Labour's increasingly pro-market trajectory, we should explore how and why that road was taken and the staging-posts along it.

Frank Dobson, Health Secretary from Labour's election in 1997 until autumn 1999, had rightly sought to focus policy on standards and quality. The creation of the National Institute for Clinical Excellence (NICE) and the Commission for Health Improvement (CHI) represented respectively the intended design of standards for care and the facilitation of improved quality in hospitals and other providers. Led by Chief Medical Officer Liam Donaldson, a quality-monger and co-author with Gabriel Scally of the Departmental paper, An Organisation With A Memory (Department of Health 1998), 'clinical governance' was launched in hospitals and indeed all Trusts to put quality as high on the agenda as financial governance. There has over time been much hair-splitting about the minutiae of clinical governance and what it means, but the best and most robust definition was in fact made at the time by Scottish Health Minister Sam Galbraith (a neurosurgeon)—'the corporate governance of the clinical process.'

All of this was an ambitious agenda—and, we should note, a developmental agenda rather than an inspectorial one. CHI (later to become the Commission for Healthcare Audit and Inspection, soon afterwards the Heath Care Commission and later still the Care Quality Commission) started off as a partner for Trusts, but—as New Labour panicked about collaboration and trust as the basis for achieving intended outcomes—became a more adversarial or at least remote inspector, as the breathless name changes listed above suggest.

The panic was in fact not induced by quality, but by some partial and rather crude data suggesting that overall NHS productivity, expressed prominently in 'waiting lists', had fallen slightly in 1997–1999. As Dobson pointed out later, this was reversed before any reversal of his own policy could have taken effect. We may moreover point out that NHS 'productivity', whether expressed through total workload ('Finished Consultant Episodes') or waiting-times, has varied in both directions under all types of governance regime (trust; central command; the market), not least because it is such a dysfunctionally crude measure.

But for the Blair government and the Prime Minister himself, insecurity and near-panic were the order of the day. A parliamentary majority of nearly 200 was not enough to persuade 'the man' that time and a steady course were both required for NHS improvement. With some justification but not as much as he thought, Blair was in fear of 'Tory England' even when at his zenith, and he saw anything which might savour of Old Labour or of feather-bedding the public sector as poison. For Blair, the 'forces of conservatism' were the source of the 'scars on his back', and the former conveniently flagged up both right-wing obstruction to his more left-wing supporters and yet also obstruction by professions and labour to his more right-wing supporters. Another useful triangulation. In fact, Blair had had in mind the medical profession specifically when he had talked of the 'forces of conservatism.' The implication for the NHS was that reform would be a leitmotif, a restless process of which the symbolic value was more important than the destination. For the latter changed over time, as we shall see.

'Targets Before Breakfast, Lunch and Dinner … and Breakfast Again the Next Morning'

Thus, with the convenient replacement of Dobson (who was not a Blairite 'moderniser') with Alan Milburn (who had become one) towards the end of 1999, New Labour moved from the pseudo-Third Way in health to a modernised and much more top-down version of the First Way—hierarchy, command, and also (unlike from 1948 until the market dawn in 1991) control. This meant governance by targets. Gordon Brown's dominant Treasury was virtually the executive office of the government for domestic policy, and its Public Service Agreement with the Department of Health was translated via the Department's own Performance Assessment Framework into detailed performance indicators for the NHS. And for quality, the emphasis was now to be upon inspection, rather than facilitative external aid from CHI. An even more formal approach—accreditation of providers—was floated by the PM's Political Secretary, Robert Hill, who was, perhaps appropriately given the need to spot the nuances of the different jargon-laden approaches to performance management, a theology graduate.

The new hierarchy was not like the caricature of the First Way (hierarchy and state control) which had seen history rewritten in order to develop the 'narrative' of the Third Way—a 'narrative' meaning the reconstruction of the past in order to serve the purposes of the desired future. For the NHS from 1948 until the 1980s may have looked like a hierarchy when one looked at a nice tidy organisational chart of its structure—from the Department of Health in England to Regions, to Districts and then their constituent service providers. The parallel in Scotland, for example, was from the Scottish Office, at this time, to Scottish Areas, then Districts (which were abolished in 1984.) In Wales, the Welsh Office was in charge of Regions and Districts.

But these structures masked the reality that the centre articulated policy objectives and took certain decisions about national services, but then left the lower tiers to manage and implement, which de facto meant making regional policy to boot. Additionally, the professions—especially the still-powerful doctors, at this time—were not subject to control within the hierarchy; they were not even subject to command, let alone the follow-up known as control.

Ironically this is the opposite of the caricature. It was with the rise of the market in 1991—in the myth of the Third Way, the so-called Second Way—that we saw the centre, the Department of Health and its executive partners and bosses, strengthen its executive powers and seek to command and to control. This was opposite to what the rhetoric suggested—that the market was a part of devolution away from central (or regional) control.

In the NHS, the Griffiths reforms of 1984 onwards, following Roy Griffiths's misleadingly short 'Letter to the Secretary of State' dated 6 October 1983 (DHSS 1983), had attempted to make the NHS more of a genuine corporate hierarchy, in the mould of public corporations, with a central head office and regional and lower tiers which not only 'reported up' but also incorporated the professions as never before. But this was always a compromise at 'street level' between NHS managers and doctors (nurses and other less powerful professionals were easier to corral.) Ironically if the 'new hierarchy' of Milburn had had the Griffiths structures without the subsequent market reforms as its context, then things might have been easier. But one of the problems with the new hierarchy was that it inherited the purchaser/provider split.

Giving separate commands to purchasers (commissioners) and providers respectively became a major bugbear of New Labour's tenure from 2001 to 2006 and beyond. Not only did it make genuine collaboration between the PCTs and hospitals almost impossible, but it also led to system disintegration when—despite all the significant new money—the NHS financial crisis of 2005–6 hit home (House of Commons Select Committee on Health 2006).

One of the innovations which had some merit but which sowed discord in practice was the system of 'star ratings' which operated from 2001 to 2005. Hospitals and also the 'commissioning' PCTs were rated from zero to three stars, with one incentive being greater autonomy for high-performers. This latter feature was however trivial, and much less important than the reputational effect of the ratings and indeed the 'blame culture' which percolated outwards from the NHS village to the tabloid press. For example, on one occasion, the ten Chief Executives of 'zero star trusts' were portrayed as handsomely paid turnip-heads on the front page of a well-known tabloid.

Irrespective of the merits and demerits of such whole-institution ratings, one of the biggest problems in practice was the fact that purchasers/commissioners (the PCTs) and providers (hospitals and mental health providers, primarily) were subject to a different set of performance indicators each—some indicators were the same for each, but many were different. This meant—for example—that a high-performing hospital which was capable of achieving a three-star rating depended upon its local PCT's funding it adequately so that its waiting-times passed muster in terms of the target criteria. By 2005, this meant that all patients admitted to Accident and Emergency had to be treated, admitted, or discharged within four hours, and there were increasingly demanding inpatient and outpatient waiting-time targets for elective operations. Yet one or more of the local PCT might be hovering around the one-star rating, without hope of meeting access targets at three- or even two-star level on behalf of its share of the hospital's catchment population. It might well be more interested in funding its own directly-managed providers (community services, and/or small peripheral hospitals), or in achieving other targets—than helping the hospital achieve its ambition. In other words, performance management was not 'joined up' (Paton in Exworthy et al (Eds.) 2011).

Now this could of course be mitigated by removing all provider functions from the commissioner. But that would still not solve another conflict—between the commissioner's target to make a financial surplus or at least 'break even' and the provider's obligation to treat emergency and other admissions which were referred by GPs who were part of the commissioning organisation on paper but who were making referrals outside the contracts agreed for funding by that commissioner. All arcane stuff. And it got even more complicated: at the end of each financial year, in an attempt to meet its targets, a large hospital dealing with many small PCTs would be forced to shuffle the pack of cards to see where it could make compromises (i.e. allow a PCT not to pay for patients already treated) and where it could not. This was hardly rational patient care according to need.

Overload: The Unnecessary Deficit

And when the whole English NHS was facing a deficit of £1.2 billion, in 2005–6, despite the generosity of additional funding, the buck-passing between purchaser and provider took the form of both cost-shifting and patient dumping. Hospitals were ordered to cut budgets in order to fulfil their statutory obligation to 'break even' annually, despite the NHS now allegedly being on a three-year planning cycle, one of New Labour's meaningless boasts. Patients were therefore passed back to the PCT, so that care could be provided in the 'community' instead. But this was a euphemism for care denied, especially since the PCT also had to cut its own budget.

It might be argued that, if a financial deficit was looming, these are necessary hard choices. But the issue was the irrational means of proceeding, seen from the viewpoint of the whole system and the prospect for clinical prioritisation of patients' needs. What is more, the costs of the purchaser/provider system, with its duplication of administrative functions on both sides of the fence as part of the contracting process, were a significant component of the 2005–6 deficit. There were, to boot, far too many small PCTs, each with the full panoply of management structures and costs. Add to this the botched pay awards of 2004, the emerging payback costs of various PFI schemes and the fact that national priorities were snowballing, with money for each double and triple-counted, and we see that New Labour's policy regime was both overloaded and contradictory.

It was in this context that the next reorganisation loomed—in part, to undo the damage of Alan Milburn's 2001 Shifting the Balance. But first we should consider albeit briefly the NHS Plan of 2000 (Department of Health 2000) and its more significant rider—the formal resurgence of the market as presaged in 2002 through what was formally an extension of the NHS Plan (Department of Health 2000) in the misleadingly slim and informal Departmental paper entitled, 'The NHS Plan: Next Steps for Investment, Next Steps for Reform' (Department of Health 2002).

THE NHS PLAN AND BEYOND

The NHS Plan was itself a Janus-faced document emphasising both (in the government's mantra), 'investment and reform.' Initially, it was the investment which registered. Blair and Milburn sought to create a 'big tent' to launch it—nearly all the clinical and managerial 'great and good' co-signed the preface, and it seemed (indeed was) mostly about investment in new kit for the NHS—a kind of letter to Santa come true in good time for Christmas 2000. The backdrop had been a damaging political row following the outburst from Lord (Robert) Winston, Labour peer, eminent embryologist, and TV personality, who had decried British healthcare in 1999 in an article in the left-of-centre New Statesman as being 'worse than in Poland'—under-funded and creaking. Blair's Director of Communications was literally sent round to extract a 'clarification', but the damage had been done.

Soon after, in January 2000, Blair announced on David Frost's Sunday morning TV programme that NHS spending was to rise to the level of the 'European average.' Just as Mrs. Thatcher had announced the NHS Review in January1988 on TV unknown to her Ministers, one of her 'sons' (in the words of former Times Editor Simon Jenkins) (Jenkins, 2006) was now doing the same. It was this which led Chancellor Gordon Brown to burst in on a subsequent private meeting being held by Blair and accuse, 'You've stolen my f***ing budget.' One suspects that Brown was also riled that his erstwhile comrade had also stolen his f***ing announcement: Brown liked personally to deliver any domestic largesse going, as he later showed when he commissioned the Wanless Report into NHS funding and later accepted its conclusions which he interpreted as endorsing both the NHS model and the need for more money (which he found by increasing that surreptitious tax, National Insurance.)

The other side of the NHS Plan was 'reform'. It was stated in generalities at this stage, but a significant marker was put down in terms for the so-called concordat with the private healthcare sector, which was now to be a partner rather than an awkward guest. More significant than this however (even in 2015, genuine private provision of NHS-funded healthcare—as opposed to private management and leadership of clinical networks and 'integrated care' federations, and of course the infamous PFI—is less than 10% of the total) was the move to the new market which emerged in 2002 through the 'Next Steps' paper.

NEW LABOUR'S NEW MARKET

The rest is history, as they say. The New Labour market reforms were heralded in 2002, and were to consist in 'patient choice' (so-called) with money following the patient in a scheme misleadingly called 'Payment by Results' (what was actually meant was payment by workload, i.e., the money following the patient—the original technical motivation which underlay the non-political dimension of the Thatcher internal market.) It was correctly argued that under the internal market, money had not followed the patient but that the patient had followed the contract—with the purchaser (an NHS agency) rather than the patient deciding which providers were to be allowed for referral. What was incorrectly argued, or rather unknown to the Blairites, was that the NHS had allowed open, free referral since 1948, and that it was ironically the contracting system of the internal market which had prevented this. It was certainly true that there were financial barriers to realising this free referral, but these were technical (see Chap. 1) and indeed what was now to be called 'patient choice' was equally hamstrung by a shortage of money (despite the real increases after 2000) to allow it to operate as advertised.

Interestingly, the rest of the UK—without the market—ended up with just as much (or as little) 'patient choice' as in England, by the time Labour retired hurt in 2010. The slogan had always been at base an ideological weapon which the Blairites used to protest (too much) that they were reformers rather than Old Labour. The content of the 'reform' mattered less than the symbolism—and this could be the epitaph for much of what went wrong in New Labour's health policy, which oversaw real improvement in the NHS but (for the money) less than there could have been if about half the valuable real extra resource had not been frittered on the 'reform' lottery.

The new market was only implemented after 2006, which had been a watershed year for the NHS in terms of a loss of financial control throughout England. This was not as severe as what happened after 2015 under 'austerity', but there was much less overt reason at a time of plenty: the covert reasons were mentioned above. Health Secretary Patricia Hewitt had inherited the pressures in 2005, which were swept under the carpet in election year, and subsequently presented a reinvigorated 'Health Reform Programme' (Department of Health 2005) as the solution. This was nonsense, however: the cause of the pressure had been an overload in policy and 'initiative', not a lack. Hewitt sought longer term financial planning by Trusts, with new market regulator Monitor (the overseer of the 'Foundation Trust' sector at this stage, until the Lansley reforms brought it centre-stage more than five years later) charged with obliging—without seemingly twigging that a reinvigorated market made this less possible. If the rug could be pulled from under hospitals' and indeed any provider's financial solvency by capricious 'market' purchasing decisions, then what hope stability—and complex hospital services needed both stability and buy-in from strategic 'commissioners', not the banana market which Ministers were naively encouraging, repeating the mistake of the early 1990s.

'CRISP IS TOAST'

But in 2005, Hewitt had a more pressing, although less long-term, problem on her plate. Aware that her predecessor-but-one Alan Milburn had created far too many small PCTs in his ill-fated 2001 reform, shifting the Balance of Power, she sought both to merge PCTs in yet another policy reversal and also to begin the process of making PCTs divest themselves of their in-house providers in order to remove the 'conflict-of-interest' (it was always market language now).

Whatever the arguments for these initiatives (and some of them were compelling), the process was botched. On Hewitt's behalf, NHS Chief Executive and Department of Health Permanent Secretary Nigel Crisp (the posts had been re-merged in 2000 when Crisp took over, reflecting the reality of political control of the management agenda, despite the aspiration of Roy Griffiths in 1983) sent a 'letter' inter alia to all PCTs in July 2005 with the anodyne title 'Commissioning a Patient-Led NHS' (Department of Health 2005). The non-executive community was livid. PCT chairs, mostly local worthies with local political connections, had been recruited and marched up to the top of the hill only to be marched down again. It is widely believed that Crisp resigned in March 2006 because of the NS financial crisis, but in fact this was more instrumental. He was given a seat in the House of Lords for falling on his sword ('Crisp is toast', announced Gavin Esler on BBC2's Newsnight in March 2006) and saving the hapless Hewitt, who survived little more than another year in any case before being sacked by Brown when he formed his Cabinet on Blair's forced exit in summer 2007.

Crisp was succeeded by his deputy, self-styled hard-man David Nicholson, a career NHS manager and a former Communist party member (who, to his critics, had ditched the ideology but not all of the method!) He had been the iron hand within Crisp's velvet glove, and now his time had come. His primary mission was 'financial turnaround', as it had been when he was briefly Chief Executive at the re-created West Midlands region (or Strategic Health Authority as it now was called) following the 2005–6 're-re-organisation', where he had also been concerned to implement the Foundation Trust policy as best he could. This double preoccupation was later to lead indirectly to his nemesis—the fallout from the Mid Staffordshire NHS Foundation Trust (Stafford Hospital) debacle.

I explore the Foundation Trust policy in Chap. 5 below, as it is best seen as a significant lead into the Coalition's later, post-2010, reforms. The Foundation Trust (FT) policy was part of New Labour's high noon in Blair's second term, when 'public service reform' was his domestic mantra, but it was also one of the harbingers of New Labour's end-game, also considered below, as it re-opened Blair-Brown conflict and came to represent the excesses of Blairism in the eyes of the Brownites. The Brown-Blair compromise on FTs had emasculated the intent of the policy, in the eyes of Health Secretary, former Trotskyite-turned-Blairite-outrider Alan Milburn—which was of course Brown's intention—and Milburn resigned in frustration in autumn 2003 to be replaced by loyalist apparatchik John Reid, another former Communist. It seemed that just as many neo-conservatives in the USA were former far-Leftists, so more than a few neo-liberal-leaning Blairites were also former far-Leftists in the UK.

Subsequently, after Blair had resigned, the FT policy itself was left alone but first New Labour during Brown's Premiership and then the 'post-New' Labour party under Ed Miliband (leader from 2010 to 2015) and subsequently leftist Jeremy Corbyn, elected leader in September 2015, rowed back from the market as a cornerstone of policy. Brown's last Health Secretary Andy Burnham (2009–10) described the public NHS as 'the preferred provider', for which he was pilloried by former Milburn and Blair adviser Paul Corrigan (a former Trotskyite like his boss Milburn) and by recent Department of Health Minister of State (under Patricia Hewitt), Lord Norman Warner, an adviser to Social Services Secretary Barbara Castle in the 1970s but long since turned Right, and who was to leave the party in 2015 on account of its leftwards direction of travel. While Labour did not seek a formal reintegration of the NHS as in Scotland, for example, by the time that Green MP Caroline Lucas proposed the NHS Reinstatement Bill late in 2015 (to do just that), Labour was split on whether or not to support it. Either way, Blairism and the market was dead in the realm of health policy at least.

REFERENCES

Ambler, W. (1995). *MBA health executive dissertation*. Keele: Keele University.

Commission for Social Justice. (1994). *Final report*. London: Institute for Public Policy Research.

Department of Health. (1997). *The new NHS: Modern, dependable*. London: DoH.

Department of Health. (1998). *An organisation with a memory*. London: DoH.

DHSS. (1983). *Letter to the secretary of state, October 6 (the Griffiths report)*. London: DHSS.

DoH. (2000). *The NHS plan: A plan for investment, a plan for reform*. London: DoH.

DoH. (2001). *Shifting the balance of power in the NHS*. London: DoH.

DoH. (2002). *Implementing the NHS plan: Next steps for investment, next steps for reform*. London: DoH.

DoH. (2005). *Commissioning a patient-led NHS*. London: DoH.

Exworthy, M., et al. (2011). *Shaping health policy: Case studies in health policy and management*. Bristol: Policy Press.

House of Commons. (2006). *NHS deficits*. London: The Stationery Office.

Jenkins, S. (2006). *Thatcher and Sons: Revolution in Three Acts*. London: Allen Lane.

CHAPTER 3

Political Explanation of Labour's Initiative-itis

The complex New Labour policy agenda requires a whole chapter of political explanation. How can this story of restless, in many ways circular, policy-making be characterised in terms of the three dimensions discussed at the end of Chap. 1? These, to recapitulate, were: rationality versus arationality; comprehensiveness versus piecemeal incrementalism; and unitarism versus pluralism, elitism, or conflict. Recall that arationality is not irrationality: policy may simply not be envisaged or designed with rationality in mind, at least rationality in the sense of overt choice of policy 'ends' and then the selection of 'means' to meet these ends using as much evidence and judicious choice as possible. That is, no party, politician, adviser, or particular interest is going to be deliberately irrational (in normal circumstances) and indeed all are going to have an end in mind which they assume that they are purposively pursuing. Let us leave aside the sort of psychological theory which interprets such as ends as post-hoc rationalisations for deep-seated patterns of behaviour or choice which do not fit the model of the purposive agent so familiar to most of economics and indeed much of political science.

New Labour's policy went through the following phases: the diminution of the 'market' and the 'Third Way' of collaboration, 1997–2000; the high noon of central targets, the 'new hierarchy', from 2000 onwards; the new decentralisation, 2001–2005; the new market, signed in 2002 and including the Foundation Trust policy of 2003, the patient choice policy, and the accompanying tariff-based 'Payment by Results', codified further

© The Author(s) 2016
C. Paton, *The Politics of Health Policy Reform in the UK*,
DOI 10.1057/978-1-137-47343-1_3

into the relaunch known as the 'Health Reform Programme' of 2005; the 're-re-organisation' advertised in 2005 and implemented in 2006, to reverse the mess created by Milburn's 2001 moment of madness; and then the end-game under Brown, in which new policy was not forthcoming and the 'ethos', such as it was, was less overtly enthusiastic about the market: Health Secretary Alan Johnson, from 2007 to 2009, stated that market jargon had demoralised NHS staff, and Andy Burnham then sought to steer a more 'pro-NHS' course than before, while still implementing the Blairite policies on competitive tendering for services and related issues

Each phase can be seen as a part-rational, part-arational, and occasionally part-irrational reaction to what had gone before. The Conservatives in the 1990s had 'rolled out' first general policies to promote the market and then various specific 'primary care purchasing' policies. This is what started the ball rolling. When New Labour took office, there was a rational element to their policy. The extremely modest 1997 manifesto promises (a deliberate attempt to make promises believable and achievable) had included saving £100 million from reducing 'the market's' administrative costs and ploughing it into reducing waiting-lists. There was also a reasonable judgement that the perverse incentives inherent in purchaser-provider relations had got in the way of both legitimate, indeed necessary, service planning and an emphasis upon quality of care as opposed to bean-counting.

An arational part of policy can best be summed up as the continuation of primary care purchasing, now called commissioning. Labour in opposition, in 1995, sought to combine what was hostility to the 'internal market' with a kind of unconscious, visceral belief that 'primary care' and/ or 'locality commissioning' was also desirable, as a private meeting of academic advisors with Shadow Health Secretary Margaret Beckett revealed. But there was no evidence which called for 'primary care commissioning', which was in any case often rhetoric rather than reality: it had simply become an emerging orthodoxy, not least because of the 'insider' policy community which was on the one hand advising the Conservative government and/or the NHS community and on the other hand building bridges to an opposition which looked very likely to take power soon. Such an approach—accepting the direction of travel and then positioning oneself as a 'constructive critic'—can of course be justified as pragmatism in seeking to influence government of whatever hue, but in succeeding years too, this 'pragmatism' extended to engaging with all degrees of market reform. Papers entitled 'Where Next for the NHS Reforms?' (Ham et al. 2011) and 'Beyond Fundholding' (Smith et al. 1996) catch the essence of the approach at different times, which might of course alternatively be called, 'having it both ways'. One of the reasons why this phenomenon was to grow further in salience later, in the twenty-first century, was that the traditionally independent think-tanks, the King's Fund and the Nuffield Trust, became closer to the dominant policy agenda, not least as a result of becoming 'providers' of government-sponsored research as well as charitable commissioners and agents of independent research.

This focus on primary care purchasing was the basis for Labour's initial policy. At first the new government experimented overtly with GP commissioning groups, which were area-based—drawing on the outgoing Conservative government's 'total purchasing' (Miller et al. 2012). But soon this was superseded. The December 1997 document, 'The New NHS. Modern, Dependable' (Department of Health 1997) heralded the creation of Primary Care Groups within each Health Authority area. There were 100 Health Authorities in England, organised within Department of Health Regional Offices, which had replaced the 14 more independent Regional Health Authorities in 1996 as central government paradoxically took tighter control of the 'market' agenda through making the regional tier a directly managed subsidiary of the Department of Health. This was replacing limited decentralisation with mere deconcentration (Rondinelli 1983).

The primary care focus actually represented continuity with the final years of Conservative reform, when GP Fund-holding groups had merged both with each other and in some cases with non-Fund-holding GP practices, to form larger consortia. Such developments included the so-called Total Purchasing Pilot (TPP) groups, which were given budgets by regions for all care, including emergencies, and which in hindsight bore some significant similarities to the GP (later Clinical) Commissioning Groups which emerged from Health Secretary Andrew Lansley's White Paper 13 years later in 2010. I say in hindsight because there is no evidence that Lansley built upon this model deliberately.

The idea of 'primary care commissioning', sometimes erroneously conflated in policy discussions with 'locality commissioning' (which may or may not be dominated by primary care clinicians), suited Labour at the broad level of symbolism, including keeping different factions happy. It should however be noted that, as New Labour's policy developed, the so-called primary care commissioning was not actually GP-led but manager-led.

The new Primary Care Groups (and later the PCTs) were intended to emphasise, not least in their name, that hospital care should be considered a last resort, with the PCGs organising care as locally, and as much in the 'community', as possible. Why else would bodies holding budgets for all care, in which the hospital would always be the largest part overall, have the designation 'primary care' in their title? The progressive movement has always had an anti-professional, anti-'high technology' strain, in some ways traceable to the 1970s anti-professional guru Ivan Illich but wider than that, reflective of an almost puritan mindset—and which in some cases has been buttressed by the kind of feminism which sees professions and management as male-dominated and grey-suited respectively. As with 'care in the community' for the mentally ill and mentally handicapped, 'primary care commissioning' acted as a dog-whistle for progressives, yet often in practice an anti-hospital ethos was convenient for the Right's agenda of closures on financial grounds. Lenin's infamous term 'useful idiots' comes to mind. We were to see a repeat of the pseudo-progressive version of the subtly anti-hospital case again in 2006, when Health Secretary Patricia Hewitt published 'Our Health, Our Care, Our Say' (Department of Health 2006). For former progressive leftists such as the feminist Hewitt, now reinvented as a managerialist Blairite, such symbolism was a useful genuflection in a seemingly radical, 'right on' direction. But in practice it meant little. For New Labourites more generally, of course, increasingly on a pro-market journey, primary care commissioning was a useful means of showing that they were wedded to reform and to the purchaser/provider split: that is, it would signal to the right-wing press that they were not 'Old Labour' statists (however statist the market was in practice!)

The argument that the NHS should be a *health* service, not just a health*care* service, an illness service, or a hospital service, sounds, and indeed may be in intention, progressive. But to this author, it would be more sensible to distinguish between the NHS as a healthcare service and wider social policy as the source of health promotion and illness prevention. For to load all 'health' aspirations onto the NHS is, like the anti-hospital virus it may well contain, at the end of the day a pathology which suits the Right. It loads prevention and promotion—most of which is outside the scope of the NHS—onto an already-stretched NHS budget, instead of ensuring that other government departments and policy sectors take the strain. This is one of the reasons why I opposed, at the time of the Thatcher reforms, one of Labour's putative policy responses, which was to give the health/healthcare budget to local government. Quite apart from the fact that this would make NHS funding (even) more of a political football than at present, with local variation growing to boot, it would, under the progressive-sounding guise of 'unified budgets', load too much weight onto one budget. Better to be upfront: the NHS is an illness service and the wider health service is a wider responsibility, commensurate, it should be noted, with the long-researched and acknowledged wider causes of ill-health.

Such was the wider underlying ethos to the debate. But to return to the 1997 specifics: Primary Care Groups were intended to follow one of four models: advise the Health Authority on commissioning care for the localities they represented; become formal committees so to do; hold shadow budgets for such; or become authorities themselves with real budgets, if they successfully applied to become Primary Care Trusts independent of the Health Authority. This last stage was wholly voluntary, it was claimed—which soon was shown to be a myth in 2001 when Health Authorities were abolished and replaced with statutory Primary Care Trusts. Thus 'seeking Trust status' became just as compulsory for commissioners as it had been for providers, steered under the Conservatives to become 'Self Governing Trusts' after the NHS and Community Care Act (1990). In both cases, there was a genuinely farcical requirement for 'local consultation', which would have been better described as informing local actors of the inevitable. To say this is not to support or oppose the policy—just to point to the disingenuous and schmaltzy means of promoting it, which did so much to bring 'reform' into disrepute under both parties in the 1990s and 2000s.

So-called primary care commissioners and especially the later PCTs were however given an unfair advantage, given that they were both budget-holders for hospital care, that is, purchasers and also the first port of call for provision. If they had owned or directly managed the hospitals (for which role they would have had to be much bigger organisations), then they would have had to keep hospitals viable and adequately funded. But in the context of the retained purchaser/provider split, they could simply pass the buck to the separately organised hospitals, over which they had financial power but no responsibility. This was the main perverse incentive of the split between purchasers and providers in a nutshell.

One political explanation, separate from ideological or national policy-based explanations, as to why it became popular over time in this new form under Labour is that non-executive roles on local PCTs gave local Labour loyalists a civic role. Indeed the excessively large number of excessively small PCTs from 2001 can be explained in part by lobbying by local 'worthies' during the consultation period. Thus in North Staffordshire, for example, one Health Authority was replaced by four PCTs, with a row that there were not five—all with a similar management structure and cost to the Health Authority.

Meanwhile however, from 1997 to 2000, the idea was that local PCGs/PCTs and Health Authorities would collaborated and cooperate with their 'sister' hospital Trusts. The question therefore arises, why did the government change emphasis after 2000? Again, one can find a plausible explanation which is part-rational and part-arational. There was a moderate panic in No. 10 Downing Street at slightly longer waiting-lists in 1998–99, and it was not unreasonable to think that the so-called Third Way (an economy-wide ideology which had no relevance to health policy beyond the level of rhetoric) was neither clear enough nor capable of offering clear incentives for delivery. Such was in the realm of rationality, whether evidence-based or not, although it beggared belief that after 18 years in opposition, Labour was only sorting through such dilemmas now. But in fact such a panic may have been premature.

The arational (note: not irrational) part of the explanation lies in the application to the NHS of the government-wide adoption of delivery targets, with implications for NHS governance. Instead of local collaborative management, central government was now to call the shots with local PCTs and provider ('self-governing') Trusts agents of delivery. Both the Treasury and No. 10 Downing Street were in favour of delivery targets, although tensions over content and timing existed.

The irony is that, had collaboration been given a surer footing through a reintegration of the separate purchaser and provider agencies into one organisation, then the delivery of targets could have been a focus for that collaboration. Targets per se are not a denial of collaborative culture, professionalism, or altruistic motivation. It was the target culture and structure of administering it which soured the concept.

As emerging evidence was later to show, the 'targets' phase of policy was what was responsible for the achievements in heath service out*put* as measured not only by performance indicators of waiting-times in particular, but also in terms of some out*comes* (i.e. improved health as a result of faster treatment for cancer, heart-attack, and stroke). Many doctors attacked targets, but they failed to separate the wheat from the chaff. Yes, there were inappropriate targets and yes, there were sometimes distortions of sensible clinical priorities (e.g. playing the numbers game by treating easier cases and lengthening waiting-times for more serious, if admittedly non-emergency, cases.) But these were a problem with either poorly designed targets or over-zealous implementation by naive or ruthless politicians, to whom management too often 'kissed up' by 'kicking down' below in the (mostly hospital) hierarchy.

It was hardly the proverbial rocket science. Measuring and managing to target meant that what was measured and became the 'P45' target (the criterion for job-preservation and avoidance of the sideways move or the sack) was, by and large, achieved. Monkey see, monkey do. Not only in England but in Scotland and Wales too, with a time-lag of two or three years, 'targets worked' (Bevan and Hood 2006a, b; Connolly et al. 2010; Alvarez-Rosete et al. 2005). It is a myth that it was 'the market' which produced results—at the time of greatest achievement, not reintroduced in practice, and of course never reintroduced, quite the reverse, in Scotland and Wales.

So why herald the new market in 2002? Admittedly it was not implemented until four years later, if then (Paton 2006), an inconvenient truth which even Ministers at the time did not understand. Ministers genuinely thought, in many cases, that the announcement *was* the policy, and that the policy *was* the implementation, that the medium (on the bridge in Whitehall) was the message delivered (to the bunker in the bowels of the NHS.) With 'patient choice', for example, they did not understand how it was (not) operating at street-level. But the question remains: why the restless search for a new, or revived, policy just as the previous policy stream was beginning to flow?

Indeed there were two new streams of policy, after 'targets', emerging by the early 2000s—related but conceptually distinct. In 2001 the 'Shifting the Balance' reform (Department of Health, op.cit.) created more than 350 PCTs to replace 100 Health Authorities; 29 'Strategic Health Authorities' (SHA) to replace eight regions; and four 'Regional Directorates of Health and Social Care' to oversee the middle-tier of SHAs. This was an ill-thought-out and unwieldy reform, which Ministers soon came to regret. Shifting the Balance was announced by Milburn at a press conference appropriately on April Fool's Day in 2001, and—incredibly for a government with a record majority of nearly 200 which was to be renewed at the general election that summer—the immediate motivation was the 'intelligence' that the Opposition Conservative Health spokesman, Liam Fox, was going to announce the abolition of health authorities in an 'anti-bureaucratic' initiative.

At the time, with the Conservatives so down-and-out that Charing Cross Arches would have been a step up for them, Liam Fox could have announced the Second Coming and it would not have deserved any attention. But the supreme insecurity of Blair and some of the Blairites, as to what they always felt was the fortuitous position in which New Labour found itself in 'Tory England', meant that the culture of 'instant rebuttal', and pre-emption, which was the rock (or sand) on which New Labour had built its house in opposition pre-1997, was still all-pervasive. The government had to get in first. Of course this immediate explanation is the tip of the iceberg, to be fair. The underlying reason was the search for 'primary care commissioning.' But its form, and timing, was thanks to the government indulging in Fox-hunting (incidentally, another self-made difficulty for New Labour at this time).

This policy was not born in rationality, and indeed bordered on the truly irrational. As well as the PCTs, the SHAs were a near-disaster. Eight or ten Regions were about right; 28 SHAs were neither fish nor fowl. They were too big to represent natural healthcare catchment populations, yet too small to do the wider regional planning which all efficient public healthcare systems need. Additionally, it was unclear whether they were to be developmental organisations on behalf of their constituent PCTs and provider Trusts, or 'policing', top-down performance managers. The latter role, unsurprisingly, quickly crowded out the former. But even this was not well carried out—for the lack of legitimacy of the SHAs (not only unelected but centrally appointed) and the lack of formal powers to reshape healthcare within their boundaries (there were cumbersome procedures for reconfiguring services) meant that they monitored performance but could not manage it.

They were, in short, a very expensive post-box, a clockwork mechanism in an electronic age, for transmitting central orders. Just as Monty Python's Flying Circus was so named because there was nobody with the name Python, it had nothing to do with flight and it wasn't a circus, more than a few Strategic Health Authorities seemed to have been so named because they could not handle strategy; they were bad for the health of those forced to work with them; and they had no authority.

The four Regional Directorates were unwieldy, and were abolished the following within two years, in one notorious case even before permanent premises had been found. One Region meandered from North Staffordshire to Hertfordshire and made no sense in geographic or substantive terms. Overall, Shifting the Balance was a monumental and expensive mistake, and should have been a serious discredit to Milburn, incredibly the erstwhile hammer of the cost of the internal market in the 1990s. But such mistakes are below the waterline of 'high politics' (although not far in this case), in which policies reach the public eye and personalities' reputations are recycled, and so Milburn escaped scot-free to continue his reinvention as a Blairite thinker. Gordon Brown was more accurate as and when, in 2005, he allegedly demanded Milburn's head as election campaign director (he was now a possible Blairite leadership candidate) if he, Brown, were to agree actively to help out in the 2005 general election, describing Milburn as a '****ing lightweight'.

This type of debacle was not unique for New Labour. Part of the problem was that no one had experience of being a Cabinet Minister, prior to 1997, and even former Ministers of State were thin on the ground, with Jack Cunningham being a sole exception in Blair's first term. Moreover experience of government, such as it was, was of local government—where amateurism reigned. Milburn was but one example: he had been a trade union organiser, a councillor, and had run a Trotskyite bookshop in Newcastle called Days of Hope, known locally as Haze of Dope.

The only rational explanation for Shifting the Balance is that it was geared to bringing clinicians directly to the 'frontline' (the subtitle of the White Paper which launched it, continuing the prose which increasingly coloured such documents.) But even this is to be charitable, for there was no evidence that the 'frontline' (whatever that in fact meant) was the right place for clinicians. If it meant being close to patients, it was a tautology. If it meant that doctors and other clinicians should be planning, contracting for, and running the service, it was highly contestable, although 'politically correct' in the policy and management communities, not least because of the 'opportunity cost' of clinicians' time, which might be better spent with patients, and also because of the related point that doctors and other clinicians (apart from that minority of enthusiasts) were neither trained nor necessarily skilled in management.

Milburn's new NHS Leadership Centre, part of the Department of Health's Modernisation Agency, also created in 2001, spent a lot of money on 'sheep dipping' about 5000 Medical and Clinical Directors through leadership programmes, but these were often de facto an exercise in therapy and, more seriously, there is no evidence that they 'worked.' One of the problems was of course the term 'leader': it seemed that, to the politicians and Departmental top managers, what was surreptitiously intended was 'followership.' When Milburn's resignation was announced to the annual conference in 2003 of the British Association of Medical Managers (now the Faculty of Leadership and Management)—the self-created professional group for those doctors most enthusiastic about management, it should be noted—a cheer rang round the hall.

Such activities were not irrational, but they were half-baked and knee-jerk. And whatever the intent, doctors did not take over the 'frontline' of management. The new PCTs were run by traditional managers, and their 'Professional Executive Committees' (PEC), supposedly the locus for systematic medical input, were soon marginalised and seen as the metaphorical Friday afternoon chore for those doctors who had been bothered to be involved in the first place. In 2005, the demise of Shifting the Balance was announced, in the 'Crisp suicide note' discussed above.

When it came to the second prong of post-'targets' policy, the new market (as it was not then called), a more lasting legacy was created. The partly rational logic for yet another 'initiative', so soon, again lay with Alan Milburn—he began to feel that his Whitehall target regime could not maintain improvement for the long term. It was as if the NHS's very own 'Roi Soleil', who had appeared to beleaguered NHS managers and doctors to believe that 'L'etat, c'est moi', now wanted to abdicate. Self-sustaining improvement (also the slogan of the Lansley reforms eight years later) came to be seen as necessary, and a market driven by patient choice was seen as the route to this. The arational part of this new initiative lay in its origin—a separate but related panic about outcomes, just as the previous panic had been about waiting-lists and waiting-times. Again, time had not been allowed for previous action to work its way through the system. And there was, as usual, no evidence that 'more market' was the answer or the 'solution'—not least because the question or problem was not articulated, if indeed there was one at all.

Not least in order to 'sell' renewed market reform to its supporters who had until recently celebrated Labour's so-called abolition of the market, New Labour now conflated the market with 'patient choice'. This was not just cynicism, as the government naively thought that this was a new phenomenon for the NHS and also, even more naively, thought that their policies would make such choice a reality. In 2003, the Department of Health published 'Building on the best. Choice, responsiveness and equity in the NHS' (Peckham et al. 2011). It is also worth noting that there was now an explicit requirement to offer a choice of a private provider—opening up choice to a required number of providers (four or five, it was to become) including the private sector. This was based on the belief that the public sector needed a shake-up, a wake-up call, if you will. The direct engagement with overseas private companies by the government reflected a belief also that the traditional British private medical sector was stuffy and complacent, and itself needed a shake-up.

Whatever the partial truths of these assumptions, all the above policy strands provided examples of New Labour approach to policy-making—policy-making by announcement following informal policy deliberations conducted on the No. 10 and Health Department sofas, the so-called sofa government (Butler 2004). It was not a structural cause, rooted in the nature of British political institutions, which produced this 'irritable bowel syndrome' in policy, although the centralised executive-dominated parliamentary system enabled it. It was a cultural phenomenon—a kind of cod post-modernism in policy, ironically presided over by a rather po-faced modernist government which believed its own soundbites about its grandiose mission of 'modernisation'.

But even this is not enough to explain the ever-changing, ever-accumulating policy. We must add in a number of three related factors—the captivation of the insider policy community (Ministers, Special Advisers, think-tanks, academics, tame managers, and doctors) with the 'reform' agenda in general and 'the market' in particular; the susceptibility of a government which fervently feared the Conservatives even at this time and the right-wing media to 'solutions' which signalled that Labour was not Left; and the interests and actual interest-groups created by the legacy of already-extant reform. All this created a mobilisation of bias to more reform, even when the latter became not only cyclical but circular.

One need only compare Scotland and Wales (and Northern Ireland in a different way). These countries had parliaments and assemblies which were equally 'structurally' capable of permanent revolution, but the above three factors were largely absent. The opposition was not Conservative; there was no significant insider policy community, let alone one organised around the 'London consensus'; and reform had not progressed to the extent of special interests (e.g. fund-holding doctors, Trust federations et al) putting down both markers for the future and constraints upon the direction of future reform, that is, lobbying.

Taken together, the above factors enabled the conditions for the 'garbage can' model (Cohen et al. 1972; Kingdon 1984) to operate in policy-making: frequent 'decision-points', based on political 'panic' in the face of 'problems' requiring action; and a constant supply of 'solutions' from think-tank-land. My own adaptation of the theory of the 'garbage can' posits that policy-making is not rational, although it may contain elements of rationality by design or by chance. Instead, policy is driven by the 'selling' of solutions to decision-makers, at times and for reasons which rationality cannot necessarily explain. Problems, 'solutions' (i.e. policies-in-waiting) and politics are not related linearly, although politics is the source of decision-points and may be influential in shaping, if not defining, problems: problems may crystallise as the result of media portrayals, interest-group activity, and their inter-relation, but at some stage, politicians will frame choices or make decisions as to when to create new policy, with varying degrees of autonomy from the agendas of others.

In the 'garbage can' model as commonly applied in the USA, the essence is lobbying by special interests. It should be noted, in applying it to the NHS, that the British context is less the lobbying of individual and diverse centres of power in a decentralised legislative system, as with the US Congress, and more the lobbying of central executive decision-makers. Furthermore, lobbying may be conducted to sell products or ideas—we may be referring to private healthcare interests lobbying for market reform of the NHS, but we are more likely to be referring to the 'sale' of ideas from think-tanks et al. That said, the two are related, as ideas-factories tend to be funded by commercial interests.

The same applies to ideology. The 'garbage can' model does not operate in a vacuum and is not immune to the way the ideological wind is blowing. The hegemony of neo-liberalism in the context for the last 25 years of NHS reform and more, when even the 'left-of-centre' think-tanks were tacking in this direction (in a mirror image of the 1960s and 1970s when Conservative thought had been 'semi-socialist', according to Sir Keith Joseph, Margaret Thatcher's initial mentor). For example, the IPPR (Institute for Public Policy Research) was founded in 1988 to counter the influence of the neo-liberal think-tanks during the Thatcher heyday, but failed to develop a new ideology or vision, as opposed to acting as a brake on the more right-wing applications of neo-liberal ideas. Its staff were memorably described in an IPPR newsletter as 'earnest young compromisers' by Gerald Holtham, its Director in the 1990s. In a different vein to similar effect, Demos became captured by a 'post-modern' approach in its heyday, which prevented any systemic critique of the prevailing political tide.

So it was 'garbage can' policy-making, but situated in a neo-liberal environment. The former meant frequent new decision-points; the latter meant that this led, in the main, to frequent re-assertions of neo-liberal 'solutions.' This can be called a 'path-dependence', but that would be misleading. Path-dependence means either that 'history matters'—which is a truism—or, more specifically, that, when a path has been chosen, it is irrational to move off it and start again, as an internal logic has been established in policy, implementation or both. The latter may simply be untrue, as are many analogies from economics and systems theory. But more importantly, why and how a path is maintained takes us beyond technicality into politics. There are examples of paths being abandoned at great cost as well as of paths being maintained. The more interesting question is: when and why does 'path-dependence' apply and when and why does it not? Some key episodes of NHS reform can be read as path-rejecting, even if the phase of implementation may contain some characteristics of path-dependence.

Meanwhile, we may note that, overall, the type of policy-making which has characterised reform—combining elements of rationality in an arational context—tends to create an overall process of reform, over time, which prevents progress to a goal or set of goals. For the raison d'etre for reform is different from episode to episode, and any rational kernel within the reform tends to be vitiated owing to an unfavourable context. To take but one example, paying hospitals 'by results' could make sense in a system in which hospital care was part of an overall care which was 'integrated' around the patient's needs. But it was part of a policy to make some hospitals more autonomous than before—Foundation Trusts—and therefore created budgetary inflexibilities through the nature of contracts with such Trusts. Yet additionally, those hospitals which were not given Foundation status—which includes some of the most specialised teaching hospitals in England; by no means just struggling or 'unviable' hospitals—did not receive enforceable contracts, and so could simply not be paid by a commissioner if the latter could not afford to do so, or presented itself as such. The system was riddled with perverse incentives, as a result of reform being neither comprehensive nor adequately rational at each stage.

Progress implies that the criteria for the success of policy at each stage of reform are comparable and commensurate with the previous stage (although this requires sympathetic interpretation, as such criteria are rarely supplied by reforming politicians). Consider a succession of reforms, that is, movement from A to B to C to D, say, and so on (and it was on and on). Yet health policy 'reform' from B to C, say, was generally in pursuit of a different objective from that which inspired A to B. For example, the move from the internal market to 'local collaboration', A to B, was in pursuit of coherence and reintegration of the NHS, as well as saving administrative costs; yet the subsequent move from local collaboration to 'central targets', B to C, was in pursuit of 'delivery'. If we then consider the move from C to D—which in our case was the move to 'decentralisation' (in name only, as it turned out) in the form of the 2001 Shifting the Balance reform—the criterion for success was clinical engagement and active clinical involvement with improvement (to put words sympathetically into Mr. Milburn's mouth). The extension of D to E was the addition of the 'new market', geared to patient choice as the driver of both productive efficiency and improvement of quality, the latter supposedly induced by a standard tariff for paying hospitals, but also including the Foundation Trust policy. Then came the move from E to F, which was inter alia the merging of PCTs so that the number was reduced from c. 350 to c. 150 (it was always slightly varying as adjustments were made over time), the reduction in number of 'Strategic Health Authorities' from 29 to 10 and the beginning of the divestment of PCTs' provider function (i.e. the small hospitals and community units which they ran). At the same time we had the 'Health Reform Programme', which codified a variety of extant initiatives into a 'programme', in an attempt to relaunch a confusing cacophony of policy noise. F to G was New Labour's half-hearted and partial recreation of GP Fund-holding: 'Practice Based Commissioning' (Curry et al. 2008) gave indicative or quasi-real budgets to local groups of GPs within the now-larger PCT, and could be described without too much cynicism as the recreation of the smaller PCTs which had just been abolished.

Thus by stage G: the combination of ever-changing policy objectives and an unsurprising failure to demonstrate achievement through reform, yet a continuing ability of both 'the market' and 'primary care commissioning' to mesmerise policy-makers, created a wasteful and meandering policy process which came to resemble a circle more than a straight line over the ten years of Labour reform before Brown's accession to power swiftly followed by the banking crisis led to a quieter period for the NHS in terms of re-re-re-organisation but the beginning of the 'NHS funding freeze' which followed fiscal crisis. But reorganisation was not off the agenda for long, as Chap. 5 explains.

REFERENCES

Alvarez-Rosete, A., et al. (2005). Effect of diverging policy across the NHS. *British Medical Journal, 331*(7522), 946.

Bevan, G., & Hood, C. (2006a). Have targets improved performance in the English NHS? *British Medical Journal, 332*(7538), 419.

Bevan, G., & Hood, C. (2006b). What's measured is what matters: Targets and gaming in the English public health care system. *Public Administration, 84*(3), 517–553.

Butler, R. (2004). *Butler review.* London: The Stationery Office.

Cohen, M., March, J., & Olsen, J. (1972). A garbage-can theory of decision-making. *Administrative Science Quarterly, 17*(1), 1–25.

Connolly, S., Bevan, G., & Mays, N. (2010). *Funding and performance of health-care system in the four countries of the UK before and after devolution.* London: Nuffield Trust.

Curry, N., et al. (2008). *Practice-based commissioning: Reinvigorate, replace, or abandon?* London: King's Fund.

Department of Health. (1997). *The new NHS: Modern, dependable.* London: DoH.

DoH. (2006). *Our health, our care, our say.* London: DoH.

Ham, C., et al. (2011). *Where next for the NHS reforms?* London: King's Fund.

Kingdon, J. (1984). *Agendas, alternatives and public policy.* Boston: Little Brown.

Miller, R., Peckham, S., Checkland, K., Coleman, A., McDermott, I., Harrison, S., & Segar, J. (2012). *Clinical engagement in primary care-led commissioning: A review of the evidence.* London: Policy Research Unit in Commissioning and the Healthcare System (PRUComm).

Paton, C. (2006). *New labour's state of health: Political economy, public policy and the NHS.* Ashgate: Avebury.

Peckham, S., Sanderson, M., Entwistle, V., Thompson, A., Hughes, D., Prior, L., Allen, P., Mays, N., Brown, M., Kelly, G., & Powell, A. (2011). *A comparative study of the construction and implementation of patient choice policies in the UK.* Southampton: National Institute for Health Research Service Delivery and Organisation.

Rondinelli, D. (1983). *Decentralization.* Washington, DC: World Bank.

Smith, J., et al. (1996). *Beyond fundholding.* Birmingham: Health Services Management Centre.

CHAPTER 4

England in a UK Context: Diversity of Governance

STANDS SCOTLAND WHERE IT DID? THE REST OF THE UK DIVERGES

Meanwhile, in Scotland, the internal market was abolished in two stages and in Wales, in three stages. In Scotland, devolution in 1998 produced a Labour administration with Donald Dewar as First Minister. Although Dewar was personally an erstwhile Cabinet Minister close to the Westminster government, the divergence between the governance of the different UK NHSs began, building on an already-separate heritage. The territorial offices of state for Scotland, Wales, and Northern Ireland had always been responsible for inter alia health, not the London Department of Health which was the UK Department in terms of dealing with the rest of the world but the English (and in some cases Welsh) Department for the NHS and other domestic health policy.

In 1999, Scotland, having followed England (at this stage) in rejecting market culture on Labour's election in 1997, simplified NHS organisation further (Scottish Executive 1999; NHS Management Executive 1999). Scotland's NHS was overseen by Health Boards, the approximate equivalent of England's health authorities, although varying much more in population from Greater Glasgow at the large end down to the outlying areas. Each Board was to contain one acute Trust and one non-acute Trust, including mental health and various community services. GPs were to form advisory groups on a territorial basis to feed in advice to the Boards. Thus, while England after 2000 began to develop complex

© The Author(s) 2016
C. Paton, *The Politics of Health Policy Reform in the UK,*
DOI 10.1057/978-1-137-47343-1_4

and expensive purchaser and provider agencies and relationships, Scotland applied Occam's razor.

In 2003, Scotland, still at that time run by Labour, removed the last vestiges of the UK Thatcher reforms, by abolishing separate statutory governing Boards for the Health Board, that is, the planning function (what would have been called the purchaser or commissioner in England) and providers (Scottish Parliament 2003). From now on acute and community Trusts would have management Boards to run them, separately from the overall Health Board planning and governance activity, on which they would be represented. But these management Boards would not be statutorily separate from the Health Boards, that is, there would be no purchaser/provider split. Planning and management would however be distinguished.

This was in essence the UK model after the Griffiths general management reform but before the internal market, and was de facto what Labour had proposed at the 1992 UK general election, at a time when the Thatcher reforms were still seen as reversible in England—irrespective of what then-Labour leader Kinnock subsequently said.

In Wales, the process of 'de-Thatcherising' was more roundabout, or rather zig-zagging—occurring over the course of three reorganisations, with primary care in the end having only an advisory role, although with local primary care commissioners existing at earlier stages along the way. These different staging posts, unlike the more direct market abolition in Scotland, were reflective of changing approaches and arguably of less confidence in the robustness of the system. But the ultimate destination was similar: an end to the purchaser/provider split and governance through territorial unified organisations (Welsh Assembly Government 2009; Health and Social Services Directorate General 2009), called Local Health Boards in Wales.

In Northern Ireland, the on-off nature of devolution meant bluntly that health had less autonomous focus than elsewhere in the UK. Health and social services had always been run together in the NHS era, and while the structure of the Thatcher reforms had been aped, the reality was very different: in essence there was and is an administered system.

Greer (2004) has rightly analysed the 'territorial politics' of UK difference. Moreover there has been a double-edged sword to the process of differentiation from England (Timmins 2012). On the one hand, the absence of Conservative hegemony in Scotland and Wales has enabled the equivalent in health policy of the football chant, 'Anyone but England', that is, 'Anything but England('s market NHS)'. Yet there has been definite nervousness that the English model might produce results unseen elsewhere. As a result, management initiatives in England such as targets to reduce waiting-times have been aped elsewhere in the UK—with similar results. Additionally, the Scottish approach of encouraging and facilitating rather than 'inspecting and demanding' quality improvement through NHS Quality Improvement Scotland saw a sea change after 2008 with the Crerar review of regulation in government—which, all in all, implied a move from service-specific regulatory initiatives to a 'one size fits all' approach. This arguably suggested a replication of England's own experience—in moving, for example, from the partnership approach of the Commission for Health Improvement in 1998, in working with hospitals and other providers, to the more austere inspection and 'shaming' approach of the Care Quality Commission ten years later.

There was a time early in the 2000s when it was argued that England had 'delivered' in those areas (Alvarez-Rosete et al. 2005), and some hubristically claimed that it was because of market reform. But their aping in Scotland in particular gave the lie to this (Connolly et al. op.cit.), as more significantly did the sober fact that English achievements in cutting waiting-times predated the implementation of so-called market reform. Wales is more complicated, but—prior to 2010—a target regime had similar success there too, albeit to a slightly lesser extent probably because the regime was less draconian in command and control than England's so-called targets and terror. After 2010, the real reductions in the Welsh block grant from the UK had a deleterious effect throughout the NHS there, although—as in England—local management may bear some responsibility for the more egregious scandals and shortcomings.

Overall, it seems that outcomes—and even processes, such as managing 'patient choice' -have been similar across the UK. There has been less consumerism, or at least citizen involvement, in England than the rhetoric suggests, and more elsewhere than the avoidance of such rhetoric would suggest. 'Choice' in England has been heavily managed (Peckham et al. 2012), even after 2008 when it supposedly became wholly free, and with Jeremy Hunt replacing Andrew Lansley as Health Secretary midway through the Coalition government and then continuing after 2015 in the Conservative-only government, choice has almost disappeared from the dominant policy agenda.

The question therefore becomes: has the substantial cost or continual reform (both the one-off, start-up costs of each round of reform, and the recurrent, annual costs of the complicated purchaser/provider systems thereby instated) been justified in England? And, if not, why has England's trajectory of reform been so relentless?

TYPES OF GOVERNANCE

We may also ask: as New Labour's restless reform in England continued apace, did the overall view of governance, to the extent there was one, change with it? The broad answer is yes. It had been implicitly assumed up to the 1980s that the public services were qualitatively different from private industry, and that public administration had its own norms and nostrums. It was the 'new public management' which challenged this. In New Labour's first health policy incarnation, it rejected the market without rejecting the need for 'business management'—although ironically what it gradually developed was a new hierarchy of public administration rather than a devolved 'new public management.' Yet early New Labour, seeking a Third Way for the NHS, also decried the diminution of collaboration inherent in a market model, and seemed to imply that trust underlay such collaboration.

Some academics, most prominently Julian Le Grand (2003, 2007) have implied that it is no longer tenable, if it ever was, to run public services on the basis that professionals and providers can be trusted on the assumption that they are altruistic. However this pristine stance creates a straw man, in my view. It is perfectly reasonable to assume that people are motivated by and large for the public good, as NHS professionals, yet that their activities may require to be steered—either through performance management or by targets, or both. That is, the view that performance management is the same as top-down 'command and control', effected on the basis that managers and professionals are 'knaves', is mistaken. Performance management may be of this ilk. But it need not be.

As it gave up its early belief in collaboration, New Labour settled upon a neologism—'the new public management' but at the point of a politician's gun, which meant that it was not really the new public management at all. It was the 'new hierarchy'—hierarchy as central command and control rather than the traditional hierarchy of planning relationships. This new hierarchy cut out the middlemen—or rather, used them as agents of the centre. Ironically, this control-freakery was accentuated by the fact that the failure to abolish the purchaser/provider split had left the meso-level institutions of the NHS diffuse and uncoordinated. What was in theory market structure was in practice fragmentation. And so the centre had to bypass these structures (local purchasers and the like) with direct command to the frontline.

An early if subconscious intimation of this came in October 2000 when the man who had been a safe pair of hands as NHS top manager during the Conservative internal market, Alan Langlands, retired and the new

Chief Executive of the NHS, Nigel Crisp, was also appointed as Permanent Secretary to the Department of Health. This dual appointment drove a coach and horses through the 1983 Griffiths report's recommendation of a separation of the management apex of 'NHS plc' from political control. But at least it was honest and pragmatic: there was no longer to be a pretence of a divide between political command and managerial implementation. Crisp had the personality to combine both elements of the role, and to polish some of the cruder target-chasing of Health Secretary Milburn, but the logic of the change was fully realised under his successor from summer 2006, David Nicholson, a 'delivery' man with a 'kiss up and kick down' reputation whose mission was not to counsel Ministers as to policy complexity but to force through financial solvency as a seeming one-club golfer. Only much later, when faced with a bridge too far, did he speak out about the conflict between politics (Ministerial re-structur-itis) and service objectives (enough stability to allow necessary change both to be promoted and achieved), describing Health Secretary Andrew Lansley's reforms after 2010 (which Lansley ludicrously denied were a 'top-down re-organisation') as so big a reorganisation 'you can see it from outer space'.

When the new market developed, New Labour no more gave up its belief in central control than did the Coalition and then the Conservatives alone, after 2012 and 2015 respectively. So even after 2006, it was not plausible to attribute improvements to 'the market', let alone before then. And in terms of the present discussion, whereas performance management and trust were compatible, as against the formal economist's view, central control and the market were not. In this environment, the market was not an invisible hand but a visible fist—a technical means of carrying out political transactions couched in market language but managerialist logic. The language was all-pervasive: even when it came to closing or shrinking hospitals (as with the Mid Staffordshire NHS Foundation Trust), it was 'insolvency' which caused it and 'the administrator' who carried it out. But this should not have fooled as many as it did.

Overall, New Labour sought to move from trust to managerialism to the market, with a dash of hindsight thrown in, for reality was messier than that. Ironically, while it was wrong to see only one type of governance alone as 'the' answer, it was equally wrong to accumulate too many types. One was too little; three or four was too many. And by the mid-2000s, there were four extant approaches to governance: the inherited purchaser/provider split, which saw NHS bureaucratic agencies as the purchaser; the new market, allegedly driven by patient choice located at the GP referral; the new hierarchy which predated but continued with the new market; and the still-necessary and sometime-exhorted collaboration between 'partners' both within the NHS and beyond the NHS, especially with local government's social services.

The tensions between some of these were significant. For example, if contracts were made by commissioners yet patient choices were made without regard to these, which was to prevail—the former, including the cost-control inherent in restricting patients to providers with which contracts existed, or the latter? And if the latter, what was the point of commissioning at all, with its contracts based on priorities and 'hard choices' (i.e. rationing, whether formal or—more likely—informal). This was in essence the question which had arisen when the internal market had been created. Hitherto, there was no restriction upon where patients could be referred. But upon the rise of the market, with its contracts between purchasers and providers, a patient could only be referred to a provider with whom no contract existed through an 'extra contractual referral' (ECR.) But now, under New Labour, the government actually thought it was creating choice where none had existed previously. History was indeed bunk, to the Blairites.

One of the reasons that New Labour Ministers erroneously thought they were inventing choice was that, between 1997/8 and 2001/2, especially after GP Fund-holding was abolished in 1999, the working assumption was that patients would be referred locally unless there was a reason to do otherwise (e.g. a requirement for specialised services which were not locally available). This was not *de rigeur,* and what were called 'Out of Area Transfers' (OATs) were generally enabled where reasonable. Note that OATs were not the same as ECRs. You could be referred within a contract out-of-area; equally, you could be referred locally without a contract, during the internal market. But in the brief 'anti-market' interregnum after 1997, when contracts were replaced linguistically with the term 'service level agreement', such nuances did not seem to matter much anymore.

It was just that an end to overt market competition seemed (wrongly) to imply an end to non-local provision—although from 1948 to 1991 GPs had been free to refer where they pleased. As a result of this historical ignorance, New Labour—when it reinvented the market in the name of choice—brought these two concepts closer together than ever in the mind of the health management community and the chattering classes.

This wrong-footed those Labour loyalists who saw it as their business to enforce the party/government line come what may. For example, Labour's choice as Chairman of the West Midlands Regional Office after 1997, redoubtable Birmingham local government leader Clive Wilkinson, had intimated in 1999 to the author that competition had been abolished and that he would not tolerate it if 'I find anyone competing' (an intriguing vision). Such certainty had to be reversed with the introduction of New Labour's market, complete with Foundation Trusts, of which Wilkinson perfectly understandably became the Chairman of one: such loyalists were pragmatists in the name of loyalty. But the Damascene conversion (or eventual revelation of their hitherto-concealed preference) by Blair and Milburn to the market made many Labour activists, by no means just the Left, uncomfortable.

Conflating choice with competition suited an ideological purpose too, of course, after 2001: if you opposed the market variant of choice, then you were 'Old Labour' or the 'forces of conservatism'—in the eyes of both Blairites and the succeeding Coalition and Conservative governments Yet as we saw in Chap. 1, allowing free referral of patients without the market paraphernalia introduced respectively in 1991, 2002, or 2010–12 was perfectly possible. The barrier to making free referral instantaneous was financial, not structural: perfectly effective ways existed to allow financial flows to follow referred patients.

Policy-Based Evidence?

The million-dollar question of course was: was the policy of market competition any more evidence-based than it had originally been? For it had been introduced without evidence. The best the Department of Health could come up with, both in 2005 and again in 2012, was a so-called Programme Theory of how the Health Reform Programme, so-called, worked—both when Hewitt re-launched New Labour's market in 2005/6 and again when the Coalition's Health and Social Care Act (HSCA) was passed in 2012 and seen, revealingly but mostly correctly, by the Department of Health, as continuing further down the same road as that started by Labour while in government. This view was reiterated by Blair's former health adviser from 2003 to 2005, Julian le Grand, who saw the 2010 White Paper as evolutionary rather than revolutionary, as did Labour's first pro-market Health Minister, Alan Milburn. Both indeed deplored the compromises inherent in eventually passing the HSCA, which they saw as a sell-out to those who opposed market reform.

The 'programme theory' simply stated that the elements of the Health Reform Programme were the variables which brought about the desired changes, and that the mechanisms by which this happened were in a kind of black box which it was the responsibility of implementers and tame researchers to bring to life. This was risible. Firstly, this was at best a hypothesis, not a theory. And if it were to be tested, it could not simultaneously be assumed to be true. Yet it was, and the 'Health Reform Evaluation Programme' was geared to implementation, not to testing the validity of what was to be implemented. At best, it was policy-based evidence, not evidence-based policy: the policy was not to be challenged, but learning how it could best be implemented—shorn of the warm words, how its pitfalls could be minimised and problems ameliorated—was the best that could be achieved.

This very British gentle abuse of officialdom, with which the health policy research community was fairly complicit, was in fact a specific example of a general problem. The market's effect was unknown, and to assume it was benign, design a pro-market policy then seek to 'improve it' while evaluating it, was incoherent. Yet this had been the basis for the internal market as well as New Labour's reforms—assumption; passage of a law; then either assume success without evaluation (the Conservatives in the 1990s) or 'evaluate' yet in a manner which prevented evaluation (New Labour in the 2000s; the Coalition subsequently.)

It was revealing that Jeremy Hunt, Conservative Health Secretary, rowed back on evaluation after 2013, annoying the academic and 'think tank'-based community of evaluators, of course, in the process. He probably realised that if it was to mean anything at all, it could prove awkward in debunking his predecessor Andrew Lansley's clunking reforms, which the Tories now wanted to forget as a prominent and unnecessary policy disaster. But more sensibly too, he probably realised that, at a time of scarcity as opposed to plenty, 'choice' was an unaffordable luxury. It has indeed been deemphasised and barely mentioned at all after 2015. Yet 'competition'—that is, tendering to allow the private sector to lead 'integrated care' consortia—is now emphasised more than before. So just as Labour, with historical awareness and confidence, could have had patient choice without market competition, the Conservatives, in a fatal inversion, have prioritised market competition over patient choice.

What evidence has emerged has most centrally been concerned with the question as to whether 'more choice means better outcomes'. One prominent study suggested that this might be the case (Cooper et al. 2011). But this study, on closer examination, is puzzling and paradoxical. Even if methodologically valid, which is a big 'if', it is unclear what, if any, is the causality in operation. The study correlates increased choice for elective services (non-emergency surgery) in one region of England with improved outcomes in a wholly different area, indeed the opposite type of service— Accident and Emergency care following heart attacks. This correlation's validity is a moot point; as is the question as to whether any such correlation may be association rather than causality.

Defenders of the hypothesis that choice in elective services produces improved outcomes in a non-elective service could at a pinch argue that it comes about because, through increased choice, patients choose those better or larger hospitals which are able to cope with *both* the government's choice agenda for elective *and* improvements in emergency care. It is not that choice directly improves emergency care, where choice is not applicable, but that improvements in emergency care over time are possible to a greater extent in certain hospitals which are also those favoured through increased choice.

Or, perhaps more likely if one is bending over backwards to accommodate the hypothesis of the study, it can be argued that those hospitals which are, or become, fitter to promote choice actively and successfully as a result of better management are also those hospitals which are managerially equipped to improve quality in emergency services. But demonstrating such would require detailed qualitative research, which did not in fact accompany the purely quantitative study. Continuing to bend over backwards: if valid, such results would not be insignificant.

Overall, caution is required. A corollary of the conclusion that hospitals which 'win' in the marketplace are the better ones might be that weaker hospitals can only maintain a toe-hold by cutting corners. An analogous result—worse care in weaker hospitals as a result of having to compete in a 'market-ised' NHS—was derived in a study (Propper et al. 2004) of the 1990s internal market (care again being required, in that it was a study of one specific specialty.)

What might 'cutting corners' mean? In the internal market of the 1990s, where competition was generally price competition, the argument was that the need on the part of weaker hospitals to compete and have a chance of winning contracts from purchasers meant that they had to offer lower prices than 'better' hospitals; cut costs internally to break-even financially despite such lower prices; and skimp on quality. But, in the new market of New Labour after 2002, price competition was overtly forbidden, in one (rather unusual!) example of awareness of the past being factored in to policy-making (One cannot go as far as to say, 'evidence', as the study suggesting quality concerns in the internal market only came out in 2004). Prices were regulated by a tariff and therefore competition was supposedly on the basis of quality. But if a weaker hospital can only break-even financially at the regulated 'tariff' price by cutting its higher costs somewhat arbitrarily or hastily, then quality may be at risk. Simply designating market competition as 'quality competition rather than price competition' does not guarantee the desired result.

Note that talk of 'weaker' hospitals is not to impute necessarily worse management or a lower standard of clinician. It may be that the hospital in question is unable to compete on a 'level-playing field' as a result of many factors—such as historical inheritance, including under-investment; the nature of its catchment population; or the attitude of, and available finance from, its main purchasers (commissioners). Indeed it is important to remember more generally that the necessary conditions which lie behind successful 'neo-classical' market competition are highly unlikely to be realised in a public health service, even with effort made by government and regulators (usually at high cost) to bring about those successful conditions. Merely two illustrations follow.

Firstly, NHS hospitals are unlikely to be 'maximisers' ie seeking the highest profit or, in the public sector, surplus. For example, the Board of a hospital whose central mission is to provide specialist and emergency care may decide that it is better to concentrate upon that than to seek to be a 'winner' in the elective choice 'market'. Albert Hirschman (1970) talked of the 'lazy monopolist' which, if it has a market secured through the impossibility of competition, may seek to avoid extra business. Moreover, such a monopolist—or public sector organisation not concerned with profit-maximisation—when faced with a standard tariff price, may allow costs to rise as long as overall loss is avoided. Thus the assumption that competition under a fixed-price business model will lead an NHS hospital to maximise efficiency (i.e. the price-cost differential), creating a surplus which can be used to improve quality, may simply be wrong. Note that this is not because the hospital is venal or knave-like. It is just that it does not see itself as a quasi-private profit maximiser—and why should it? This is the story of many regional specialist hospitals in the English NHS.

Secondly, policy-makers have to decide if the market is a means or an end. If it is a temporary means to achieving what might in a previous age (different ideological regime) have been called planning objectives (e.g. a changed hospital configuration over a region), then if it works 'too quickly', it may not give poor performers which are nevertheless pivotal to the NHS time to improve and become financially viable in the market-place. In a nutshell, the wrong hospitals may close, or important hospitals may become locked into a spiral of financial decline. We have seen this repeatedly in the English NHS in the twenty-first century.

If on the other hand, the market is seen as a permanent source of 'constructive discomfort' (a phrase used at the time by Simon Stevens, adviser to Milburn then Blair between 1999 and 2003, and much later the Chief executive of NHS England from April 2014) then planning objectives are likely to be unrealisable. Throughout all the three main phases of the NHS market (the Conservative 1990s; New Labour; Coalition then Conservative government post-2010), Health Ministers have—rightly—had more pressing priorities than the operation of a textbook-inspired neo-classical market, which in practice they have found to be expensive and disruptive but have usually found themselves unable to admit to be so publicly, for political and ideological reasons. These more pressing priorities are of course the real policy objectives which a rational policy-maker would pursue: the appropriate mix of hospital and community services; appropriate funding for specialist hospitals; integration between preventive NHS care, acute NHS care ,and post-hospital social care; and so on. But the story of permanent revolution in the English NHS has been the story of rational priorities being periodically forced off the agenda, or demoted, as a result of senior managers having to try to digest the latest political confectionery usually without the ideological wrapping having been removed.

The use of limited pseudo-evidence for the market by politicians grateful at least to have some justification for their already-decided policy was graphically illustrated in 2011 by Prime Minister David Cameron during the 'pause' in passage of the Health and Social Care Bill. He trumpeted the LSE study of market choice (Cooper et al. 2011) as justifying the Conservative-led further 'marketisation' of the NHS.

REFERENCES

Alvarez-Rosete, A., et al. (2005). Effect of diverging policy across the NHS. *British Medical Journal, 331*(7522), 946.

Cooper, Z., et al. (2011). Does hospital competition save lives? Evidence from the English NHS patient choice reforms. *The Economic Journal, 121*(August), 228–260.

Greer, S. (2004). *Territorial politics and health policy.* Manchester: Manchester University Press.

Health and Social Services Directorate General (Wales). (2009). *Impact assessment work—NHS reform programnme.* Cardiff: Welsh Assembly Government.

Hirschman, A. (1970). *Exit, voice and loyalty.* Cambridge, MA: Harvard University Press.

Le Grand, J. (2003). *Motivation, agency and public policy.* Oxford: Oxford University Press.

Le Grand, J. (2007). *The other invisible hand.* London: Princeton University Press.

NHS Management Executive (Scotland). (1999). *Health Act Scotland 1999.* Edinburgh.

Peckham, S., et al. (2012). Devolution and patient choice: Policy rhetoric versus experience in practice. *Social Policy and Administration, 46*(2), 199–218.

Propper, C., Burgess, S., & Green, K. (2004). Does competition between hospitals improve the quality of care? Hospital death rates and the NHS internal market. *Journal of Public Economics, 88,* 1247–1272.

Scottish Executive (Scottish government). (1999). *Designed to care* (White Paper), Edinburgh.

Scottish Parliament. (2003). NHS Act. Edinburgh.

Timmins, N. (2012). *Never again.* London: King's Fund and Institute for Government.

Welsh Assembly Government. (2009). *Written cabinet statement by the Welsh Assembly Government.* Cardiff: WAG.

CHAPTER 5

From New Labour's End-Game to Coalition Re-invention of the Wheel

As reform progressed over the decades from the 1980s to the present day, a seemingly superficial but rather revealing trend in policy presentation could also be noted. There was a move away from sober and descriptive presentation of policy through traditional government documents, to glossy documents characterised by warm words, purple prose, and incidentally poor grammar and punctuation—in particular, verb-less slogans rather than sentences. It might be called 'policy by powerpoint'.

In the latter years of New Labour's regime, we had the hubris inherent in departmental papers with titles such as 'World Class Commissioning' (Department of Health 2008), the name allegedly the brainchild of long-time NHS manager Mark Britnell, who was by 2008 the Department of Health's Director of Commissioning and later went on, like so many in the 'market' era, through the revolving-door linking public and private sectors, to sell healthcare 'solutions' back to national healthcare systems. Rather as the audit and inspection of NHS hospital Trusts were often a surrogate for genuine quality initiatives, the World Class Commissioning tick-box was extensive and bewildering: the idea was that commissioners should be 'accredited' as 'fit-for-purpose' (an infamous and continually reappearing NHS phrase which reeked of tautology) just as providers had to be, for example in the exercise conducted by Monitor to 'diagnose' the capacity of Trusts for Foundation status (of which, more just below).

This was a perfectly reasonable aspiration, sponsored by NHS Chief Executive David Nicholson who was even more reasonably worried about

© The Author(s) 2016

C. Paton, *The Politics of Health Policy Reform in the UK*,
DOI 10.1057/978-1-137-47343-1_5

the capacity of 'commissioners' (PCTs up to their final demise in 2012 and then the new Clinical Commissioning Groups) but the devil was in the detail. Indeed, the detail crowded out the strategy and provided a field-day for management consultants selling the 'implementation' of World Class Commissioning to bamboozled PCTs whose first port-of-call was to outsource rather than master.

Indeed it has been a major source of waste in NHS management—whatever the need for high-quality management, which is self-evident—that large amounts of money were spent on major 'leadership and management development' programmes within the NHS, yet the major challenges for leaders and managers in the NHS, especially post-2001, post-2005, and post-2010 (commissioning, commissioning, and commissioning) were outsourced either de facto to management consultants or formally to private organisations. One cannot blame only the politicians for this: senior managers, with honourable exceptions, are very good at keeping hold of 'strategy' and outsourcing the boring bits. This phenomenon of outsourced commissioning applied especially after 2010, when the 2012 Health and Social Care Act gave the formal commissioning power to groups of GPs in Clinical Commissioning Groups and at the same time restricted the amount of CCG money which could be spent directly on management to £25 per head of population. This was a charter for out-sourced private commissioning, either by naivety or intent on the part of policy-makers (with some in each camp.)

TRAMPING FURTHER DOWN THE MARKET ROAD: BLAIR'S LEGACY TO HIS HEIR CAMERON

The Coalition government's NHS White Paper of July 2010, Equity and Excellence (Department of Health 2010) was another example of egregious language attempting to conceal half-baked content. It was produced only two months after the 2010 general election which had made the Conservatives the largest party yet failed to produce an overall majority—hence the Coalition with the Liberal Democrats. The road to this policy initiative can be separated into three sections: firstly, the way in which it did or did not build on what had gone before; secondly, the peculiar politics behind, and embodied in, the White Paper itself, and the road from that to the 2012 Act; and thirdly, the Health and Social Care Act of 2012 itself, the final resting-place of the 2010 White Paper. Regarding the second of these three, the political emergence of the 2010 White Paper has been dramatically and brilliantly described by Timmins (2012), and therefore that part of the road will be discussed and analysed principally in terms of the origins and implications of the White Paper as regards actual health policy, and the road from it to the 2012 Act.

In this chapter, I consider those aspects of Labour's pre-2010 policy upon which the 2010 Coalition White Paper, Equity and Excellence, built, and in the next, I consider that White Paper's travails and the eventual emergence of the 2012 Health and Social Care Act.

New Labour as Lansley Lead-in?

So what had gone before? I have waited to consider some key aspects of New Labour's 'reform' policy here, in order to relate the most market-oriented initiatives to what followed under first Coalition (2010–15) then solely Conservative (post-2015) government. In particular I refer to the Foundation Trust (FT) policy and relations with the private sector—from contracting with private providers to the Private Finance Initiative.

Foundation Trusts: A Foundation Built on Sand?

The FT policy was—at a stretch of the sympathetic imagination—a rational accompaniment to, or component of, the new market announced in 2002. In other words, it was seeking to ensure that this new type of organisation, called Foundation after Alan Milburn had learned of the 'Fondazione' model giving some hospitals so-called autonomy within the Spanish NHS, would be a lean, mean machine capable of competing effectively in a revived market-place.

But there was a puzzle. Had not hospitals been made into 'Self-Governing Trusts', between 1991 and 1993 in 'three waves', to give them exactly the operating freedoms which the new FTs were supposedly going to have? Well, yes. But the arational part of policy was about signalling and initiative(–itis). This would concentrate minds wonderfully, it was believed. To be fair, it could be argued that the freedoms for 'Self-Governing Trusts' as advertised at the beginning of the Thatcher reforms had never been realised, and indeed that those which had had soon been whittled away as governments, and the Treasury, sought control. What was absent from the FT initiative was any hard-headed analysis of why control was reasserted, in order to prevent recent history repeating itself. In truth, some of it was natural governmental control-freakery but some was a necessary attempt by managers to keep the healthcare system coordinated, that is, to do the implementation which did not interest headline-seeking politicians.

The FT policy was unpopular in the parliamentary Labour Party (what was Labour doing relaunching the Thatcher reforms with additional bells and whistles?), but this was (Iraq excepted, and the fallout from that had not yet seriously weakened Blair) Blair's second-term high-noon, and the policy was passed with an admittedly narrow majority, given New Labour's huge majority in parliament, in 2003. Yet even this was only achieved when Brown—who had angrily opposed the policy in a long and detailed memorandum to Cabinet—called off his parliamentary dogs after a compromise with Blair which Milburn felt (with justification, whatever one thinks of the policy) emasculated the policy. If this was the Self-Governing Trust story all over again, with the emasculation even before parliamentary passage this time, then what was the point?

The original intention had been quite radical. When asked in a private meeting in 2003 what the difference was between the Thatcher internal market and New Labour's reforms, Milburn's special adviser Paul Corrigan replied revealingly, 'We're serious; they weren't.' The aim was that FTs could raise capital from high street banks outside the Treasury process, decide their service-mix within certain limits and be governed outside the NHS structure altogether. Another revealing answer to a question, at the same time, in the Department of Health, showing both the potentially radical nature of the policy yet also the confusion within the top echelons of the bureaucracy as to exactly what it meant, came when—an hour apart, separately—the Permanent Secretary and NHS Chief Executive, Nigel Crisp, and the Chief Nursing Officer, Sarah Mulally, were both asked if FT would be part of the NHS. 'No,' said Mulally. 'Yes,' said Crisp.

After the Blair-Brown compromise, FTs were no longer allowed to raise capital independently of Treasury limits; were restricted as to the private income they could raise to a small percentage of their whole income; and were clearly NHS FTs subject to some of the regulatory machinery passed down from the Department of Health to the Strategic Health Authority, including targets (although formally they were regulated by Monitor, a new quango created for this purpose, which some wags suggested should be called, after the energy and other economic regulators (Ofwat, Ofcom, et al), 'Offsick'.

Their governance structure sent contradictory signals. On the one hand, they were supposed to be nimble market competitors. On the other hand, they were to have governing bodies which were composed of local stakeholders and citizens, who could pay one pound annually to become a 'member' of their local FT. The model in the minds of government advisers such as Corrigan was the Nationwide Building Society, and maybe the old friendly societies: these were non-profit but also, of course, private. There was a lot of naivety here. People in general did not want to govern, let alone help run, their local health service 'providers'; they paid taxes so that professionals (executives) could do that, and lay experts (non-executives) could oversee the process. New Labour sought to appeal to the older 'community self-organisation' ethos of pre-statist Labour, in an attempt to go beyond the pointy-head neo-liberals to appeal to a wider Labour constituency. Beyond this, Ministers and MPs actually believed their own rhetoric. In a different context, former Tory Health Secretary Kenneth Clarke, when asked what the difference was between Conservative health reforms and Labour's, perceptively remarked that his lot didn't believe their own rhetoric but Labour did.

The problem was that an FT could not be free to make unpopular decisions in a tough market with limited resources (e.g. to disinvest in services or change strategy) yet also be the creature of local activists or interests, that is, risk being 'stakeheld to death'. This also mirrored what had been a problem with the original Self-Governing Trusts: the concept 'sounded' as if it promoted business efficiency but the reality was that it was easier to reconfigure district and regional services—according to changing needs, the search for better quality and also economies of scale—if hospitals were not preserved in aspic as formally autonomous 'self-governing' organisations with their own governing structure and, at least in the short and medium terms, a veto upon change.

Add in a third dimension—the need to collaborate both with other hospitals and with other NHS organisations to ensure that services developed appropriately—and the FT policy was an ill-thought out mess. Later evaluations suggested that there was no significant difference between FTs and hospitals which were not FTs in terms of quality and/or economic performance, and that any slight difference in the latter probably reflected the situation before FT status had been granted (a similar result to an earlier evaluation of the productivity of Self-Governing Trusts and directly managed hospitals in the early days of the 1990s internal market.) Later data, from 2008 to date, on excessive hospital mortality, sought in the wake of the Stafford hospital crisis, revealed a fair proportion of FTs on the danger list.

Additionally, implementing both the 'payment by results' tariff as a means of reimbursing FTs in practice (and hospitals in general in theory) and the FT policy prevented 'integrated' reimbursement for 'integrated' patient care, as noted above.

A DANGEROUS FT FALLOUT

The FT policy came back to bite Labour in another way too, although it was not acknowledged as such and probably still is not. There was significant pressure from Ministers and therefore the 'top of the office' in the Department of Health (what used to be called the NHS Executive but latterly was called the management group) upon the Strategic Health Authorities to 'find' as many FTs as possible. There was a diagnostic process for such, intended for Trusts which had gained three stars in the star-rating system which operated from 2001 to 2005/6 but by 2005 extended to other Trusts as well. To turn down a request to go down this road if 'asked' was what Sir Humphrey Appleby of 'Yes Minister' fame would have called 'a brave decision' for a hospital Board. Among those launched on the process was the Mid Staffordshire NHS Trust which in four consecutive years had acquired 2, 3, 0, and 1 stars respectively.

Add in the mission to break even, and indeed acquire a working surplus, after the NHS deficit crisis (it was a political crisis, given the extent of the additional resource in real terms for the NHS, even if—at this stage, ten years before the unravelling of NHS finances on a different scale—it was financially recoverable for most if not all Trusts). Add further the pressure to meet the prevailing government 'access' (waiting-time) targets. For many hospitals, this created pressure to restrict recruitment and cut nursing staff in particular.

It does not require huge ingenuity, or even hindsight, to see that such pressure would in turn put pressure upon quality, not at this stage a 'P45' matter in the annual governance review. This is not to excuse a Board's behaviour in handling such pressures, but it is to explain it. The NHS at this time operated with a culture of fear in some quarters, and the national Chief Executive, David Nicholson, appointed in summer 2005, was seen as a tough operator. He had the misfortune of having overseen Mid Staffs first as Regional Director of Health and Social Care for Midlands and Eastern region, 2001—2002, and then, more significantly as Chief Executive of three merging West Midlands Strategic Health Authorities, including the Shropshire and Staffordshire SHA, from August 2005 to Spring 2006. In this role he oversaw not only the Stafford hospital but also its application for FT status.

Both Monitor and the Care Quality Commission (the Health Care Commission's successor) were rightly criticised both for being myopic and having failed to collaborate in inspecting hospitals. Monitor was only supposed to recommend the granting of FT status if a hospital was excellent in the round—not just in financial control. Its failure over Mid Staffs was spectacular, as was the Health Care Commission/Care Quality Commission (HCC/CQC). Even as a special investigation by the latter into Mid Staffs was beginning in 2008, its regular inspection arm was accrediting it as good, and Monitor granted it FT status only days before the 'alarm' was raised formally over alleged 'excess deaths.' For its part, the SHA and Nicholson were accused of being asleep at the wheel, by medic Phil Hammond, Private Eye's health correspondent, now as often a more perceptive commentator on the NHS than even the specialist press and health management weeklies—although driving in the wrong direction might have been a more apt characterisation.

There were three government-ordered reviews of Mid Staffs along the road to the Independent Inquiry called by the government chaired by Robert Francis QC—by the CQC; by the Department of Health's former Emergency Care Director, George Alberti (one of New Labour's 'Tsars', that is, National Clinical Directors, in charge of emergency care); and by the GP David Colin-Thome. These all focussed upon the hospital itself, and missed a lot of the context, but the subsequent Public Inquiry, ordered by Andrew Lansley after Labour lost office in May 2010 and also chaired by Francis, rightly investigated the external relationships, that is, the management, regulatory, and supervisory environment (Public Inquiry 2013).

The Coalition government after 2010 blamed the 'target culture' for much in the NHS it inherited, including Mid Staffs. Interestingly, after the Conservatives won power in their own right in 2015, Monitor was merged with the development body for non-FTs, the Trust Development Authority, into a new body called NHS Improvement, which seemed to be a de facto recognition that the theology of the market was no longer quite so central.

What else may we interpret as being a Blairite forerunner to the 2010 White Paper? Top of the list must be tendering for contracts to provide services. There is also the Private Finance Initiative (originally adopted and adapted by New Labour from Conservative Chancellor Norman Lamont's initiative in 1990, and in 2010 returned to its original Conservative owners), and the aspiration to situate commissioning more centrally in GP-land.

One might add patient-held budgets as a source of continuity between New Labour and subsequent governments, but these have not developed to be a significant part of the system overall despite achieving some prominence in long-term care for those with chronic conditions where future need can be predicted. One of the problems—quite apart from patients not having adequate knowledge of options in general medical care as opposed to very specific chronic conditions—is that devolving budgets to individual patients would prevent the spreading of risk (statistical and actual) across large enough populations to allow the system to be tenable. Whether a system is called 'insurance' or 'population-based healthcare funding', which individuals are going to need the care, and therefore the money, is unknown (except for those with defined needs with a clear and predictable clinical prognosis). Therefore devolving budgets to individuals generally would mean an end to needs-based funding—and some individuals unable to pay the cost of their care alongside others allocated too much funding. This is not to deny that involving well-informed and willing individual patients with defined long-term conditions in choosing their provider or, more importantly, type of care, may be valuable. But this is a long way from the ideological roll-out of patient budgets as far as possible. Furthermore, the latter would make (and is making, where it is happening) an already-complicated and expensive contracting landscape more complicated and more expensive.

PATIENT CHOICE VERSUS COMMISSIONER CONTRACTS

The emergence of 'patient choice', implemented through the 'Choose and Book' technology situated in the GP's surgery, did not of itself mean competitive tendering for contracts awarded to hospitals, community, and mental health providers. Indeed logically, if the patient and GP were to choose where to send the patient for secondary care, then it was incoherent or redundant for NHS agencies such as the PCT 'commissioners' to contract with such providers.

Contracts are by definition one of three different types. Most likely, they are an agreement to pay for a set number of people to be treated at a particular institution, albeit with the possibility of variation in that number. This is a 'cost and volume' contract. If a contract is for a large sum of money with no patient numbers specified, that is, is with a provider whom the commissioner sees as its main provider for that service, then that is a 'block' contract. Thirdly, there is the 'cost per case' contract, which tells the provider how much will be paid for each case. New Labour's 'choice market' included a nationally agreed tariff, that is, set of fixed prices for each type of case.

Therefore local contracts which simply agreed prices without stipulating numbers were redundant. The only reason they continued were that, whatever they were called, they were in fact cost and volume, or modified cost and volume, contracts, whereby total numbers were restricted. In other words, despite the rhetoric of referral by GPs to any provider chosen by the patient (after 2008; a choice of four or five up until then) for any service which the NHS offered, the reality was that there was not enough money in the system for this to happen. As a result, it was up to local managers and Boards to agree how to restrict referral, usually through little-known organisations such as 'referral centres' which mediated GPs' requests. What is fairly astonishing is that Ministers such as Patricia Hewitt (Health Secretary 2005–7) did not even absorb the implications of these necessary compromises: they genuinely believed their own rhetoric.

Over time, the tension between free referral and commissioner-provider contracting was settled with the latter generally, if not always, winning. Even after 2008, choice was 'managed choice'. If enough patients had sought to buck the system, that is, had sought in significant number to go to hospitals where commissioner-provider contracts did not exist, or did not exist to an adequate extent, then the system would have collapsed. The only reason it did not was that free choice in theory did not become free choice in practice, and also because patients and GPs behaved conservatively—a rare example of the 'forces of conservatism' saving Blairism!

What this meant was that England, despite its rhetoric (distinct from Scotland, Wales, and Northern Ireland) of the market, the consumer and individual patient choice, was actually pretty similar to the rest of the UK as regards the patient's mode of referral: it was a compromise between the individual, the GP, the funding of providers (called 'contracts' in England and simply allocations elsewhere) and indeed the technology.

It was only in a speech in July 2015 that Health Secretary Jeremy Hunt boasted that new technology, replacing 'Choose and Book', would enable more effective choice. He was referring to information about waiting-times and also the rating of the hospital by the CQC. But now as the, choice was not choice of the particular clinician, that is, usually a hospital consultant—it was choice of hospital or other provider. The CQC information was institution-wide, moreover. So it was not possible to know if one was choosing a bad department in a good hospital, or indeed vice versa—let alone to choose the particular doctor of one's choice. It was a bit like a school-leaver choosing a 'top' university without realising that he would never see the academics who had given it that rating.

Therefore we were back to purchaser (commissioner)/provider contracting as the mainstay of the system. New Labour expected commissioners to invite tenders but did not make such tendering statutorily compulsory for (nearly) all services, as did the 2012 Act. When after 2012 Shadow Health Secretary Andy Burnham, the former Health Secretary ('a shadow of my former self', as he joked) attacked the Coalition for privatisation, it was true but a bit rich: they had simply taken New Labour's stance a step further: it was evolution, not revolution, in policy, although pursued through yet another root-and-branch reorganisation which was revolutionary rather than evolutionary as regards management structures.

The Private Finance Initiative (PFI)

The PFI also was even more central to New Labour's hospital rebuilding programme than it was under subsequent Coalition and Conservative governments—principally because, by 2010, the bulk of the rebuilding was by then completed or underway. So there too, this highly uneconomical and inefficient means of providing 'jam today and pain tomorrow' saw at most a cigarette paper between Labour and the Tories. It had not always been thus. Labour had opposed the PFI in opposition, from its genesis in 1990 up to the replacement of Margaret Beckett as Shadow Health Secretary not so long after a particularly revealing event in 1995, described below.

Clearly the PFI was not a health-specific policy, but an economy-wide strategy for keeping public investment off the national accounts, and just as significantly for other purposes. If the aim was solely to prevent public investment in hospitals, roads, and schools from counting towards the Public Sector Borrowing Requirement, the easier way to do this would have been to distinguish between current account public expenditure and national investment, as many other countries do in their national accounts. Gordon Brown after all was the Chancellor who loved to talk about investment even when he meant only current expenditure. So either there was a tunnel-vision or else a hidden agenda.

There was of course a desire to avoid funding new hospitals and facilities generally through increased taxation or by 'printing money', that is, making money available to banks and then the economy through cheap loans from the central bank. New Labour had after all tied itself to the Chariot Wheels not only of an independent central Bank of England but also of a promise not to raise taxes. So if it also diagnosed the public sector estate as crumbling and neglected, which it was after 18 years of Conservative government (and indeed an economically straitjacketed Labour government in the 1970s), then it had to find another way.

Just as significant as the self-imposed rigidities of the Public Sector Borrowing Requirement (PSBR) accounting system (or Brown's desire not to tinker with it at the risk of seeming to want to spend like the mythologised 'Old Labour') was another reason for Labour adopting the PFI—the age-old political desire to provide goodies while postponing the cost. This was a microcosm of New Labour's wider political economy after 2000, when its strategy was to rely on a global capitalist boom and the role of British banks therein to spread mortgages and cash to the not-so-well-off without taxing the better-off except through minor stealth taxation such as the increase in National Insurance to fund some of the NHS budget's expansion. This 'end to boom and bust' was another example of self-delusion by politicians, misinterpreting the entry of India, China, Brazil, and the former Soviet-dominated Eastern bloc into the world economy as a kind of economic Kantian 'perpetual peace'.

So the PFI was jam today. Unfortunately the postponed pain was even worse than had been suggested by the PFI's detractors—which included the former Deputy Director of the National Audit Office, who described the calculations which allowed the PFI always to seem a better deal than the 'public sector alternative' as 'mumbo-jumbo' going on to say that if the calculations came out wrong, you didn't get your new hospital, so they always came out right! By the time of the financial crash of 2008, when real interests rates became negative, what had already been a thoroughly bad deal became a ruinous deal.

In essence the PFI meant that, instead of the government using its large-scale power to borrow, private financial vehicles were created by business consortia to borrow on the open market in order to finance the new hospitals and other developments, and they were to be paid back over a time-frame of typically 30 years from the (annual recurring) revenue budgets of NHS hospitals. This meant that NHS commissioners' allocations to these hospitals were substantially reduced in terms of the costs of actually running services. As well as borrowing at worse rates than any sensible government could have procured, substantial profit was written into the payback, and the assumed rate of interest, always higher than the market rate, was written into the contracts. After 2008, this rate of interest was pie-in-the-sky at 6%, as compared with the zero or negative prevailing rates in the economy.

Even minus the later financial crash, this policy had always been correctly seen as a bad deal by Labour pre-Blair. And then when Conservative Prime Minister John Major's PFI adviser Sheila Masters, who was au fait with the NHS as she had been seconded there as Director of Finance in the late 1980s, announced arrogantly (or was it presciently?) that Labour would retain the PFI in the NHS, the Shadow Health Secretary, at the urging of a few of us, it should be said, denied this and metaphorically slapped down Dame Sheila. But this was to fall foul of the emerging New Labour orthodoxy embodied in Blair and—on this issue—especially Brown, and Beckett, the sharpest Labour spokesman since Robin Cook, who had been succeeded after the 1992 election by David Blunkett, was replaced first by Harriet Harman and then Chris Smith, neither of whom mastered (pardon the pun) the brief to anything like the same extent.

THE ROAD TO THE 2010 WHITE PAPER: GP COMMISSIONING AND MARKET PROVISION

Labour had started by abolishing GP Fund-holding, announced in 1995, in the policy paper 'Renewing the NHS' (Labour Party 1995) repeated in the 1997 manifesto, and accomplished in stages between 1997 and 1999. By 2007, it had not come full circle—the 'Practice Based Commissioners' (Curry et al. 2008) were a damp squib and fell between the two stools of traditional NHS bureaucracy, on the one hand (they were accountable to the PCT), and real decentralised power, on the other hand—but had rather pusillanimously and expensively reasserted the alleged merit of GP commissioning. Indeed the nearest Health Secretary Hewitt came, when asked in 2007 to apologise for New Labour's expensive reorganisation-itis over 10 years, to doing so was to say that her party should have recognised the merit of GP commissioning sooner. As ever, there was no evidence to justify this, but it sounded anti-statist and New Labour-esque, as well as supposedly bringing decisions about care closer to the patient.

This was very close to what had increasingly come to obsess Andrew Lansley. He was appointed Shadow Health Secretary in 2004 to replace the abrasive and unpopular 'privatiser' Liam Fox. Fox's main contribution to policy had been to propose tax-allowances for the purchase of private insurance, a throwback to the debates in the early stages of the Thatcher Review in 1988, themselves a throwback to the review by Thatcher's first

Social Services (then including Health) Secretary Patrick Jenkin of alternative systems to the NHS in 1981–83 (McLachlan and Maynard 1982). After the 2005 general election, Cameron became Tory leader and set about trying to 'detoxify' the Tory 'brand' in order to remove the image of the 'nasty' party. His predecessor since Iain Duncan Smith's ill-fated leadership collapsed in 2003, Michael Howard, was part of the cause of that impression, fairly or unfairly—the man with 'something of the night' about him, according to his deputy when he was Home Secretary in the 1990s, Anne Widdecombe. Yet even Howard saw that Fox's approach to the NHS was politically unacceptable and he replaced him with Lansley.

The latter was quite sincere in wanting to bring the patient, or at least what he saw as the patient's advocate in primary care, the GP, more centre-stage, and his starting-point was this rather than privatisation. His sincerity gradually won him some plaudits in the NHS community. Yet he had not gone wholly soft, from the viewpoint of the Right. Although he was no longer the Thatcherite Head of the Conservative Research Department or the right-wing adviser who had previously been a private secretary to one of the founders of Thatcherism Norman Tebbit, he also wanted much more of a market in provision. He was therefore seemingly an ideal choice to appeal to different elements of the party, and to at least some branches of what he saw as the NHS family.

Yet this is a phrase which ignores to its peril the fact that most families are dysfunctional, and Lansley may have overestimated his political capital as a result of a benign hearing from unrepresentative 'reform' minded GPs and that tiny minority of hospital doctors who were attracted by the ideas of the neo-liberal think-tank Reform which set up a branch entitled Doctors for Reform. Most of these doctors—as ever, ferociously bright but distinctly naive when wading into political waters—did not realise that Reform's agenda was hostile to the NHS, and that it faced both ways when asked whether it wanted to replace, reform, or supplement the funding of the NHS. Thus, despite the extent to which Lansley worked assiduously to learn from the NHS over six years before becoming Health Secretary, it was misleading to think that he had given up on his right-wing inheritance.

Yet by 2010, he was widely believed to have 'gone native', very much in tune with David Cameron's promise in the Conservative 2010 manifesto not to entertain any 'top-down reorganisation' of the NHS. How wrong could so many people be? Or rather, how could significant continuity in policy from New Labour's tenure, which indeed there was, be sidetracked by root-and-branch reorganisation?

THE LANSLEY LEGACY

The Conservative manifesto for health and the NHS in 2010 was not radical, and indeed boasting of such—promising 'no top-down reorganisation' of the NHS. The Liberal Democrats came up with their usual fare concerning greater democracy in health authorities (by now PCTs). When the election result led to a Coalition government with the Conservatives as senior partner and the Liberal democrats as junior, a 'Coalition agreement' was drawn up in the weeks following the May election. This Coalition agreement led to a policy on the NHS which was both technically and politically incoherent, and this has been explained well by Nick Timmins.

This reflected a kind of negligence by Cameron, who as new Prime Minister admittedly had plenty on his plate, and perhaps also by Nick Clegg, the Liberal Democrat Deputy Prime Minister, who equally had some excuse. Perhaps more culpable however were the two colleagues asked to review emerging policy on behalf of Cameron and Clegg—Oliver Letwin for the Tories and Danny Alexander for the Liberal Democrats. Letwin was the son of William and Shirley Robin Letwin, both right-wing political theorists, a man with a rarified approach, a track record of gaffes (one of which had seen him banished from sight during the 2005 election campaign) and a previous memorable tribute by eminent political journalist, the late Alan Watkins, as 'educated out of his wits'. Danny Alexander's previous job before entering parliament as tourism officer for the Cairngorms National Park in Scotland. So, without cynicism, the prospects were not good for an expert, and politically savvy, judgement about health policy.

The rest is history. The self-contradictory Coalition agreement on health policy had to be rewritten, and Lansley seized his opportunity to produce what he really wanted without messy compromise as he saw it. Lansley has been described by Danny Finkelstein of The Times, also a Conservative peer and Lansley's former staffer at the Conservative Research Department, as a most unusual politician—a steamroller rather than a compromiser and interested in policy rather than politics (ironic, given the reception afforded his White Paper.) As he beavered away, this was the stage at which Letwin and Alexander could have turned the signal red. But the opportunity was missed and the White Paper was not only published before 2010 was out but also co-signed by Cameron and Clegg.

The White Paper proposed the total abolition of all agencies below the level of the Department of Health—the PCTs, the Strategic Health Authorities, and the Regional Offices. The Department of Health management group (the NHS executive) would be wound up and an NHS Board established outside the Department—something which *had* been trailed in a 2007 policy paper from the Conservatives (Conservative Party 2007) and also in the Conservative manifesto. This was an attempt to take politics out of the management of the NHS, a perennial chestnut regularly proposed over the years by the King's Fund and others, and of course tracing its pedigree back to the 1983 Griffiths Report.

Most of the NHS budget (at this stage, it was stated 80%, although later scaled down to 60% when the hasty policy was given a little more thought) would go to GP commissioning groups, with PCTs wholly abolished. Putting GPs at the centre of the process—yet again!—had also been lauded, it should be said, in the same 2007 paper, but at the time those who paid attention (not many) assumed this meant either a reaffirmation of the primary care presence on PCT management executives or simply Tory endorsement of the 'Practice Based Commissioning' which had become Hewitt's apology for a big idea—and nothing was said to disabuse them of this assumption.

Thus, in terms of governance and control, there would be the Department of Health making policy overall and commissioning specialist services (about 20% of the budget, it was assumed at this stage) and nothing other than GP groups which would now be statutory, it was assumed, although whether and how this was possible was not made clear. Putting 80% of the NHS budget of about £100 billion at this stage in the hands of GPs who were not even NHS employees but independent contractors was strange, to understate the case, and hugely irresponsible, without necessarily overstating the case.

Crucially, the most controversial aspect of the proposal was in terms of policy, For sure, the fact that an unnecessary reorganisation was proposed was controversial—one so big, according to NHS Chief Executive David Nicholson, that one could 'see it from outer space', directly contradicting Lansley's ludicrous protestation that it was not a 'top-down reorganisation'. But the privatisation, or scope for it, implied in the mandatory tendering for clinical services and, to underpin it, the removal of the Department of Health's statutory obligation to provide or secure a service—opened the door to political rejection of the White Paper as it stood, given that the Conservatives were not in government alone (see Chap. 6 below).

Was any of this justifiable—not in terms of evidence, of which there was none and could not really be any, with such a new approach, but in terms of a diagnosis of what had gone wrong in the past—in other words, judgement. For the demand for 'evidence' by academics, it must be said, can sometimes be a little po-faced: the essence of an innovation, whether clinical or managerial or policy-wise, is that conclusive evidence by definition cannot exist. That is why 'pilot projects' are often called for by academic and less ideological policy-makers.

But to bend over backwards to be fair to politicians, pilot projects may be atypical of what might later be generalised, or 'rolled out' in the infamous NHS jargon seeking to convey a business mentality. To extend the jargon and use a later vogue term in the NHS, a 'pathfinder' may be a poor indication of the nature or quality of the path later taken. It can work both ways. In 1989, Health Secretary Ken Clarke scoffed when asked if he would 'pilot' the internal market and its 'purchaser/provider split', replying, 'What? And have the BMA and the press crawling all over it' (it being the chosen region for the pilot). In other words a pilot could fail despite the policy being good. More likely of course in the 'control freak' age we now live in would be the opposite: the evaluation of a 'pathfinder' pilot project would be set up to demonstrate success.

Either way, the legitimate criticism of Lansley was not that he failed to 'pilot' his policy but that he moved from a largely correct diagnosis to a disastrous prognosis. The diagnosis had lots of insight. At the risk of sounding arrogant, let me put words into Lansley's mouth to make his *apologia pro policia sua* sound better than it did: New Labour, in its perpetual itchy-fingered 're-disorganisations' (the lovely term coined by Professor Alan Maynard), had actually accumulated a very cumbersome set of commissioning institutions and had, moreover, complicated the purchaser/provider split. Both the 'one off' costs of each reorganisation and the recurring costs of the management arrangements were much higher than they need be.

So far, both Tories and the Left who wished to abolish the purchaser/provider split could agree, leaving New Labour in a muddle in the middle uneasily holding a very expensive baby. Indeed the House of Commons Select Committee on Health produced two reports, in 2010 and 2011, which pointed to the exorbitant cost of 'commissioning' and indeed, under the chairmanship first of Labour MP Kevin Barron and subsequently the former Conservative Health Secretary Stephen Dorrell, actually cast some doubt on the validity of the 'purchaser/provider' split—tentatively, but significantly: this was the first 'mainstream' questioning of the trajectory of reform since 1991, when maverick Tory MP Nicholas Winterton had chaired the same committee and opposed the break-up of health Districts into 'purchasers and providers.' The Committee in its 2010 report quoted a York study of 2005 (Bloor et al. 2005) implying that the administrative costs of the NHS were 14%, as opposed to 5% in the early 1980s, assumed to be not unrelated to the structure and content of 'reform', to put it mildly.

Of course such an assumption was not uncontested, and to lay it all at the door of 'commissioning', as the report seemingly did, was clumsy: it was the whole panoply of reform (and, to be fair, an increased need for information—but this latter factor only explained a little). But a later report by Paton (2014), despite being based on conservative estimates, suggested that the reforms subsequent to 2005 had worsened the problem, not made it better.

So Lansley was onto something. But his solution in turn was analytically flawed and politically inept, although by the time of the 2015 election this probably did not hurt the Conservatives much if at all, and certainly less that they feared at the time.

The problem pre-2010 was that a succession of 'reforms', variously intended to promote technical efficiency, choice, and more appropriate care (what economists might call 'allocative efficiency'), had been very expensive and in many cases failed wholly in their objectives. New Labour had confused permanent change and 'constructive discomfort' with business efficiency: it seemed that the Blairites did not recognise that stability and calm improvement was the hallmark of most successful business. Yes, there would be times of rupture and change, but when necessary, not obsessively.

The term 'public service reform' had become a totem rather than a possibility to be considered critically—for both Labour and the Conservatives. The content was de facto less important than the concept: whenever a reform to the NHS failed, the answer was always 'public service reform', with the previous reform reinterpreted conveniently as the status quo, or the conservative past. Much of the media, especially leading articles in *The Times*, regularly saw 'market reform' as the answer without realising or acknowledging that 'market reform' had often been the problem. It is of course possible logically that it was an answer to at least some problem but had been mishandled or not implemented enough. But this was not the case. For example, it was as a result of a contentious piece of research on New Labour's market that Conservative PM David Cameron claimed in 2011 that 'competition worked' (Cooper et al, op.cit). So the alleged problems identified by *The Times* and others (lack of adequate productivity;

not enough sensitivity to patients) required both critical investigation and critical analysis of potential solutions to those problems which were indeed problems. Instead 'public service reform' became a mantra.

This is not just an academic point. In assessing New Labour's over-all record on the NHS, it is undoubtedly true that many good things happened. But these were mostly as a result of significant funding increases, for which New Labour deserves credit for arranging and secur-ing consensus around them which bound the Tories in to endorsing them (until the banking and financial 'crash' in 2008–9 changed everything). As a crude but useful generalisation, about half of New Labour's extra money improved services either in terms of access or quality. The other half was wasted—*not,* as the marketeers and privatisers would have it, because there was not enough market or privatisation, but because of the crippling cost of waves of redundant reform (most of which was 'market reform'.) The official—authoritative but 'sympathetic'—multi-part evaluation of New Labour's 'market reforms' commissioned by the Department of Health's own Policy Research programme concluded that they had not done any direct harm and that the costs of the reforms were unknown (Mays et al. 2001). This was hardly a suggestion of value for money. By 'sympathetic' I mean that the research was of integrity but restricted by the official remit to consider particular aspects of the reforms without challenging the over-all direction of travel.

If the Conservatives had wanted to build on Cameron's critique of Labour's NHS record, which he made perceptively in 2006 and 2007 concerning the ever-decreasing circles of Labour's redundant reorgan-isations, and consolidate their improved reputation on the NHS (with Cameron's personal experience of the NHS making his praise of it sin-cere), then they could have confounded expectations. They could have in effect said: we believe in the market in general but there are areas of public service where the costs outweigh the benefits. But in the end such a reversal of the orthodoxy since the internal market, that 'more market' was 'the answer', was a bridge too far.

This stance—opposing 'marketisation' in public services for hard-headed rather than traditionally left-wing reasons - was left for the UK Independence Party (UKIP), which in 2015 came out against the PFI, for example. This was not because its leader Nigel Farage had read left-wing critic Allyson Pollock's stinging critique of privatisation (Pollock 2005), but was for those hard-headed reasons: their leader Farage, with his expe-rience of the City, knew where the bodies were buried and how the City was profiting excessively, egregiously and otiosely from the NHS. There were overtones here of lawyer Ken Clarke refusing, as Health Secretary, to allow the new internal market's purchaser/provider 'contracts' to be legal contracts, as he of all people knew that the legal profession would dine out on the proceeds and that the more naive neo-classical 'pro market' economists would get a nasty shock. Below (Chap. 10), I sketch the possible contours of a 'new NHS politics' which gets the NHS off the hook of 'public service reform' for its own sake, as a slogan without coherent content, and yet avoids the conventional 'left' and 'right' pigeon-holes in the NHS debate.

Meanwhile, back in 2010, in what a couple of the more irreverent commentators were calling La-La-Lansley Land, the Conservatives were 'stuck' with the Lansley proposals, which had grown from a partly correct diagnosis to a harmful prescription.

References

Bloor, K., et al. (2005). *NHS management and administration staffing and expenditure in a national and international context.* York University, unpublished (embargoed by the Department of Health).

Conservative Party. (2007). *NHS autonomy and accountability: Proposals for legislation.* London: Conservative Party. www.conservatives.com/pdf/NHSautonomyandaccountability.pdf.

Curry, N., et al. (2008). *Practice-based commissioning: Reinvigorate, replace, or abandon?* London: King's Fund.

DoH. (2008). *Next steps review: Final report (the 'Darzi' report).* London: DoH.

DoH. (2010). *Equity and excellence.* London: DoH.

Labour Party. (1995). *Renewing the NHS.* London: The Labour Party.

Mays, N., et al. (2011). *The purchasing of health care by primary care organizations.* Buckingham: Open University Press.

McLachlan, G., & Maynard, A. (Eds.). (1982). *The public/private mix for health.* London: Nuffield Trust.

Paton, C. (2014). At What Cost? London: Centre for Health and the Public Interest (CHPI); www.chpi.org

Pollock, A. (2005). *NHS Plc: The privatisation of our healthcare.* London: Verso.

Public Inquiry. (2013). *Report of the mid Staffordshire NHS foundation trust public inquiry (the Francis report).* London: The Stationery Office.

Timmins, N. (2012). *Never again.* London: King's Fund and Institute for Government.

CHAPTER 6

From the 2010 White Paper to the 2012 Health and Social Care Act

When the White Paper had been published, the reaction was dismay throughout the English NHS. If the aphorism, that a fool learns from his own mistakes but a wise man learns from the mistakes of others, is true, then Scotland, Wales, and Northern Ireland must have been feeling wise. For the English government, or rather the UK government administering the English NHS, had not even deigned to learn from its own mistakes, by accident rather than design. Previous reorganisations based on idealistic new policy visions had ended up losing the vision (or worse, discovering it led to dystopia) yet had ended up costing the NHS dearly in terms of both actual costs and the effort expended on reforming structures, with all the fallout, rather than tackling the substantive healthcare agenda.

CORPORATISM BY THE BACK DOOR?

The management community, not without its self-interest in cementing its myriad roles in the new NHS but in the main simply reacting to what it saw as a juggernaut of 're-disorganisation', was pessimistic but fatalistic. As ever at such times, the NHS lost a lot of talent (House of Commons Select Committee on Health 2011). At least this time the aim was to reduce the number of managers-qua-managers, unlike (say) in 2001–2, when the Shifting the Balance reform had caused the commissioning landscape to replicate itself like the fast-multiplying little brushes trying hopelessly to manage, but ending up creating a flood of chaos in Emperor Mickey Mouse's absence, in *Disney's Fantasia*. In 2001, the new PCTs were so

© The Author(s) 2016   85
C. Paton, *The Politics of Health Policy Reform in the UK,*
DOI 10.1057/978-1-137-47343-1_6

numerous that there was a dearth of managers who were 'up to the job' of running them, not least given the new PCT structure's inadequacies as discussed above. Now, the NHS could afford wastage in terms of numbers, although it could ill-afford the cost of the large severance packages.

Hospital doctors were generally dismayed, but pretty fatalistic too. The Royal Colleges and the BMA were opposed. But in the twenty years since the Thatcher–Clarke reform initiative of 1988–90, the death of 'corporatism' had been confirmed: policy-making was seen even less now as a matter for securing agreement between the 'great interests' of business or management, trade unions or professional organisations and the state. As a result, the opposition of the medical profession, which had got a bloody nose from Ken Clarke in 1989–90, mattered less, at first, although when the Conservatives faced a rebellion by their Coalition partners, the Liberal Democrats, the resulting 'pause' in the legislative process atypically opened some doors for professional interests. Other staff professional associations and trade unions, representing nurses, other clinical grades, and ancillary workers, were wholly opposed—to the extent that it mattered. UNISON, the second largest trade union, was traditionally the main health service union, having emerged from a merger in the early 1990s of National Union of Public Employees (NUPE), Confederation of Health Service Employees (COHSE), and National Association of Local Government Officers (NALGO), and still is in terms of NHS numbers, but in recent years the spearhead of more thoroughgoing opposition to 'market reform' has come from UNITE, the country's largest union.

In GP-land, however, there was the usual small but vocal and nationally well-connected minority of 'reform junkies'. Even since GP Fundholding, some GPs had seized each opportunity to get involved in the succession of 'primary care commissioning' schemes, for reasons which varied from an altruistic desire to use greater autonomy constructively through a desire to control the money to the (probably dominant) desire to avoid control by others, from above (the government) or sideways (managers). This time around, Lansley's White Paper actually offered them—on paper—genuine autonomy, even more than in Fund-holding days, when the GPFH practices had been accountable to the Regional Health Authorities (Department of Health Regional Offices after 1996).

Unlike GP voices on PCT Boards, or more likely their 'Professional Executive Committees' and later as Practice based Commissioners, this time the GP Commissioning Groups were to have Board status, with managers employed by doctors rather than (as hitherto, with the partial exception of fund-holding) the other way around. This was attractive to those GPs who felt willing and able to hold the baby of commissioning. But there was a catch—not a conspiracy by Lansley and the government, but a consequence of their failure to think through what implementation would inevitably mean, as discussed below. Meanwhile the Royal College of General Practitioners, while sceptical about the policy, was prepared at this stage to give it a hearing. This changed later, when it became clear that the majority of GPs opposed it.

When the dismay about Lansley's White Paper, which had been picked up by the Chancellor George Osborne earlier than many others, percolated via the media right through to the whole Cabinet, it became clear by early 2011 that the dismay would translate into a failure to get the Health and Social Care Bill, based on the White Paper, passed in the Commons. Even had the Liberal Democrat leadership been willing to continue to support it, which they were not, the majority of Lib Dem MPs would not have been.

Cameron's Hand Forced: The NHS Future Forum

Prime Minister Cameron had to overrule an unhappy Andrew Lansley directly, and announce a 'pause' in the passage of the Bill. This was highly unusual, and was mainly the result of the fact that, equally unusually hitherto, there was not a one-party government with an overall majority, for the first time since 1977–79, when Labour had just lost its small overall majority. There had not been an actual coalition since wartime. This situation emboldened the Conservative sceptics in the House of Commons, one of whom was Sarah Wollaston, a former GP who had been chosen as Conservative candidate through an innovative selection meeting open to non-Conservatives. She was a member, and later became Chair, of the Commons Select Committee on Health, and was a personable and sensible voice.

Cameron attempted to make a virtue out of necessity, arguing that, unlike previous administrations (it seemed he wished opportunistically to make the contrast with the domineering Thatcher), this one was prepared to listen. But nobody was fooled. Privately the government was gnashing its collective teeth, and—the more his colleagues looked into it—the more frustrated they became with Lansley whom they now realised could have pursued his more reasonable objectives without such senseless upheaval. A committee was set up to review the legislation under the chairmanship of Steve Field, a GP with managerial experience in the West

Midlands Region as well as some RCGP clout, and containing representatives of 'establishment laity' from the voluntary sector such as Steve Bubb, the Chief Executive of the Association of Chief Executives of Charitable Organisations, and Bishop Victor Adebowale, who included some NHS Trust non-executive experience in his public service experience. This was the NHS Future Forum (2011; Paton 2012).

When the Forum reported, its recommendations were immediately accepted by Cameron, as a means of trying to 'move on'. But they were basically a mess, or at least a fudge whether deliberate or not, with warm words instead of analysis papering over the conflicts which had come to the surface as a result of Lansley's initiative. What is more, the new organisations which were proposed to 'coopt' some of the Bill's opponents would—if they meant anything; an open question—create a sclerotic rather than nimble NHS, and would 're-bureaucratise' what had at least been intended as an anti-bureaucratic reform.

This was principally because the Forum tried to have its cake and eat it on 'competition', on the one hand, and 'integration' and/or 'collaboration', on the other hand, arguing that both were possible. That may be true if defined in an arcane theoretical way of little use to the NHS (see below) but the Forum's lack of expertise in such a minefield meant that it made what philosophers call a 'category mistake' here: it confused integration as in the abandonment of competition, that is, economic integration on the one hand, and integration as in competition between rival integrated providers (each containing hospital and community services and therefore arguably 'integration' in terms of clinical services but not economically), on the other hand. It seemed to move from one definition to another in its analysis, which meant that it did not make a proper case either for abandoning competition (e.g. between hospitals) or for integrating services, that is, ending the fragmentation between hospital and community Trusts. This was of course useful to the government: it could continue with its plans but using a softer language.

If integration between different hospitals' complementary services, and between hospital and community services, was to be possible, then certain types of market reform—and certainly the type being proposed, both before and after the 'pause'—would have to be abandoned. But this was neither mooted nor did it subsequently happen (again, see below). Monitor was the body charged with overseeing the fudge: instead of 'promoting competition' as in the Bill Mark 1, it was now to 'prevent anti-competitive practices' (sounds different but means the same) and yet also 'promote integration'. Quite apart from this having no real meaning in the Forum's fudge, Monitor was culturally quite unsuited to 'promoting integration'. It was staffed by mostly non-clinically qualified young competition hawks (Public Servant 2012).

Not much of this mattered to the Cabinet, which simply wanted a face-saver which could then be handed over to the NHS Chief Executive and his team to make sense of. But a straw in the wind as to the nature of the hybrid which the Forum proposed came in the reaction of those non-Conservative figures who had been quietly, or not so quietly, sympathetic to the Lansley vision. Former Labour Health Secretary Alan Milburn and Professor Julian le Grand of the LSE, an ex-Blair adviser, bemoaned the brake put on competition and the creation of new participatory bodies such as 'Clinical Senates' which would give representation to interest-groups. It seemed the compromise would alienate market reformers while failing to please opponents of the market and 'reform', in that it still enabled privatisation and still necessitated major reorganisation to create what were now to be Clinical Commissioning Groups (CCGs) and deal with the consequences of abolishing the PCTs and SHAs. The Forum had, through Bubb and others, links to the private sector—and while this came over in the Forum's report as support for the non-profit 'Third Sector', the proposed new NHS would have its front door opened to the new for-profit health players such as Virgin et al.

So what did the Forum propose? Principally, the new commissioners were to be 'clinical' (not only medical), that is, to include the token nurses and others. Competition was not out, but it could not be allowed to crowd out integration. There were to be Clinical Senates to review local commissioning plans. And the local government Scrutiny Committees were to have a formal consultative, and possible veto role, on local health plans and especially service reconfigurations (which likely involved closures). Monitor, as we have seen, had a remit which was changed on paper.

THE LORDS STEP UP TO THE PLATE

But if the Cabinet thought the Bill could now be passed, they had reckoned without the House of Lords, where Labour, whose case was aided by the health sector expertise of former Minister Lord (Philip) Hunt of King's Heath, a former head of the NHS Confederation (representing the NHS commissioning authorities and Trusts) and its predecessor organisations, was now joined by influential peers Baroness (Shirley) Williams, erstwhile leader of the Liberal Democrats there and former Labour Cabinet Minister; Lord (David) Owen, former SDP leader and former Labour Foreign Secretary as well as Health Minister; and some independents and independent-minded Conservatives. Ironically, the Bill was supported by Labour's recent Health minister, Lord (Norman) Warner and one or two other Blairites. So what was now the sticking point—other than general disillusionment with what all now knew to be an unnecessary reform but which Deputy Prime Minister Nick Clegg (Lib Dem) as well as Cameron the PM decided could not simply be abandoned, which would have involved too much loss of face and a possibly terminal verdict of government incompetence?

Firstly, the Bill still did not restore the Department of Health's responsibility to provide a service under the NHS, which was missing from the Bill Mark 1. This may seem arcane, but it was not just a quasi-constitutional or pedantic point. To Lansley, who behaved almost robotically, it seems, in the light of criticism, and indeed to those who believed in the 'theology' of the purchaser/provider split, removing the Department's role as 'provider' was simply to recognise that decisions as to which services to 'commission' (i.e. buy) are local ones, and more importantly that provision is by quasi-commercial 'independent' providers, whether 'NHS' or not, that is, self-governing.

But this prissy view ignored the political and social realities of the NHS. It was and is a tax-funded service accountable to the citizenry via the government, which still—despite all 'purchaser/provider' theology—controlled it from the centre. It was and is therefore important that services are guaranteed by the Health Ministry. A Lords amendment, in due course passed, as opponents of the Bill in its current form negotiated with the government's spokesman Lord (Freddie) Howe, restored the Department's responsibility at least to ensure that a service was provided.

Additionally, the scope for privatisation was a major worry. The eventual passed Bill included limitations on the income which Foundation Trusts could make from private sources to 49% (still a huge percentage). Additionally, it was claimed that the nature of mandatory tendering under the Bill now meant that the EU's single market 'competition' directive could not be invoked to the benefit of private providers, although this was and is dubious—not least with the EU's Transatlantic Trade and Investment Partnership (TTIP) with the USA, which complacent commentators have equally dubiously claimed that health can easily be exempted from. This remains to be seen in the long term, even after the House of Commons insisted upon it in 2016.

Eventually the Bill was passed in 2012, and the process of full implementation (already begun by NHS Chief Executive Nicholson within legal parameters, seeking to avoid the legal case in 1989–1990 when it was alleged Ministers had exceeded their powers in implementing the internal market reforms before they had become law, and also seeking to make a difficult transition as smooth as possible) could begin, at which point it was realised that the troubles had only just begun.

Making Sense of the Insensible

Soon the NHS 'bosses', as the press call them, realised that the question of competition was going to be a running sore. Was it competition for the treatment of particular conditions (e.g. 'the hip-replacement contract'); for services (e.g. orthopaedics in general); for overall specialties (e.g. surgery); or for whole-hospital contracts? Or could it be competition for all or any of these, to be decided locally by commissioners? Crucially, if services were 'picked off' by private competitors, how would the hospital losing them stay viable—not just economically, but clinically (e.g. how would an Accident and Emergency department be competent if the hospital had no orthopaedic service?). Even before Labour lost the 2010 election, Health Secretary (2009–10) Andy Burnham had rightly defended the idea of 'whole hospital' contracts, as the least he could do to maintain the coherence of a public sector in provision. But for even this modest brake upon the neo-liberal strain of Blairism, he was pilloried by the former left-wingers seemingly turned neo-libs, Lord Warner and Paul Corrigan, his New Labour predecessors at the Department of Health.

One may go further: if competition is to be compatible with a coherent public service, then more than 'large contracts' are needed. As modernisers (in the more noble sense of the term than in the discredited version peddled as self-justifying rhetoric by Blairites in the 2000s) would urge, hospitals and indeed all services require integration—in the sense of cooperation around the needs of the patient who passes from one to the other, for example, from the GP to a community service, into hospital, then a further 'tertiary referral' to a specialist hospital, then back to a community hospital, then home with a 'care package', for example, planned home visits and out-patient follow-up. In the jargon, this is the 'patient pathway.' Simply to describe it suggests how dangerous to 'integration' piecemeal tendering and privatisation might be. Moreover, if public money has been invested in public provision, then it is highly likely to be inefficient to sacrifice the value from continuing that investment, instead running down the public service in order to contract out. Not impossible, but unlikely to form an effective strategy—rather like selling a core energy need abroad.

The next issue to confront those implementing what was now the Health and Social Care Act was the extent to which competition/markets and integration of care were in fact compatible. If care was to be 'integrated' in terms of the patient pathway (example above), then contracts would have to be *either* let for the whole pathway *or* let to a 'lead provider' to manage the pathway. If the former, then competition would be between rival regionally based 'whole pathway providers'—academically viable but seriously unaffordable in practice unless the NHS spent at Californian levels on healthcare. If the latter, which actually began to lead to the privatisation of cancer and other services from 2014 onwards, then why should the *management function* for whole services be tendered and privatised when NHS 'leadership' had been such an expensive priority for more than 30 years in one guise or another? Either the money had been wasted to an extent that Ministers should be deemed incompetent, or the agenda was ideological.

Regarding CCGs, it soon became clear that these would bring down the edifice through well-intentioned inexperience and incompetence, if they were not reined in and controlled from above. Since PCTs, SHAs, and Regions had all been abolished, the only option was for the Department of Health to reinvent them as Regions of NHS England (the renamed NHS Board, outsourced from the Department as the NHS Head Office), subdivided into Local Area Teams (LATs), soon renamed Area Teams (ATs). These were invisible to the public and yet made decisions on specialist services without accountability, as well as 'performance managing' the CCGs (BBC Radio 2014). CCGs were thus subjected to the humiliation of losing the autonomy which had been the sole reason for the minority of enthusiastic GPs to get involved.

Thus CCGs became the 'poor bloody infantry' rather than the newly autonomous clinicians in charge. Those who ignore history (even the contemporary history of the last 15 years) are condemned to repeat it. This is what had happened to the small PCTs created in 2001, and even more so to their 'Professional Executive Committees' intended to put GPs at the centre of commissioning (Paton 2006); to the 'Practice Based Commissioners'; and to all naive attempts at 'decentralisation' which ignored the need (practical not ideological) for meso-level (i.e. regional) strategy, management, and control). The iron law of ill-thought-out decentralisation in the NHS is that it devours its children and becomes its opposite.

Next, if one route to integration was for large hospitals to 'take over' community services and even GP practices, would this be allowed? Common sense said yes; market theology (and Monitor, until made aware of the will of politicians where they had of necessity to wear their pragmatic hat) said no. Initially the confusion prevented the sorts of reconfiguration which made sense on the grounds that they were 'anti-competitive', but there were signs by 2015 (with Lansley long gone, replaced by Jeremy Hunt as Health Secretary in September 2012) that competition per se was yielding to the wider and more important agenda of managing the NHS's survival when £22 billion of 'efficiency savings' were required by 2020. This meant that dilettante, ideologically based policies would look even more bizarre if they got in the way of reshaping NHS provision in search of both clinical viability and efficiency.

Overall then, the latest version of the NHS presaged more fragmentation and indeed sheer mess, as well as and indeed as a result of an unnecessary loss of continuity.

FROM LANSLEY TO HUNT

It was in some ways ironical that Lansley, who had before 2010 become committed to a tax-funded NHS as opposed to an alternative mode of financing healthcare, was seen as more dangerous to the NHS than was his successor Hunt, at least before the latter's high-handed behaviour over junior doctors' pay in 2015. The latter had after all co-authored an earlier publication calling for those who could afford to do so to save through 'health savings accounts' for healthcare needs, then to be purchased from providers in the marketplace whether public or private. Those who could not afford to do so would be protected by the state. But this would of course extend the perverse incentive inherent in means-testing for publicly funded healthcare. It would furthermore raise the spectre of 'a service for the poor being a poor service'. This would not be just because of the loss of middle-class 'voice' from the public service but also because those who had saved and created their health accounts would be less willing to redistribute to the less well-off through the tax system, if their own healthcare was more expensive in a market system, as was highly likely.

Those who consider that the privatisation of financing for healthcare is a response to the 'inefficiency' of the NHS model are generally mistaken. There is a political threat to the NHS in England not because it is inefficient but because its challenge is to be *so* much more efficient than private insurance or private payment models that those better-off who contribute to it through a mildly progressive taxation system get a better financial deal for themselves than through an alternative system even *after* they have contributed somewhat to the healthcare costs of the poorer through redistributive taxation. In other words, as the Blair government realised early on, the NHS was itself, as stated by Prime Minister Blair in the Foreword to the NHS Plan, an act of modernisation (and not an 'Old Labour' problem, it was implied, given the bouquet it was granted of New Labour's favourite 'hurrah word'), but this did not guarantee its survival in an age when a de facto majority coalition to support it had to be assembled from self-interested strata in a complex post-Fordist society rather than merely derived from a majority self-interested working-class. That is, the old left-of-centre majority in British politics had been replaced by what Galbraith (1992) had perceptively called in the 'culture of contentment'.

Having originally considered alternatives to the NHS altogether rather than being interested in boffin-esque schemes to 'marketise' it internally, Hunt—when he had to do a volte face and support the NHS model—maybe had less interest in internal mechanics than in getting on with the job. His ideological ballast was Right-wing, but his ideological interest did not extend to intra-NHS policy-wonking. If the NHS was here to stay, a pragmatic approach was required. This was also the only possible stance in any case, given that he had come in as 'anyone but Lansley'.

There had been an awkward fluttering-in-dovecotes when Hunt was in his previous job as Secretary of State for Culture, Media and Sport, when his office was suspected of being too close to the Murdoch media empire when it was his job to devise policy for media regulation especially after a series of phone-hacking scandals. But despite this he had political capital by default at the start of his tenure at Health, on the grounds of the Lansley debacle, even if there was a suspicion that whereas Lansley was all policy and no communication, Hunt was the mirror image. And for a Health Secretary, three years of 'quiet' from his appointment in autumn 2012, despite the travails of the NHS in England, is quite good going.

Unfortunately his mishandling of a major pay grievance by junior doctors which came to a head in October 2015, when he was accused with some justice of being devious and economical with the truth, squandered this capital. His offer to the junior doctors, upon whom the NHS depends 'out of hours' (i.e. at night and at weekends), created perverse incentives or at least further lowered morale, by cutting weekend and out-of-hours 'overtime' pay for junior doctors (which actually means all doctors except Consultants and non-career staff doctors) at the very time when his policy goal was a 24-hour/7-day high-quality NHS. From now on, out of hours work was mostly to be incorporated into normal shifts, with remuneration for those whose services out-of-hours were most required (i.e. emergency doctors) most adversely affected.

It was no good offering a rise of 11%, as he did, on basic pay, as the overall settlement was to be cost-neutral and the money had to be clawed back through cutting this overtime—and intensifying work on shifts for all doctors, as the same number of doctors had to cover more shifts now that the roster was to cover 7 days for elective surgery and medical treatment, including out-patient clinics, without increasing the number of doctors. This therefore drove a coach and horses through the proper funding of the 'sharp end' specialities out-of-hours, as it was doctors in 'accident and emergency', and in emergency surgery and medicine, who kept the NHS afloat out of hours—and they who would be the losers. More than this: Hunt advertised unreliable data about a greater risk of death for patients treated 'out of hours'—without adjustment for the fact that many of such patients were sicker in the first place (hence their emergency admissions out of hours as opposed to at a more convenient time) and also for the fact that the quoted studies had not isolated weekend care specifically, as Hunt claimed. It was further disingenuous to claim that the government's proposals were all about increasing quality in a 24/7 service in any case: international evidence (Feachem et al. 2002) suggested that the best way to combine such quality with efficiency (i.e. shorter lengths of stay) was to staff the out-of-hours service with substantially more senior doctors, that is, consultants—not more juniors. But advertising this would mean the government had to spend more money.

The first doctors' strikes for 40 years were the result of the government's intransigence. Furthermore, the dispute gradually worsened, with more strikes occurring from March 2016 by which time Hunt had imposed his new contract but failed to end the dispute—which threatened to sour relations between government and medical profession for many years to come. The bitterness and low morale on the part of the junior doctors, and many Consultants who saw moreover that it was they who would be called on to cover 'on the cheap' for the over-stretched juniors, was likely to mean that the 'surplus' which the NHS derived from medical goodwill would be further eroded. Hunt did not help his case by making a speech in March 2016 in which he demanded that GPs learn from Easyjet. Whatever he meant, it sounded like he was proselytising a cheap, no-frills service. So either he was lacking insight on a magisterial scale or being deliberately provocative. Of course the dispute was not only of Hunt's making: it reflected the mishandling and underfunding of the political promise of a '7-day NHS'—as if this were something new—made by Prime Minister Cameron, and the unwise translation of that problem from better resourcing out-of-hours (wise) to 'bog-standard services seven days a week' (unwise in that it was unaffordable and ill-thought-through).

Despite his slipperiness on this issue, at least on the issue of NHS reform, Hunt wore his previous NHS-sceptic ideology light, or rather shelved his core beliefs for political reasons. That is, there was no revival of his flirtation with critiquing the NHS model—unless one adopts the conspiracy theory that his handling of the pay dispute was a surreptitious attempt to discredit state medicine.

In any case, more significant than Hunt in the question of 'reform' post-Lansley was the new Chief Executive of the NHS, or as it was now styled, NHS England, the renamed NHS Board which in the purchaser-provider theology or fiction no longer had responsibility for provision of services. Indeed NHS England now had to jockey for space and influence with many other agencies responsible for the different parts of the further-fragmented NHS. Nevertheless, NHS England's new boss was a significant appointment which suggested that, despite all the rhetoric of pluralism, NHS England's boss was intended unequivocally to be the whole-system leader.

'Simon Says'

This was Simon Stevens, who took over in April 2014 from the much-maligned David Nicholson. Stevens was a high-flier, PPE student at Oxford, and former President of the Oxford Union, who—unusually for such—had become an NHS management trainee and then an NHS manager, as well as a Labour councillor, prior to becoming special adviser to Frank Dobson, Labour's market-sceptic first Health Secretary after 1997, then to his successor Alan Milburn, then to Prime Minister Tony Blair. After this, his career in the USA with United Health meant that when he came in as NHS Chief Executive, he had an authority and power base: he was not just a promoted NHS regional manager, as had been all his predecessors in the age of the market—Duncan Nichol, 1989–1993; Alan Langlands, 1993–2000; Nigel Crisp, 2000–2006; and David Nicholson, 2006–2014.

Stevens was successful in persuading Hunt and the government, in the run-up to the 2015 election, that £8 billion would have to be found—both to give the NHS breathing-space, and also as the minimum conceivable as part of the £30 billion agreed to be needed and of which a massive £22 billion would still be required to come from that lovely euphemism (or is it oxymoron?) 'efficiency savings'. (Often, promoting genuine efficiency, as opposed to economy or death by a thousand cuts, costs money, especially in the short term). It is difficult to imagine Nicholson or indeed his other predecessors being as effective in 'persuading up' as opposed to transmitting orders 'down'. That said, the overambitious statement on efficiency savings of £22 billion promised by Stevens did let the government off the hook somewhat.

Moreover, Stevens, although he had been an enthusiast for market reforms after 1999, dismaying his first political boss, Frank Dobson, in the process, was at heart a pragmatist, and now those neo-classically based academics who had seen him as their champion were equally dismayed to find no reference to markets at all in Stevens's first major document from NHS England, the rather unmemorably named NHS Five Year Forward View (Department of Health 2015), in early 2015. This was more of the 'let a thousand flowers bloom' ilk, suggesting that local health economies should be allowed to pursue 'integration' of care in their own way, without the blooming flowers being cultivated at the centre as in Mao's original version. This did not rule out market mechanisms as a means of bringing providers together, but equally it did not rule out integrated local health economies. As ever, the devil would be in the detail—or rather, in the performance management by the 'Area Teams' which were now the meso-level regulators (giving the lie to the myth that NHS England had nothing to do with provision as the latter was the responsibility of Monitor, for Foundation Trusts, and the NHS Trust Development Authority for non-Foundation NHS Trusts - brought together in summer 2015 as NHS Improvement).

De facto, the rigidities caused by the theology of the Lansley reforms began to be ignored. Perhaps the most egregious of those was the idea that the CCGs should not be allowed to 'commission' primary care. The reason was impeccable, in La La Land: GPs could not commission from themselves without a conflict-of-interest. But evaluation of the previous scheme most similar to the CCGs—the Total Purchasing Pilots in the late 1990s—had shown that, while in fact GPs were neither particularly interested in nor therefore good at commissioning in general, primary care and local community services, including mental health, was a partial exception.

The answer was surely therefore to solve the conflict-of-interest by making the new commissioning groups authorities which were wider than merely the creatures of GPs. This would have solved also a major problem with the new CCGs: whereas with Health Authorities in one form or another (1948–2001) and PCTs (2001–2012) the GP had remained at least in some senses the patient's advocate, as the ultimate 'rationing' decisions were taken by management authorities, with CCGs, the GPs themselves were the ultimate rationers. This was a conflict-of-interest much more serious than Lansley's market conundrum.

Now, post-Lansley, the conflict-of-interest would just have to be ignored. It was ludicrous that GPs had to commission hospital services, which most of them were no good at, not interested in doing and would need substantial long-term investment in order to do adequately (King's Fund 1998; Thorlby et al. 2011) and yet could not commission primary services, which had to be done by NHS England, that is, the Area Teams in practice. So new 'pathfinders' were set up to 'pilot' CCGs' commissioning all services except specialist ones—in other words, to get back to doing what had previously been done by all health authorities since the abolition of Family Practitioner Committees in 1990 and the subsequent absorption of their temporary replacement, Family Health Services Authorities, into the general Health Authorities. Along with these pathfinders came other pilots to bring together NHS and social care 'commissioning', building on the ubiquitously quoted local so-called success stories which the King's Fund, Nuffield Trust, and other insider outside bodies had been publicising for years.

As in the period from the mid to late 1990s up to 2000 and again perhaps from 2007 to 2010, we were seeing the reining in of the market obsession at least in some respects. This should not be over-estimated: the expensive PFI remains, as does the unwarranted assumption that it is necessary to 'outsource' major contracts to 'integrate' care—for example, in order to bring together hospital departments, community services, and care providers for cancer patients. But the idea of the market as the engine of the system—as opposed to the feather-bedding of private firms such as Virgin—was again in decline by 2015. Only time would tell if the gut instinct of the Jeremy Hunts of this world—that 'private is good and public is bad', as good grandchildren to Margaret Thatcher believe—would yet again lead to a threat to the NHS in the future. This is always possible: Hunt, as but one example of the NHS-sceptic type of politician in the Tory mainstream, had endorsed a book (Carswell 2002) with other right-wingers such as Daniel Hannan MEP which had decided that the

NHS was past its sell-by date. And, with Labour in meltdown by the end of 2015 and long years of Tory rule on the horizon, the next moral panic about the NHS in England might not be far away. But that is for the future, and indeed not for the rest of the UK.

So now it is time to move to political explanation of the whole cycle from the late 1980s to the end of 2015: were the cycles, the swings and roundabouts, the slings and arrows, of 'more then less' market, a necessary means of keeping the NHS show on the road, or was it more arbitrary than that? The next chapter investigates.

REFERENCES

BBC Radio 4. (2014, November 12). File on 4, 8pm

Carswell, D. (2002). *Direct democracy*. London: Change.

DoH. (2011). *NHS future forum. Final report*. London: DoH.

DoH. (2015). *Five-year forward view*. London: DoH.

Feachem, Richard G. A., et al. (2002, January19). The NHS versus Kaiser. *British Medical Journal*.

Galbraith, J. K. (1992). *The culture of contentment*. London: Sinclair Stevenson.

House of Commons. (2011). *Commissioning: Further issues*. London: TSO.

King's Fund. (1998). *Evaluation of total purchasing pilots*. London: King's Fund.

Paton, C. (2006). *New Labour's state of health: Political economy, public policy and the NHS*. Ashgate: Avebury.

Paton, C. (2012, March). Competition and integration: The NHS Future Forum's confused consensus. *British Journal of General Practice (BJGP)*, Lead Editorial.

Public Servant. (2012, September 13). Mid staffs, the NHS and the future: Complacency in the teeth of collapse.

Thorlby, R., et al. (2011). *GP commissioning; Insights from medical groups in the United States*. London: Nuffield Trust.

CHAPTER 7

Summative Political Explanation: NHS 'Reform' over 30 Years

This chapter considers possible explanations from political theory and public administration for the health policy story over nearly 30 years, and the next chapter goes into greater detail in outlining how the most plausible explanation can be applied in practice to that period.

PATH-DEPENDENCE

A term in political science which has had significant currency over some decades is 'path-dependency' or path-dependence. This comes in two variants, as Pierson (2000) makes clear. The first version is a general, almost tautologous statement that 'history matters'. What has gone before is bound to affect or condition what comes next, at least in some way. The second version is more 'analytical' or, perhaps one should say, seeks to draw an analogy either with concepts such as economic equilibrium or rationality in choice of policy. That is, once an initial decision has been made, and indeed a subsequent decision or two made to reinforce that initial decision, a 'logic' is created which makes it irrational or at least difficult to go onto a different 'path'.

A quoted analogy to elucidate the second version, which must seem quaintly ancient to younger readers versed in contemporary technology, is from the development of video technology, and how the VHS video crowded out and rendered obsolete the Betamax, after a short period up to the beginning of the 1980s when they competed in the marketplace.

© The Author(s) 2016
C. Paton, *The Politics of Health Policy Reform in the UK*,
DOI 10.1057/978-1-137-47343-1_7

It was not because VHS was intrinsically better, it is argued, but because complementary technology for various reasons was developed which was compatible with VHS and not Betamax. The very nature of this frequently quoted analogy shows what is meant by path-dependence: there is no intrinsic merit to a path, but once that path is trodden so far, it is rational to stay on it and not just for natural conservatism or the short-term, one-off costs, including the psychological costs, of change.

The application to politics, and in particular policy-making, can be made for both types of path-dependence. The first type simply says: once a policy 'track' is chosen, it is any change or significant deviation from that track which needs to be explained rather than continuing on the same track. My interpretation of the second type is as follows. If a policy 'track' is established which has significant interconnected components which reinforce each other to help make the policy 'practical', then tacking off in a different direction is likely to render the policy less coherent. It would be irrational to jump from one policy track to another, or to pile one type of policy on another—as long as 'rationality' is understood as being concerned with coherent policy which, when implemented, can be made to 'work' better rather than worse. Rationality is instrumental, not intrinsic. In this sense, sticking to the path is rational unless the change is radical enough to remove all vestiges of the pre-existing policy and so it is rational to 'start again'—which we know both from theoretical plausibility and practical experience is rare, not least because it is costly (in the conventional sense) and psychologically costly (in the sense of making policy-makers look either foolish or brave).

The first type of path-dependence is rather banal. Moreover it leaves the more interesting phenomenon—why a path is chosen in the first place—unexplained. And it also allows any later policy choice to be explained by any alternative 'theory', as long as it is understood that the explanation has to be made against the backdrop of the implicit question, 'why?'.

But although the second type of path-dependence is superficially less banal, two critical points should be made before taking the analogy of the second type further and seeking to apply it to our period of health policy. One is that there is no reason why a phenomenon from technological development or economic 'equilibrium' should be usable as a valid explanation of political phenomena. Such a case would have to be made, not assumed. In economics or business, there might be 'increasing returns' from progressing down a path (say, a technology) which is complemented by other technologies which have been chosen to match it. The example of the VHS video applies; another example might be a type of airline engine given investment by airlines in particular types of aeroplane. But there is no automatic, or even plausible, analogy in the realm of politics and public policy: a path chosen may be abandoned only at inconvenience because of complementary arrangements having been made (e.g. the revenue-raising, distributive and management apparatus to accompany state-provided medicine) but this does not mean 'increasing returns' in any analytical sense. Given this, one can in fact query the validity or durability of the distinction between the two types of path-dependence in the field of politics and public policy as opposed to business.

The second critical point is that such path-dependence still does not explain any of the following: the initial policy choice; what indeed can be considered 'initial' or primary, given that policy always has a predecessor, for our purposes at least; and when and why a radical departure, creating a new track, is going to happen. That is, the 'theory' is somewhat less than that word implies, hence the inverted commas.

Seeking to apply the idea to our period takes us into the following considerations. The 'market' policy, as in 1989–1991, may be considered a new departure, the creation of a new path. This is in effect what Tuohy (1999) argues, in a book which compares the different paths taken by the UK, USA, and Canada after World War II up to the 1990s. But she contradicts herself indirectly when arguing (correctly, in my view) that there are compelling reasons why the 'old', pre-market NHS reasserts itself in many ways. Implicitly, this is because the original path is seen as being too strong for the market to render it invalid. Therefore implicitly the 'market' is not after all a new policy, and we have implicitly different orders of policy paths or tracks, without a theory to distinguish the different levels or the basis for the distinction.

Note that much of Tuohy's policy detail concerning the UK is correct, if unoriginal: it is just that she attempts to theorise that detail in a manner which inadvertently lays bare the shortcomings of path-dependence as a theory. Admittedly her aim is not to defend path-dependence per se, but to set out empirically the necessary conditions for a new path in health policy—as well as why, in the absence of these conditions, new policy tends to be 'coopted' to the old realities. Yet, in the absence of explaining when and why these necessary conditions for a new path arise, her exercise becomes one of description rather than explanation. A country may be on a path, but there is no compelling reason as to why and when—just the fact, with its consequences for later policy. And I would contend that this is because she sticks implicitly to the path-dependence 'theory'.

It is necessary to see that theory for what it is—a secondary theory, a rephrasing of more fundamental realities into a different language, and one which obscures the political realities, what is more. Let us try a different approach to explaining the UK—for our purposes here, English—situation. (Tuohy was summarising a period in the 1990s before UK devolution, when the 'internal market' reforms applied to all the UK.) That approach goes as follows. Each time a 'market reform' has been applied, it has been necessary to moderate and vitiate the market element over time, if by market we mean competing providers and quasi-private provision, and also genuine (as opposed to symbolic) decentralisation of decision-making to allow 'purchasers and providers' to furnish the motor of the system.

That is, the nature of the NHS as a publicly planned system has been reasserted, whatever language is in use for ideological or indeed subconscious reasons. Note that private finance for new hospitals and other entry-points for private capital are perfectly compatible with this scenario: they are part of a publicly planned system, one that happens to give preferential treatment to private interests, on a basis which makes the designation of 'competition' or even a market at all highly misleading. An analogy can be made with the British railway system, which—despite various privatisations—can be correctly described as quasi-public. Overall, the NHS, even by the end of 2015, prioritises both political control and public decisions about services and their sitting over the theology of 'reform'.

One may designate this state-of-affairs as demonstrating the truth of path-dependence. But that would only be trivially true. Any system requires operational coherence, and the NHS's *modus operandi* is no different. To replace that with a wholly new 'market' system would require the dismantling of the public mission—to attempt to site services on the basis of need and equity in access at least as a goal. That would be possible as a consequence of 'market reform'—and indeed each time market reform has been attempted, there have been touchstone decisions to be made about whether to 'let the market work (more)' or to rein it in in order to ensure that public decisions are respected or reasserted. To call this path-dependence is unhelpful. It would be perfectly possible to 'let the market rip': it is just that it would be politically unacceptable—even for those Ministers who made their name inter alia being hostile to the NHS, as with Jeremy Hunt, for example.

It would also of course be difficult to chart such a new course—as the comfortable ideological assumption that 'private (or even just competition) is better' would, in any attempt to put it into practice, require painstaking design and lots of disappointment along the way. That is the sense in which NHS privatisers are often student politicians at heart, or in origin, who 'grow up' when they take office. It is however political culture, including the public ethos, which means that, when the crossroads is reached, the touchstone decisions are usually to rein in the market rather than let it rip. If this is path-dependence, then the name obscures a rich political reality in a pseudo-technical explanation.

The (Mis) Application of Applied Economics to Public Policy

A phrase from applied neo-classical microeconomics has been (over-) used since the mid-1990s in discussions about UK health policy reform, and that is 'managed competition.' In the NHS, this means only that competition, to the extent that it exists, is not free—not primarily because it cannot be (although that too) but because it is politically managed. It is an accurate phrase in one sense only—that the management of competition is not just regulation by an external regulator (although this convenient fiction keeps reappearing in policy reform, as with Monitor's alleged role as system regulator following the Lansley reforms) but actual direct management by NHS national executives acting usually at the behest of Ministers or what they second-guess to be Ministers' wishes (the inconvenient truth to set against the convenient fiction). That is, it is indeed management and not (just) regulation. Such 'management' usually crowds out the 'competition', as it is management of issues such as where to site services, and whether or not hospitals are to cooperate or merge, et al., which are at stake. We saw this issue in the discussion above about the reining-in of the internal market in the mid-1990s.

It is therefore fair to describe the phrase 'managed competition' (Enthoven 1987) as an oxymoron—when applied to NHS (Beveridge) systems such as that in the UK. The phrase was coined by Enthoven to apply to a very different situation—the need for the US system, in his view, to be reformed so that consumers would have the choice between competing insurance plans. The analogy with Europe is with the social insurance (Bismarckian) systems, where reform ideas, as in the Netherlands, also influenced by Enthoven, often involve competing insurance companies.

It is simply lazy elision to apply the concept and phrase to the need for political or managerial direction within an NHS—an example of trendy concepts being superficially applied, indeed misapplied. The only use such a term should have in England is if reform is intended to create competing purchasers/commissioners, amongst which citizens would choose, thereby loosening the one-to-one correspondence between a commissioner and its geographical location as at present. This idea has been mooted, but it is in essence a solution in search of a problem—and one usually raised by commentators, who tend to deal in the fashion of the day.

In practice, then, managed competition has been a phrase which conveniently covers Ministerial blushes that, with each cycle of reform, their pro-competitive market reforms have come in with a bang and gone out with a whimper. The question arises, therefore: why is the cycle resumed so regularly in England? Surely this is the opposite of path-dependence: despite a policy being demonstrated to be 'out of synch' with the complex systems which make the NHS strategically and operationally functional, it keeps reappearing?

SO… BACK TO PATH-DEPENDENCE?

The answer must be sought in ideology, and in the mutual embeddedness of ideology and party political behaviour (see below.) Party politics refers both to externally focused electoral politics and to internal party behaviour in response to either failure to get into government or experience of government. The two would be positively linked in a rational world (if rationality is defined in terms of maximising the prospects for electoral success) but, as recent behaviour by the British Labour party has shown, this is by no means the case. The effect on health policy is indirect but significant. Conversely, the Conservative party may be more electorally attuned (with the exception of the period from 1997 to 2003) but still subject to 'unnecessary' health reform policy.

Of course one can redescribe all this in the language of path-dependence. For example, one can designate market reform itself as a 'path' at the policy level, even if it is vitiated at the level of implementation. But this is not the intended meaning of the term, and indeed it extends it to embrace so much that it becomes well-nigh-meaningless. An ideology (such as neo-liberalism, or just pro-market competition) which takes hold over a significant period, originating it should be remembered from well outside the realm of health policy, may condition and constrain thought and policy ideas. But to call that path-dependence is not helpful.

Taking the policy/implementation divide further: in one sense, policy and implementation are part of the same continuous process, but, in another sense, it is useful to distinguish between policy at the level of ideas (say, from a think-tank, or as adopted by Ministers and advisers 'wonking' on the Ministerial sofa) and implementation as what must happen to such idea-based policy to make it work. Note that the latter is not the same as a 'betrayal' of policy by hostile civil servants in the Department of Health or managers in the NHS. The latter may happen, but it is not what I am talking about here—which is pragmatism, in the sense of rescuing a public service from hare-brained schemes which do not work well, if at all.

In any case, the Department of Health is noteworthy, following its evolution and reform since the 1980s, accentuated in the 2000s, as the 'Department of Delivery' (Greer and Jarman 2007), which saw the sidelining of the traditional 'Sir Humphrey' style top civil servant in favour of the manager promoted to make implementation the priority. Such implementation, what is more, should not be seen as a means of deliberate weakening of policy reform, but as constructive engagement with the political agenda by 'top managers' who owe their position as the 'new civil servants' to their political masters. The civil service, in other words, has been politicised—the opposite of the old mandarins insufficiently motivated, because of their institutional independence, to obey their political masters.

Thus policy may be entirely free of institutional path-dependence, whatever its ideological provenance or conditioning. Implementation may be 'path-dependent' in the sense of adapting to the prevailing track—but only in that, and if, policy to furnish an alternative is not well devised and/ or radical enough. This requires explanation well outside the limitations of path-dependency theory.

Interestingly, both proponents and opponents of market reform could agree that it is not comprehensive enough in design (i.e. taking account of both intentions and the needs of implementation) and radical enough (in the sense of embracing all necessary complementary policy, e.g. genuine freedom for providers; pluralism in financing to avoid monopsony) to succeed. The difference of course between proponents and opponents is whether the market road should be trodden or not, but both may agree that treading it in a half-baked manner is costly and unlikely to produce benefit (Civitas 2010).

RATIONALITY?

Pro-market academics and policy-makers may point out that, had a version of the market in policy been designed and implemented which was both rational (i.e. designed to tailor means to ends as much as possible, not simply a 'knee jerk' political reaction) and also comprehensive (i.e. a 'big bang' or 'silver bullet' reform) then the costs of the cyclical and indeed circular tale told in this book could be avoided.

That may be true in the abstract. But it ignores the whole realm of politics and political culture, which is relegated to a footnote as something to be avoided rather than something to be acknowledged. If the NHS is popular for good reasons, then 'marketising' it in one fell swoop will be neither politically possible nor desirable. So, if the market route is to be trodden, then it is inevitable that it will have to be done 'softlee, softlee, catchee monkey'. As a result, it is misleading to suggest that there is a better, less costly route to a marketised NHS, or one in which the private sector is at the heart of commissioning and seriously involved both in service provision and capital provision. And it would be even more misleading to suggest that the motivation for market reform has been rational as opposed to 'political'.

ASSUMPTIONS ABOUT HUMAN BEHAVIOUR: RATIONALITY IN POLICY DESIGN?

An explanation for health policy reform which goes deeper than mere cost and benefit and which perhaps deserves (in the abstract) the designation of rationality starts with the fundamental motivation or motivations underlying human agency as the basis for interpreting the motivations of health service staff. This type of argument usually starts with doctors, although such an approach should include all staff in principle, including managers and those who steer and govern the system that is, policy-makers themselves. Le Grand (2003) for example argues that, while altruism is not wholly absent from the motivation of doctors, a more realistic assumption is self-interest. He seeks to apply a version of Adam Smith's well-known approach to economic enterprise and the social good, as well as David Hume's portrait of man as best understood empirically, rather than through a religious or doctrinal Rationalist lens, as motivated by his self-interested appetites. Thus Le Grand and others argue that, in order to derive the public good from private vice, we must assume that agents are motivated by material incentives. For Le Grand, this means the market. As a result, much of Le Grand's work on health policy in particular and public policy in general concerns defining the conditions for a market to work successfully in promoting competition between providers of services, so that from their self-interest may come the public good (i.e. the lower-priced or higher-quality supplier will win the contract with the purchaser/commissioner).

But a significant number of significant objections and qualifications to this stance exist. Firstly, the provision of material or other incentives to individuals does not necessitate market competition between suppliers of services such as hospitals or hospital departments. Instead, it may mean material incentives to individuals. Indeed one of the problems with market reforms to the NHS is that they assume that NHS hospital and other Trusts, Foundation Trusts et al, are motivated as unitary enterprises to maximise profit, surplus, or income, or some such easily agreed variable. This is far from the truth for a number of reasons.

To begin with, NHS and Foundation Trusts are not allowed to make profit, and surpluses are very strictly regulated—as a managerial tool of financial viability rather than as a fundamental motivation for Trust Boards, that is, the governors of the organisation. Secondly, doctors and other clinicians, workers, and staff generally are not, as in more simply defined business organisations, motivated by the 'corporate' objectives which any assumption of competing providers necessitates. It is true that they may have to be concerned with financial viability 'at the end of the day', to prevent their goals for services, patients, and research being thwarted. But that is a very different thing in terms of daily motivation. The hospital, for example, is a 'disconnected hierarchy', in which corporate objectives are not enforceable from the 'top' to the bottom or from the centre to the periphery. Making the hospital a kind of workers' cooperative run by the doctors is one way to square this circle. But as economic theory tells us, the workers cooperative—even were such acceptable to doctors in general, which is highly unlikely—operates according to different incentives and with different results from traditional neo-classical 'perfect competition'.

In essence we are challenging the possibility that the necessary conditions for a successful market can apply in a public NHS where, at the very least, other policy priorities exist which vitiate the possibility of a market red enough in tooth and claw to allow 'private vice' to operate clearly enough to produce the public good. On the one hand, policy-makers want providers to compete; on the other hand, they are expected to collaborate. More centrally, on the one hand, purchasers/commissioners and providers are expected to be in adversarial relationships; on the other hand, they are expected to cooperate.

As argued above, the pro-market reply—simply ramp up the radical nature of the pro-market policy—is likely to be a non-starter for both (legitimate) political reasons and for logistical reasons to do with the nature of the healthcare 'product', such as the need for regionally based cooperation amongst providers especially where specialist services are concerned. To those who think that denying markets is somehow quasi-Soviet, it should be recalled that the problem with the Soviet Union was that it could be first in space yet poor at supplying bath-plugs. Specialist health services are more like space technology than bath-plugs, to use constructive hyperbole.

Such considerations bring us to the nub of the issue. The market policy for the NHS was not and is not promulgated as a result of rational policy advocacy by the likes of Le Grand, helping government to create the conditions for a successful market. Instead the policy was—and is—pursued for arational reasons in an evidence-free zone, and then idealists such as Le Grand sought and seek to rationalise the policy ex post facto. The conditions required for a successful market were modelled by Le Grand and others (Le Grand and Bartlett 1993) *after* the event of the internal market in 1989, and subsequently the market policy was attributed a rationality it never possessed—not least because these necessary conditions have never pertained. Such conditions include perfect competition based on free entry and exit to and from the market; infinite or adequate numbers of alternative suppliers; free or economically obtainable information about providers' products by purchasers; and an unambiguous 'profit-maximising' culture on the part of providers.

Simply to state these minimal but exacting conditions for effective competition is to show how many light years are health services from satisfying them. Moreover such conditions have never been sought properly by policy-makers, in practice—partly because they are rightly seen to be chimerical or, if to be sought sincerely, hugely expensive. To make this latter point another way: if the cost of creating and retaining markets (excess capacity in hospital beds; counteracting the natural tendency of 'industrial' as opposed to 'banana' markets to monopoly; etc) were simply to be allocated to expanding available services, more benefit by far would be obtained.

Market-oriented analysts such as Propper in the mid-1990s have from time to time been drafted in by the NHS Chief Executive to help design a coherent market—leading for example in 1995 to the Departmental paper, 'Local Freedoms, National Responsibilities' (Department of Health 1995), which was a blueprint for a localised market in the NHS subject to national guidelines—but this has always been a sideshow when it has come up against more pressing political realities. The absence of stable, lasting, and rational design of the conditions for a market to operate successfully is one of the main reasons why the policy has faded regularly, only to re-emerge again for reasons which we will explore below. Yet there is no way that a public NHS can co-exist with a genuine competitive market (as opposed to centrally or regionally controlled tendering for specific services). While there are of course many opposed to the market on ideological grounds, the present assertion is not an ideological one: it is an acknowledgement that the nature both of health services in general and a universal and comprehensive NHS which combines equity in access with financial control makes 'the market' an unaffordable diversion.

Other, arguably even more substantial reasons for doubting the relevance to policy of a systemic market approach should be noted. While self-interest applies to most human beings, it applies in different ways to different degrees at different times—both in the life-cycle or employment-cycle and in different components of one's life. Self-interest, altruism, professionalism, and organisational loyalty or 'obedience'—all different things, although some overlapping—may all apply.

Simply assuming that agents are 'knaves' may become a self-fulfilling prophecy, which is another way of saying that marketising and contractualising relationships may lead to the loss of loyalty and trust and the surplus which they create. Employees may need material incentives later in their employment life, when initial energy and altruism is reduced—but this is exactly when a market-based contractual approach to professional employment may value them less. Ironically, the now old-fashioned 'increments for seniority' may provide a better incentive than the short-term contract or the salary re-assessed annually in terms of the individual product, which in any case makes little sense in terms of health service teamwork.

The various market reforms may have been introduced in the context of a vague belief that markets are efficient, but this is a long way from allowing them to be designated as an exercise in rational policy-making. As argued above, there have been part-rational episodes, but that is a very different thing. Both the Thatcher reforms and the Blair reforms were introduced as part of a public sector-wide set of policies which applied across the board, not only in health but also in education, social care, and beyond.

Yet this itself is indicative of an ideological approach—for distinctions between different public services should be made in terms of the suitability of markets for meeting the intended objectives. While these objectives may legitimately be generalised across the public sector even if contested (e.g. choice and responsiveness; diversity of product etc.), it is a hard fact that 'choice' in, for example, education may both make more sense and be both more viable and more affordable than in healthcare. Choice of school by parent and pupil is the choice of a predictable and regular need. Choice of hospital is the choice of an unpredictable and irregular need. To expect the choice, or policy for choice, to be similar in both cases is, irrespective of the availability of information, naive.

Furthermore, the nature of the choice is different. 'Choosing a hospital' is meaningless if one is not choosing the particular doctor in the required speciality, whereas choosing a school generally means access to the teachers whose performance have created the information and 'ratings'—whatever the shortcomings of both the information and the 'ratings' or 'league tables'—which influence the choice. Only the dogmatic or ideologically motivated policy-maker would conflate all 'public services' in policy design. Yet that is what happened in the UK in the 1990s and, following devolution in 1998, in England thereafter. Neither in origin nor in post-hoc improvement can we adequately explain the NHS market reforms in terms of rationality, just as path-dependency, a very different type of explanation, also is inadequate. Let us therefore turn to more plausible explanations.

THE INSTITUTIONAL EXPLANATION: POLITICAL STRUCTURE

Political structure refers to the shape and nature of the political institutions through which policy has to be passed into law. Thus the UK (as well as perhaps New Zealand, which aped UK health policy reform in the early 1990s yet reversed that market policy a few years later) has been described as 'the fastest law in the West' as a result of its centralised polity, with its political executive (the Prime Minister and Cabinet) situated in, and in control of, the constitutionally dominant chamber of the legislature, the House of Commons. The opposite case exists in the USA, where the passage of domestic policy is cumbersome and subject to multiple veto-points in a decentralised system where not only is Congress separate from the executive (the Presidency) but also decentralised itself within both its equally powerful chambers, the House of Representatives and the Senate, which operate independently of each other—and all are subject to a Supreme Court which interprets laws as consistent (or not) with a written Constitution according to the political and ideological composition of the Court.

The UK structure enables policy to be made 'because it can'. This is an important necessary condition to explain the continual restless reform of and in health policy. In the USA, the attempt to establish universal access to health insurance has been repeated since 1912, and only in 2011—admittedly following the significant policy of 1965 which established Medicare and Medicaid (Marmor 2000) was a very partial and incomplete success achieved with President Obama's Affordable Care Act, which was in essence a 'Republican' plan, consisting in incrementally increased access to the existing, mostly private system of healthcare provision in the context of continuing multiple-payer private insurance (Paton 2013). Meanwhile, in the UK, we had not only had the NHS itself established in 1948 following the 1946 Act, but a number of significant policies to restructure the NHS in 1974, 1982, 1983, 1989/91, 2001–2005, and 2010–2012.

Clearly these policy reforms are not of the same order as the creation of the NHS, and clearly also the US has passed federal (national) reforms of one sort or another over time. But the UK legislative output shows the capacity of the political structure to enable national policy and reform which 'commands' the whole healthcare system, even if its attempts at 'control' are inevitable subject to the complexities and vicissitudes of implementation. Even in the latter case, however, problems with implementation tend not to stem from lack of effect, but from perverse effects of policy. The UK's political structure enables 'top down' policy at the swing of a Thatcher's handbag or a spring in a Blair's sofa (Butler 2004) as excited policy wonks and special political advisers come up with the latest wheeze.

But we need to take account of devolution since 1998. In Scotland, Wales, and Northern Ireland, the story post-1998 has been of significantly less, and significantly less erratic, reform than in England—with little difference in outcome, when one takes account of both the available money and the existence and timing of other policies (e.g. centrally mandated 'waiting-list initiatives'). In 2005, it was claimed that the English reforms had led to shorter waiting-times (Alvarez-Rosete et al. 2005). This was never attributable to 'the market', in any case, despite the best efforts of pro-market enthusiasts to claim otherwise—which only began in practice after 2005, and was attributable to top-down command in the form of waiting-time initiatives.

In Scotland, as soon as similar (if less brutally policed) central initiatives were taken, Scottish waiting-times fell, as had England's (Connolly et al. op.cit.). In 2015, English waiting-times are indeed longer than Scotland's, in the round, taking into account 'A and E' waits, waits for operations, waits for out-patient appointments, waits for ambulances, and waits for GP appointments.

The same occurred to a lesser extent, with lesser money, in Wales, now reversed as—unlike Scotland—Wales has seen a significant reduction in its block grant from Westminster. In Northern Ireland, while political and (health service) organisational circumstances are different, a similar story applies: achievement occurs in areas where measurement and management are politically mandated.

In the UK other than England, there have been 'reforms'. But in both Scotland and Wales, these have taken the form of a gradual movement to reverse the internal market (more gradual in Wales, but completed in 2008, whereas in Scotland the reintegration of the NHS as a public entity occurred in 2003). In Northern Ireland, where heath and social services are unified in one organisational structure, the 1990s internal market was always a paper exercise more than a meaningful policy, and subsequent policy has not been on the market/non-market continuum so much as seeking to develop more effective organisations such as the Health Boards.

This is not to imply that policy in these countries has always been 'rational' rather than 'political'. In Scotland, there has been a political attractiveness to 'not following England', and in Wales there has been a focus on community health and public health, whatever the success of such initiatives, it should be admitted. But, in terms of political structure, the point is that what are unicameral legislatures (the Scottish parliament; the Welsh and Northern Ireland Assemblies) with their executives located therein have not had the itchy fingers to act continually ('we can so we will') in promulgating policy reform to anything like the extent in England.

Before we explain this, we should dismiss an alternative explanation—consisting in the presence or absence of coalition government. It could be argued that policy reform has been slower or less frequent elsewhere in the UK because of coalition. In Scotland, since the revival of the Scottish Parliament, there has been a coalition administration (Labour–Liberal Democrat) between the initial Labour and subsequent SNP administrations, and in Wales a Labour-Liberal Democrat coalition. In Northern Ireland, at those times when the Assembly has not been suspended, there has of course been a permanent coalition across the politico-religious spectrum; but in any case the unique Northern Irish position, which diminishes the import of party political conflict on health policy in any case, makes the case less relevant to either side of the argument.

But the periods of coalition outside England are irrelevant in this case, as there has been no dispute over health policy in terms of market reform between these coalition partners. The main feature has been the absence of the Conservative party from either government or influence, and broad agreement between other parties (on a left-of-centre basis in Scotland and Wales; and a non-partisan basis in Northern Ireland) that market reform is undesirable—hence its reversal in Scotland and Wales.

We may also point to the presence of coalition government affecting health policy in England from 2010 to 2015, during which the most disruptive reform of all occurred, despite the government being a formal coalition between Conservatives and Liberal Democrats. Against this, it can be claimed, with truth, that the presence of coalition led to compromise over what became the 2012 Health and Social Care Act, not least because the Conservative part of the government, and in particular the Health Secretary, behaved as if the government was wholly Conservative. It was when the Liberal Democrat leadership woke up and realised that its backbenchers would not vote for the Health Bill in 2010–11 that the brakes were applied. But this period may have been an aberration, and in any case it did not mean an end to reform, quite the reverse.

Since the political structure in the rest of the UK made it at least as easy to continue to indulge in health policy reform of the 'market' variety as in England, we must therefore look to a different explanation as to why it happened in England and not elsewhere. That explanation lies in the interaction of the prevailing ideology of 'market reform' in England, what I have termed the 'London consensus', on the one hand, with the electoral battle in England, on the other hand. The latter has seen the Conservatives as the dominant party except during the Blair interregnum, which—despite its large majorities in 1997 and 2001—was characterised by a fear of Conservative revival and a tailoring of policy to seek to prevent this.

Ironically, Blairite Labour's preoccupation with 'public service reform' has been more about sending a signal to the electorate via the media that Labour is 'New' and not 'Old'; 'modern' and not 'socialist'. The electorate in general is oblivious to the nuances of health policy, as opposed to the state of the NHS. But if the predominantly right-wing media characterises Labour as left-wing or 'dangerous', then that part of the electorate composed of swing and floating voters will be scared off. Paradoxically, sending signals of reassurance on this basis need not involve 'market' health policy, as the latter is quite unpopular even with Conservatives (from voters to businesspeople who take up lay positions on NHS Boards). One can signal Right on the economy without being neo-liberal on public service reform. But add in the Blairite view which apes the Thatcherite view that state services ('statist', according to Blair's outrider, Alan Milburn) are likely to involve the 'forces of conservatism', and a neo-liberal flavour in health 'reform' became part of the package from 2000 to 2007, indeed 2010 if one depicts the period of Gordon Brown's premiership (2007–2010) as one in which Blairite policy remained by default, with Brown preoccupied with the banking crisis and its aftermath.

The Conservatives, for their part, have had a more natural and deeply-founded belief in 'market reform', as we have seen in the 1990s and again from 2010 when they returned to government after thirteen years of New Labour. But there is an irony here too: just as in the mid-1990s, they have found by 2015 that their own market reforms are a distraction from the real challenges facing health policy (see the last chapter below.) They are never likely to come out and say so, but if we look at how they 'walk the walk' as opposed to 'talking the talk', that is the most reasonable way to interpret the periods after 1995 and 2014.

Both parties could have quietly dropped the unhelpful rhetoric, especially with the third parties which might in principle be needed for coalition—first the Liberal Democrats, then UKIP—uninterested in market reform within the NHS (for different reasons, of course). But this was never likely, as electoral differentiation (especially when, up until 2015, the real differences were less than ever) made health policy a useful political football. The election of a left-wing Labour leader in 2015 obviously reduces Labour's interest in market reform, although the conflict within the party even on this sort of issue should not be underestimated: very few non-Blairite but mainstream Labour politicians were interested, for example, in supporting Green MP Caroline Lucas's NHS Reconsolidation Bill in late 2015, which would have 'done a Scotland' to the English NHS. It is too early to tell if Labour's leftward trajectory will leave the Conservatives free to downplay market reform, or leave them freer to revive more radical ideas about privatisation in and of the NHS.

Labour, in our 30-year period, has suffered from its tendency either to fight the previous general election or to react against its previous leadership stance. From Blair's election as leader, it gradually tacked further to the right than needed, paranoid about losing again as in 19092 despite its seeming popularity then—with this rightwards journey picking up speed after 2001. Thus it could easily have won in 1997, 2001 and 2005 without its 'public service reform'—where the latter was symbolic and cost-ineffective as opposed to necessary, as with much of health policy reform. Inversely, the Corbyn leadership victory in 2015 reflected an over-compensating rejection of the Labour Right in its modern form, albeit aided by a bizarre electorate in the said leadership election.

In general, health policy has not mattered in general elections in our period. What parties have done in terms of such policy has been more about helping shape the mood music of such campaigns. David Cameron used his 'love of the NHS' as part of his attempt to detoxify the Conservative brand up to 2010. Blair used 'public service reform' to show the *Daily Mail* and middle England that he was no lefty. But when push has come to shove, despite the NHS seemingly being salient, it has been other factors which have won and lost elections—from fear of Labour taxation policy (1992) to disillusionment with the Conservatives' longevity and the economic humiliation of leaving the ERM (1997) to blaming Labour for economic complacency in the run-up to the crash (2010 and 2015). Ironically, this leaves the parties more wriggle-room on health policy than they realise—as long as that policy does not contradict the major sources of appeal to the floating voter.

In England, then, ideology and political culture have shaped the environment which has been fertile for continual health policy reform. Ideology may refer to the specific interests of a class or group generalised into a world-view. One should not underestimate the revolving door between business and government in London, and the resultant opportunities for private interests to lobby, which then becomes generalised into an 'ideology' or market reform. Both Conservatives and New Labour have been close to business: indeed even Tony Blair's close associates, such as his former Director of Communications Alastair Campbell, have been surprised at his tendency to be dazzled by businessmen.

But ideology may also refer to the content of the narrative which gains currency in 'insider' policy networks, including the Civil Service. This is less conspiratorial but arguable more pervasive. Rhodes's (2011) studies of the civil service has shown how the dominant 'narrative', rather than evidence based on any extrinsic evaluation, shapes how top civil servants consider policy options. Up to the 1980s, the narrative in the Department of Health meant that market reform was seen as eccentric or at least impractical. Since the 1990s, rejecting market reform has been seen as eccentric or at least impractical. This is not because of any evidence-based sea-change, but because of a changed narrative, itself brought about by wider ideological change, as the tide of public planning went out to be replaced by a tsunami of anti-'statist' initiatives. From the early 2000s until 2015 at least it was common for leading Labour politicians and special advisers to associate with neo-liberal think-tanks such as Reform, where the likes of Paul Corrigan (special adviser to Milburn and Blair) and Norman Warner, Minister of State at the Department of Health from 2005 to 2007, made policy suggestions which would have seemed from far-Right shores to Edward Heath, Conservative Prime Minister, in the 1970s. One need only read the latter's memoirs, and the chapter on the NHS, to see the difference. It is remarkable how the fall of the Soviet Union and the rise of global capitalism can inform changed public service policy by osmosis rather then evidence-based rationality.

But let us conclude this chapter with a final factor causing continual 're-reform'. What else explains this constant re-reform? Having explained the politics of 'policy reform', we should also note that implementation—the need to make sense of what are at heart ideological and 'political' policies in practice—leads to instability. Each successive reform is likely to mean that new governance, regulatory and management structures are created (e.g. to 'regulate the market', or to 'ensure quality' in the absence of direct control). Yet the previous mechanisms remain: not only is there policy overload, but there is also administrative overload, on the ground, as it were. One need only read the report of the Public Inquiry (2013) into Mid Staffordshire NHS Foundation Trust to get a vivid sense of the confusion—overlap and yet omissions—of regulatory, supervisory, and administrative bodies seeking to govern quality as well as to seek more general control, including financial.

As problems mount, the reaction then is to seek a new reform, rather than to recall the advice that when is in a hole, it makes sense to stop digging. This is where the 'narrative', the ideology, comes in. A new reform is drawn from the 'market' stable, in most cases. This process was aided, at least up to 2014–15, whatever the future holds, by supposedly external and independent but increasingly 'insider' think-tanks such as the King's Fund and the Nuffield Trust, which are well-intentioned but, in an effort to be 'relevant' censor themselves to fit within the dialogue of the day. There is always a fine line between pragmatism and inadequate challenge, but the fact that the King's Fund could only decide that the Lansley reforms were a mistake about four years after nearly everybody else is a clue to the point which I am making.

As a result, policy-makers are fishing in the same pool each time. Primary-care commissioning and provider markets, then later, the same plus contracted-out commissioning and compulsory tendering: they are all recycled repeatedly. The next chapter considers how ideology in general and the messy politics of each reform episode have interacted.

REFERENCES

Alvarez-Rosete, A., et al. (2005). Effect of diverging policy across the NHS. *British Medical Journal, 331*(7522), 946.

Butler, R. (2004). *Butler review.* London: The Stationery Office.

Civitas. (2010). *The impact of the NHS market.* London: Civitas.

Department of Health (DoH). (1995). *Local freedoms, national responsibilities.* London: DoH.

Enthoven, A. (1987). *The theory and practice of managed competition.* Amsterdam: North-Holland.

Greer, S., & Jarman, H. (2007). *The Department of Health and the Civil Service: From Whitehall to Department of Delivery to where?* London: Nuffield Trust.

Le Grand, J. (2003). *Motivation, agency and public policy.* Oxford: Oxford University Press.

Le Grand, J., & Bartlett, W. (Eds.). (1993). *Quasi-markets and social policy.* London: Palgrave Macmillan.

Marmor, T. (2000). *The politics of medicare* (2nd ed.). New York: Aldine de Gruyter.

Paton, C. (2013). Hyper-stasis as opposed to hyper-activism: The politics of health policy in the USA set against England. *International Journal of Health Planning and Management, 28*(2), 216–227 (April-June).

Pierson, P. (2000). Path-dependence, increasing returns and the study of politics. *American Political Science Review, 94*(2), 251–267.

Public Inquiry. (2013). *Report of the mid Staffordshire NHS foundation trust public inquiry (the Francis report).* London: The Stationery Office.

Rhodes, R. (2011). *Everyday life in British Government.* Oxford: Oxford University Press.

Tuohy, C. (1999). *Accidental logics.* Oxford: OUP.

CHAPTER 8

Garbage-Can Politics Yet Neo-Liberal Ideology

The garbage-can theory of decision-making, originally employed to describe a university (Cohen et al. 1972), has been adapted into a theory of policy-making, with notable emphasis upon the health sector (Kingdon 1984; Paton 2006.) A particular type of garbage-can framework helps to explain the nature and form of the persistence of 'market reform' in the English NHS over the last 25 years—while also suggesting that the initial and ongoing 'market reform' per se has derived from the ideological hegemony of neo-liberalism in general rather than any evidence-based application of the ideas contained therein to health policy. The prevalence of the market as the main idea in reform has led to a form of ideological closure in English health policy today within the health policy elite.

'Market reform' does not mean that the NHS has been fully—let alone successfully—'marketised', or indeed that such an aspiration is either coherent or indeed possible. Here, as explained in Chap. 7, it is taken to mean that, when the 'groundhog day' of reform to the NHS recurs with striking regularity, it is the 'market solution' which dominates the policy agenda. What happens in the final design, and/or implementation of policy, is a different matter—and may often consist in sweeping up the mess left when a garbage-can is overenthusiastically raided by amnesiac policy hyenas advocating what amounts to permanent (organisational) revolution in the NHS.

The chapter thus combines the insights of a garbage-can approach—geared to analysing the policy trees within a political wood—with wider explanations of ideological hegemony, that is, of the nature of the wood

© The Author(s) 2016   121
C. Paton, *The Politics of Health Policy Reform in the UK*,
DOI 10.1057/978-1-137-47343-1_8

itself, and of how short-term politics may contribute to longer-term political biases, leading to ideological closure. It reviews the NHS reforms described above, from 1987 to 2015—in the UK from 1987 to 1998 and in England up to 2015. It traces the interplay of 'problems', policies, and politics in explaining not only individual health policies but also the trend of policy over time.

In so doing it raises the vexed question of 'evidence-based policy' and suggests that the very concept is limited in proportion to the limits of the 'rational' interpretation of the policy process. In the 'insider' world of intrinsic policy evaluation, evidence is sought as to the effect of already-determined policies, not as to the relative validity of policy alternatives. While this is understandable from a pragmatic viewpoint, it limits the role of evidence in a conservative direction, that is, 'policy-based evidence' which evaluates policy at the margins of an unevaluated direction-of-travel. The 'stories' which policy-makers and advisers tell each other are within the language of 'public sector reform, which is understood to mean 'more market forces' (and 'reform' is taken to be a *sine qua non* rather than something to be examined critically: reform as a hypothesis is superseded by reform as self-evident).

THE POLICY PROCESS: THROWING RATIONALITY INTO THE GARBAGE-CAN

The 'rational' interpretation of policy-making suggests to the present author, as described above, that policies are developed as means to an end, and that this 'end' consists in the solution to a problem which is generally accepted to be salient in the sense that a solution is necessary. This was *ipso facto* true of Allison's (1971) depiction of the 'rational actor' in his original study which concerned the Cuban Missile Crisis, and which, as it happens, was—like its alter ego, the original garbage-can study—a study of a decision rather than a policy. In the succeeding 40 years, his framework has been used and abused to analyse policy of all sorts, all over the world, although arguably it was a framework geared to its time and place (i.e. US foreign affairs decisions, or at least central executive **decision**-making as opposed to wider **policy**-making).

This fairly broad definition of rationality is compatible with 'neo-pluralism', which follows classic pluralism in that different interests are represented in the policy process but which also incorporates the state viewed as a separate interest rather than merely an inert forum for the interplay of social/economic interests.

This view of the state argues that, while there may not be unanimity of approach within the state, the state, in some respect, represents the public interest, problematic as that concept is, and seeks to promulgate policy which 'evidence' suggests is best suited to the end in question, which is moreover articulated overtly and is not 'essentially contested.' The fact that non-state bodies (e.g. in the English NHS, commercial interests; trade unions; professional interest-groups such as the BMA) may have different primary interests does not alter this fact necessarily (although it may come to do so over time, if the state is 'coopted' by the power of external interests).

Pluralism, to recall, is an alternative to unitarism, which argues that different actors, groups, and classes have the same interest, and to uni-tarism's alter egos—elitism, ruling-class theory, and the 'radical view of power': all of which claim in different ways that unitarism is manufac-tured rather than based on 'rational' or 'autonomous' choice. Pluralism may of course involve different views of rationality, that is, different ends sought by different interests which go beyond 'economic maximisation', whether these ends are self-consciously partial, altruistic, or neither (e.g. professionalism).

To that extent, it is a half-way house to the garbage-can approach now to be described. What pours pluralism into the garbage-can is the substan-tive and procedural arbitrariness to be described below. In policy-making, the 'rational' view has one important corollary: problems are primary; policies are secondary, or consequent; and politics (in the sense of agendas to which politicians subscribe, consciously or otherwise, other than solv-ing problems through appropriate policy) is not significant, or rather is an 'add on' in the model. The garbage-can approach, on the other hand, sees 'problems', 'policies', and 'politics' as three separate 'streams' each of which has a logic (and chronology) of its own. Only when the streams 'come together' do we get a (policy) decision, and the factors which bring the streams together are 'non-rational' (meaning that they will lead to the solving of problems rationally only by chance). It thus goes beyond even the more anarchic brand of pluralism in that the primacy of problems dis-appears from the model.

A modified garbage-can approach suggests a model of how the three logics of the three separate streams might create a chronology over time, that is, it looks at the cumulative effect of garbage-can (policy) decisions over time. We must also ask what else is necessary to explain policy biases which lead to ideological closure (especially in 'insider' policy circles) over time. The model is suggestive rather than definitive.

The model may illuminate the interplay of 'rationality', arbitrariness, and ideology in policy-making over time, and the relative roles of national political structure and political culture in accelerating or retarding the phenomenon of 'initiativitis' in policy whereby new policy for, and in, the NHS comes around as often as 'groundhog day', as detected for England increasingly over the last 30 years. This is very different to the USA, for example, which *ipso facto* has need of more policy activism (Paton 2013) to solve its health policy problems—not less, as a sceptical view of recent English incontinence in health policy-making might suggest.

Ideology in Policy

We might christen this model 'ideologically biased arationality': policy is substantially non-rational (not the same as irrational) as it is made piece-by-piece, but contained within ideological tramlines which are reinforced over time.

The notion of 'received wisdom' (i.e. what the prevailing 'policy elite' believes or wants to believe, or what the elite's channels of communication transmit to media which do not fundamentally challenge this account) is relevant in the case of 'market reform' to the NHS. In the 1970s and early 1980s, neo-liberal theory/ideology when applied to health policy was seen as impractical fringe extremism. By 2012, rejecting market competition, and particularly the purchaser/provider split, was seen as impractical nostalgia or ultra-Leftism ('Old Labour'). There has been no commensurate change in 'the facts'—indeed arguably no salient change at all. Some would argue that the facts indeed point to the failure of the market, the purchaser/provider split, and 'commissioning', singly and collectively (House of Commons 2010)

This 'mobilisation of bias' (Schattschneider 1960) affects new policy proposals. In other words, perception matters as well as 'reality'. The 'health policy elite' has interpreted things in a certain way, and advised politicians accordingly. And such 'policy insiders' may have aided an 'ideological closure' which has excluded 'policy outsiders'. To take merely one example: Keep the NHS Public, and its earlier sibling, the NHS Support Federation, were led by doctors such as the late Professor Harry Keen—fully as eminent as those 'on the inside' such as his old sparring partner from Guy's Hospital, Lord Ian McColl—but they were not in tune with the spirit of the age, and therefore were dismissed in 'mainstream policy circles' as irrelevant, despite being more in tune with public instinct than the elite comprising a 'London consensus' (Paton 2012)

Perception in other words may be filtered through an ideological lens. This is not the cod post-structuralist claim that there is no such thing as external reality but only language-created versions of reality. To apply this dubious insight to the real world of policy is to make a category-mistake. There are such things as real consequences of policy (e.g. increased access, higher costs et al.). Post-structuralism is a relativist fetish and a blind-alley; a wrong turning for those who wish to explore the very real role of ideology. How 'cause' and 'effect' are attributed, and how cause and correlation often fail to be distinguished, are affected by ideology, and this feeds into a narrative, affecting future options. But this is not to deny the real world out there. Rather than resorting to the egregious academic self-indulgence of post-structuralism or its better-known consequence, post-modernism, it is better to think of ideology, or to 'managed perception' by ideological thinkers, as a mobilisation of bias, a creation of orthodoxy and its subsequent acceptance as 'common sense', as with John Maynard Keynes's 'practical men' who think they are free of theory but who are in fact 'slaves to some defunct economist'.

One can note the strangely parochial and insular nature of health policy evaluation in England. This may seem a surprising judgement, as alleged lessons from other systems are frequently held up by would-be reformers. But true comparative work should be well-structured and thoughtful. It should compare, firstly, in order to understand one's own system; then to see which features present and absent in different polities seem to explain differences in healthcare systems; and then—and only then—to suggest modestly which, if any, features of one's own system might be susceptible to improvement, and how (i.e. what political implications are raised). To be sure, there are reams and reams on policy and reform in different countries. But most of these are structured descriptions (i.e. different healthcare systems compared in terms of some characteristics, such as mode of financing, mode of provision, and recent reforms) rather than structured critical analyses.

And facile, superficial comparison is common. This ranges from the simply wrong (statements such as 'Germany and France show that systems with more private financing and/or provision are more efficient and/or more capable of pleasing the consumer' : the sort of claim made repeatedly by think-tanks such as Reform and the Adam Smith Institute) to the misleading or partial, for example, concerning lessons for the NHS from the Health Maintenance Organisation known as Kaiser Permanente, in the USA (Feachem et al. 2002). Our political masters receive 'evidence' from senior NHS managers seeking to please their masters and ending up merely confusing them. But rigorous comparison is almost entirely absent—whether across the UK countries, across Europe, or beyond. Sometimes this does not matter. 'Fact finding trips' by health service managers abroad, led by the academic industry living off reform, usually latch onto fads which are here today and gone tomorrow.

Yet facile comparison can be highly dangerous. For example, when there was perfectly legitimate, indeed overdue, worry in 2010 about how the NHS's 'administrative costs' had risen from about 4% in the 1970s to about 14% by 2005 (even before the more egregious of New Labour's and the Coalition's reforms), then-Nuffield Trust Director Jennifer Dixon (House of Commons Select Committee 2010) implied that there was little to worry about as this seemingly high percentage was about the average for comparable systems. Yet the whole point was that surely a comparative advantage of the public NHS model is its potential for, and history of, much lower administrative costs (without this being a source of harm)—because of its single-payer public financing, absence of the costs of markets et al. In other words, such 'reassuring' comparison is mindless—mindless of the reasons for differences, and the desirability of being different on this dimension at least.

DEBUNKING A 'THEORY OF PROGRESS' IN POLICY?

In *Man and Society*, his review of classic political theory, John Plamenatz (1975) rejected the idea of a theory of progress for society—not on the now-trendy 'post-modernist' or 'post-structuralist' basis that all discourses are relativ(ist), but on the grounds that the criterion for progress changes over time.

In a nutshell: one society, or group, at one time, may consider the move from social state (time) A to social state (time) B to be progress, because it advances goal X, considered the most salient value or objective, or what we might call the most important element of the ethos of the age. Later, society (a different, although perhaps overlapping, population, at a later time) may consider the move from B to C to be progress, on the grounds that it advances goal Y. Yet, comparing A to C, goal X may not be advanced, and (comparing A to C) goal Y may not be advanced. 'Progress' is not cumulative in terms of either value (X or Y); nor is the decision-maker necessarily the same one. The reason for moving from A to B is different from the reason for moving from B to C, and so on. The part of B which led to its being judged more attractive than A is not the criterion for judging C more attractive than B, and so on.

While this view can be challenged regarding social or ethical progress over time, it has insight as an analogy for the policy-making process. Policy made at time A may be part-arbitrary, part-rational. Policy then made at time B may be likewise, but in 'rational' pursuit of different goals and with arbitrary ('political') elements which may or may not stem from the same source as the arbitrariness at time A.

There may well be a 'rational' input into each episode of policy-making, but it is unlikely to be determinant and, moreover, it is unlikely that cumulative policy-making episodes follow the same 'rational' path (i.e. pursue the same goals logically, defined as systematically in an evidence-based manner). Different values, goals, or mechanisms/modes of governance/incentives/institutions may be sought at different times. While it is possible to construct a 'rational'mix of these different values et al, and seek to realise that through the policy process over time (whether incrementally or not), the argument or hypothesis is that that is not what happens in practice.

For example: even while agreement may be attempted in terms of the 'mix' of values, through some sort of political consensus process (as with the parties brought together to 'agree' the NHS Plan of 2000, or the NHS Future Forum's (2011) attempted management of the 2011 'pause' in passage of the Health Bill), this is likely to be at the level of 'motherhood and apple pie' and to dodge the meaty questions about what this means in practice, in terms of funded priorities, the role of the market, the governance of providers et al. Thus there is no route-map, or compass, in empirical terms, to steer the policy process 'rationally' over time.

REVIEWING THE REFORMS: POLICY AND IMPLEMENTATION

The Thatcher Review of the NHS began, following the 'NHS winter of discontent' of 1987, in January 1988, although the resulting NHS and Community Care Act, passed in 1990, was formally implemented on 1st April 1991. What followed was the initial era of the purchaser/provider split and then the gradual development of 'primary care purchasing' in various forms from GP Fund-Holding after 1991 through to Total Purchasing by the end of the Conservatives' tenure. New Labour's reforms, after the period from 1997 to 2000 which stressed cultural but not structural reintegration of the English NHS, consisted in a flurry of centralist performance management, decentralisation of purchasing/commissioning agencies (Shifting the Balance 2001), the 'new market' (prefigured in 2002, Implementing the NHS Plan: Next Steps for Investment, Next Steps for Reform, but only implemented after 2006), a relative, limited but significant (in terms of tacit acceptance of error) re-centralisation of commissioning in 2006, prefigured in Commissioning a Patient-Led NHS, 2005, only three years after the original decentralisation, and then tacit planning through a new approach to reconfiguration (the Darzi (2008)period), from 2007. The Coalition's 2012 Act was the culmination of a chaotic period of policy zig-zagging, but in the general direction of 'more market'. And one may detect, by 2014 and 2015, the familiar back-peddling on market doctrine and its language ('competition'; 'choice') to which all governments so far have yielded when doctrine comes into conflict with other, more sensible, priorities in health policy and in the strategic management of the NHS.

Whether or not the pragmatic accommodation of different policies over time stemming from different policy regimes, that is, politics (e.g. from the internal market of the early 1990s through New Labour's gyrations to the Coalition's failed 'big bang'), occurs through compromise in the policy-making process or through disguised policy decisions in the process of implementation is a matter of empiricism. In the USA, for example, it tends to be the former; in England, the latter.

That said, 'Coalition politics' in 2011 may provide an example of the former, with the Health and Social Care Bill amended after the so-called pause, which would have been alien to the restless executive-dominance of either Thatcher or Blair. Even so, one must be careful. Firstly, the politics of coalition may after all turn out to have been an aberration. Secondly, political compromise resulting in policy compromise is not the same thing

as 'making something work in practice' through the implementation process. For example: the Health and Social Care Act of 2012 was just as
incoherent as it was before, indeed more so, after the 'pause' in its legislative passage in 2011 brought about by coalition politics.

Before the pause the Bill was more purely a pro-market bill, with all the
difficulties that would raise for the NHS as witnessed for example in 1995
and in 2006, only to a greater extent. That is, the incoherence lay in the
incompatibility of the market with other necessities. But after the pause,
the incoherence lay in the intrinsic confusion within the Act—which was
both pro-market and pro-'integration' without the latter being properly
defined. Unless integration meant 'integrated providers' (spanning hospital, primary, and community services) competing for contracts from commissioners, integration and the market were incompatible. And yet the
former would be a purely doctrinal—and unaffordable—solution to an
unnecessarily posed problem.

So it was in the implementation process that the 2012 Act would have
to be made coherent—and then, ironically, the ambiguous warm words
of the NHS Future Forum, and their footprint in the Act itself, would
be useful for politicians and NHS top managers in giving themselves the
necessary licence to make things work. Incidentally, we might therefore
note here that, although the phrase 'policy process' points to the fact
that policy and implementation are both part of one story, it still makes
sense to distinguish two processes within: the politics/policy process
points to how policy evolves, and the implementation process refers to
the rendering coherent, at least in some minimalist way, of the inherited
policy mix.

The aim here is to weigh rival explanations of policy-making and implementation. Consider firstly how problems and policies emerge, in order
to draw a comparison between the garbage-can and its counter-factual,
'rational policy-making.' In principle either might apply, or each might
apply at different times, involving different policy episodes. At one time,
problems may be pseudo-problems manufactured by politicians, the
media, think-tanks, other interests or a combination thereof. At another
time, problems may be 'real'. One is not concerned here with the point
that different people prioritise different problems differently, which is a
truism, but the pragmatic distinction between 'real' problems perceived
in terms of the stated aims of public policy (e.g. reducing long waiting
times for NHS care) and pseudo-problems which are emotive but poorly
quantified and/or unqualified (e.g. 'state medicine wastes money and is

PROBLEM	POLICY OPTIONS	POLITICS	DECISION
Winter 1987: NHS financial shortages leading to alleged deaths in baby units	More money Reform of NHS delivery Replacement or supplementation of NHS by private or public insurance	Thatcher rampant after third consecutive election victory Right-wing and neo-liberal think-tanks influential	Internal market (PM's Review 1988 & White Paper Feb.1989

Episode 8.1   Actual policy-making: Initial primacy of problem overtaken by politics; re-definition of problem by dominant political actors and ideology; policy options and decision dominated likewise, but without regard to evidence. This produces a dilemma and a new decision soon—Episode 8.2 below

unresponsive'; 'the market is destroying the NHS'—to offer two from opposite ends of the value, or political, spectrum).

The analysis below lists key policy episodes since the internal market was mooted in 1988, and therefore draws on the discussions in previous chapters. These can reasonably be considered the main 'reforms' to the governance and management of the NHS—deriving either from the realm of 'high politics' in the sense of politically instigated reforms which have courted attention beyond the health policy community or from the 'insider network' which brings together 'policy wonks', politicians and NHS leaders both clinical and/or managerial.

For each episode, we may ask what was the real objective of the policy, or what were the different objectives of the different actors who made the policy; what happened in practice; and what were the consequences, either of the policy or of the period in which the policy was seen as the dominant feature of the political-policy landscape.

The Internal Market

What were the real objectives of the policy? There is now a huge literature on the internal market—see for example the literature reviews conducted in Le Grand et al. (1998) and Civitas (2010). Here, let us note that the internal market's immediate cause was the need for the Prime Minister's (Thatcher) Review of the NHS (February 1988–February 1989) to find a 'big idea'.' The Thatcher Review in turn had been born in the PM's frustration at the 'media panic' over NHS funding in the winter of 1987/88. She wished to change the terms of debate to one about efficiency (Paton 1992.)

Efficiency is not necessarily the same as cost-control, but an important wing of the ruling Conservative party wished to do more with the money allocated to the NHS. Paradoxically, another wing of the Party, on the Right in the main, argued that more needed to be spent on health (care) but that a tax-funded service could not achieve this (either because they opposed more taxes or because they thought this would be inefficient). Thus there were contradictory motivations feeding into the Review, which left the Secretary of State up to July 1988 (John Moore) marginalised in the middle.

Much comment, especially by non-British commentators comparing health sector reform in different countries, suggest that the Thatcher reforms were about consumerism and patients. But this is to rewrite history. Neither the public nor the Thatcher government were exercised by this. It is true that those of neo-liberal bent in the Tory Party were (as were, more than ten years later, both Blairite policy-advisers and also 'Orange Book' Liberal Democrats such as Nick Clegg and David Laws) sceptical that the NHS could embrace 'consumerism' (without ever defining it very rigorously). But those Tories in 1988–1990, when the Health Act creating the internal market was passed—unlike the Blairites but akin to the Orange (neo-) Liberals—saw alternatives to the NHS as the best hope for 'consumerism'. Within the NHS, the agenda was more bang for the buck, through a centralist reform, despite the rhetoric. There may well have been 'underlying' social trends—less deference; more consumerism; in the NHS, more informed patients (more active and less patient patients!)—but these were not responsible for the reform initiative, nor for the shape the reforms took in practice.

Another potential explanation is of course 'policy showboating'. Later reforms under New Labour probably deserve this explanation more, as the Conservative reforms were born in the need to find an answer having asked the question—or rather, (at last, when the pragmatic Kenneth Clarke had replaced the hapless neo-liberal John Moore) having found an answer, to re-ask the question.

All this is important in understanding what actually happened. There was no competitive market, but rather three layers of planning to which 'the market' was subservient. This coincided with the Treasury's belief that 'the market' could be used to achieve certain planning goals which planning per se had not been able to achieve, given medical power and local parliamentarians' opposing service reconfigurations.

The first layer concerned the 'super-services' of the future, that is, the specialised and/or 'monopoly' providers which District 'purchasers' had to support, under regional or central tutelage. Second came the 'losers', mandated by a politicised market for downsizing and reconfiguration (e.g. a local DGH loses its A and E and becomes a community facility)—closure then (as now) being a 'bridge too far' except in mental health under the euphemistic guise of 'care in the community'.

The third layer was the contested middle area where planners had an open mind, and where the market could work in allocating hospitals into either of the first two categories, or alternatively leaving them as they were.

In this environment, the 'internal market' did not lead to a real market, let alone a competitive one. It could be called the 'old system in new garb'—crucially, in which conurbations with lots of hospitals within small areas were categorised by researchers as 'competitive.' But the behavioural features of competition were not usually present. Pluralism in provision and the web of decision-making based on tradition and GP- hospital links continued as before.

There is no real evidence that 'losers' in the market lost income any more than they would have under a planning system which invested in 'winners'. Loss of income by hospitals, where it happened, was more down to new priorities and the policy of 'tipping the balance' to primary and/or community services.

When it comes to consequences of policy uncovered through evaluative research, the key questions are therefore: what happened, when, and attributable to what (most likely, a plural 'what')?

Some research has suggested that the macro-productivity of 'self-governing' hospitals increased more in the early 1990s than previously (Le Grand and Robinson 1994). Some research however has suggested that 'market losers' had quality problems (Propper et al. 2004). Some has suggested that GP fund-holders had impact upon factors such as waiting times (Duscheiko et al. 2004). And some has pointed to the high costs per se of the policy. Interestingly, in this pre-outcome era when outcomes of care were even less available and robust than now, the faux-surrogate used in the 2000s—waiting times—were not used systematically in research about the internal market, only being used in a few local studies comparing wait-times for patients of GP fund-holders with patients whose contracts for care were handled by the Health Authority.

To what can we attribute outcomes; indeed, how can we interpret them? Here, I take the two most general system-wide outcomes associated potentially with the internal market—productivity and health outcomes.

The research on productivity is both simple and simplistic. It is simple in that it focuses on 'the whole NHS', using extant data such as Hospital Episode Statistics, to measure things like 'consultant episodes'. In seeking to correlate change in this aggregate measure with an intervention (an explanatory policy change), there are real difficulties in defining and demarcating the policy. Was there a 'market' in the NHS? Possibly. Of what sort? No consensus here. Was it consistent in form over the period? Almost certainly not. What was the period when 'market forces' were more salient? Possibly 1993–5, but by judgement and qualitative measures. In this context, it is simplistic bordering on ludicrous to correlate the market with macro-productivity.

Some empirical studies have been of high methodological quality but dependent upon dubious judgements. For example, in Le Grand and Robinson (1994), the new 'Self-Governing Trusts' were seen as a little more productive than hospitals which had not become Trusts. Understandably, given the fact that the 'internal market' had only just begun, this work could not conclude whether Trust status had been a success, or whether the already-more productive hospitals had become Trusts. This edited publication also explored how different regions of England had more or less of a proto-'market'. Yet the definition of a 'market' was simply in terms of plural provision of services within a given (size of) catchment area. This did not allow examination of whether referrals either were, or were capable of, being changed as a result of market choices as opposed to a range of other explanations (e.g. networks of provision; 'monopolistic competition' as opposed to 'perfect competition'; behavioural relationships; varying cultures in terms of travel to care; et al.)

One might respond: what about later studies? Le Grand et al. (1998) usefully reviewed some evidence on the by-then-defunct 'internal market'. But, again, the 'independent variable(s)' in the studies reviewed were not specified adequately. (To be fair, maybe they could not be.) For example: were the years 1991–1997 characterised by the same means of control and the same salience of the same incentives to providers? To this author, certainly not. Was 'the market' cover for increased central control? Arguably yes. These debates were not resolved empirically, but neither were they

PROBLEM	POLICY OPTIONS	POLITICS	DECISION
The mid-1990s: the 'internal market' at the crossroads: more or less market?; the role of GPs in purchasing also at the crossroads	More competition between hospitals/commu nity trusts More collaboration led by strong health authorities Expansion and transformation of GP Fund-Holding	Major as PM rather than Thatcher Market potentially closing hospitals GPs and new 'interests' lobbying	'Managed market'; regional plans by backdoor More primary care purchasing, larger-scale

Episode 8.2   Actual policy-making: Problem is actually a political problem: politicians fear the effects of the 'free market' upon local facilities, especially hospitals, and in making short-term decisions which are not warranted in terms of longer-term objectives; decision reflects this; scene is set for Episode 8.3: New Labour inherits an NHS in which the 'internal market' has already been reined in

factored in to the production of 'evidence'—in the sense of defining 'independent variables'. Was the period from 1997 to 1999 a 'period of stagnation' with Health Secretary Frank Dobson somehow cast as a latter-day Brezhnev by NHS Sovietologists? Not really, but one would think so from the accumulating 'conventional wisdom, including sneers from Dobson's successors as Health Secretary (e.g. John Reid referred to 'Old Dobbo' rejecting advice on 'modernising' the NHS in a speech to NHS decision-makers in Birmingham in summer 2004). Did 'targets' end in 1995 and 'the market' begin again? Clearly not. And so on.

Primary Care Purchasing: Total Purchasing After the Mid-1990s (A Prototype for the Coalition from 2012)

Some of the most detailed research concerning the latter part of the internal market era (1995–1997) was into the purchasing of healthcare by primary care organisations, in particular, GP practices involved in the different types of 'fund-holding' and also consortia of practices (both categories independent of the local Health Authority) and larger-scale 'total purchasing' by larger groups of GPs across geographical areas, responsible to a parent health authority (King's Fund 1998). The research on the so-called Total Purchasing Pilots did not test hypotheses about markets per se, but sought to evaluate outcomes, understandably not in terms of mortality or morbidity data but in terms of new modes of behaviour and 'processes', of innovations in particular services, and of perceptions by those involved of success and failure.

The focus was upon evaluating not whether markets worked or did not, but upon the costs and benefits (liberally construed) of different types of 'primary care purchasing'. To simplify from a rich vein of research, the main conclusion was that there was no simple conclusion, but that primary care purchasing seemed to work best where it: concerned itself with primary care, community services and the overlap between these; was expensive (i.e. success did not come cheaply); and reflected the interests of 'product champions' (GPs and others) and enthusiasts—meaning that it tended to be partial rather than comprehensive as regards the range of services, in its successful application, and (a related point) was in the main, although not without exceptions, relatively unconcerned with the wides-cale purchasing of hospital services (secondary or tertiary.)

Thus the research, in the view of the present author, to the extent that it had import for policy-makers and strategic managers, gave contextual guidance in the event that GP purchasing/commissioning had to be done—not conclusions as to whether this was or was not a good thing per se, although it would not be to extrapolate too boldly to conclude that there was *little evidence for, and much against, making GPs responsible for purchasing/commissioning* 'in the round'. Here, we might note that the Coalition's agenda for re-reform of the NHS, 2010–11, was formed in an evidence-free zone, it seemed, despite the existence of—for once—a corpus of research from an earlier phase which had insight for the newly determined approach more than ten years later. Thus evidence was (probably) unknown (with no excuse) or (possibly) not only ignored but turned on its head.

The evidence was less important, either way, than the ideology of competition (GPs could not commission primary care, because—*if* a market was deemed to operate or it was thought desirable to foster a market culture—then this would be a conflict of interest). Equally, GPs 'should' commission hospital services (even if the evidence said they should not) so that a market could operate (hospital competition) without New Labour's 'bureaucracy' (abolish PCTs as the latest policy from the garbage-can), that is, market plus garbage-can equals policy.

PROBLEM	POLICY OPTIONS	POLITICS	
		New Labour beats Tories	
Longer waiting times; tight funding; Tories mistrusted on NHS	'Abolish internal market'; end purchaser/provid er split	Blair vows to 'govern as *New* Labour'	**DECISION**
	Maintain split but end 'market' culture	NHS in 1948 seen as 'greatest act of modernization by a Labour government'	Temporary relegation of market Abolish GPFH
	Spend more money		
		Lack of appetite for ideological or structural regorganisation	

Episode 8.3   Actual policy-making: Politics prevents more money (the new Chancellor sticks to Tory spending plans to assuage financial markets); abolition of internal market a hollow policy, as market radicalism already reined in and/yet market mechanisms remain (purchaser/provider split, with separate NHS trusts) as sword of Damocles for the future; abolition of market therefore merely a symbol of Labour's 'love of the NHS'; modest financial gain from this to go to modest waiting-list initiative. Scene set for Episode 8.4

In one respect, it makes sense to distinguish between the last years of the Conservative government (1995–7), when a more collaborative form of behaviour was confirmed, and the first phase of New Labour, when the internal market was allegedly 'abolished'. In another sense, they are organically linked: the Total Purchasing Pilots transmogrified into Primary Care Groups, and then Trusts, and the change after 1997 was evolutionary in the main—not least in that the last years of 1990s Conservative government saw a 'dampening down' of the market and the first years of the 1997 Labour government saw a move away from the market culture. That said, the years 1997–9 marked a real belief that the culture of the market was damaging, and that local 'collaboration' should replace market relationships—which led to the withering of the schemes which relied not so much on market forces as 'letting a thousand flowers bloom', for example, the variations within the Total Purchasing Pilots (King's Fund 1998).

For present purposes: if the 'intervention' or independent variable is 'collaboration' or 'local initiative across service boundaries' or both, how can we quantify, or rather qualify, that concept in order to find a causal, or at least correlated, link to 'outcomes' such as health service productivity, health outcomes (quality), or whatever?

The short answer is, we cannot in practice and only with a leap of the imagination in theory. Different policy consequences, or new institutions and structures, can be studied at the local (micro) level, to seek explanations through qualitative research, perhaps including 'case studies', of 'outcomes'. But these are very unlikely to be the 'ultimate' outcomes, that is, health status change, relative health status change, or redistribution of health status et al.

There is no systematic research on the 1997–99 're-integration' of the NHS in terms of the macro-factors which have featured in evaluations of 'the market'. The 1997 White Paper, the New NHS, Modern, Dependable, did not prefigure a 'sexy' reform which could be characterised in terms of economics-textbook theory, or in terms of what could be measured quantitatively. Some research has sought so suggest that productivity started to fall in this era. However research would need to specify some hypothesis about the time-lag, if any, between policy change—or diktat—and such an outcome. How can we compare six years (1991–7), with two (1997–9), moreover? Perhaps more importantly, given the argument of the pages above, we cannot posit the replacement of one 'regime' (in terms of governance) by another in 1997, at least unless we are willing also to posit changes of regime *within* the periods usually treated as one (e.g. 'the internal market' 1991–97).

To put it another way: if there was higher productivity in the years of the market, how do we attribute this to a 'market' which varied across the country and during which the levers of control may have lain outside local market institutions?

Post-1999, the NHS presided over by the new 'Sun King of Health', Secretary of State Alan (l'etat, c'est moi) Milburn, was a 'new hierarchy', that is, less a Weberian or traditional bureaucracy than a centralist 'command and control' system, albeit using cumbersome institutions derived from the internal market era (1991–97) which diminished the coherence of the 'control', if not the command. When Milburn came to renounce centralism in theory if not in practice, it was difficult to know whether the problem perceived both by Milburn and his opponents at the coal-face who resented his restless string-pulling was centralism per se or the labyrinthine routes central command had to follow.

PROBLEM	POLICY OPTIONS	POLITICS	DECISION
Waiting lists/times rising (despite promise to cut modestly in 1997) in 1999	Central targets	Blair turns attention to NHS	NHS Plan
	More money	Scornful attack on his own party by Lord Winston in Jan 2000	

Episode 8.4   Actual policy-making: 'Moral panic' at waiting-list rise (temporary, as it turned out); central initiatives lead to apotheosis of 'targets' and the 'new centralism' in the NHS; not strong ideological element at this stage, but scene set for Episode 8.5 as the quasi-neo-liberal modernisers (Milburn et al.) replace the left-of-centre (Dobson) and put down a marker in the NHS *plan* for 'reform to accompany investment'

The abolition of the 'meso' tier (regional health authorities) in fact had left strategic management having to operate from the centre or localities, with the latter option often retarded by fragmented local NHS institutions jostling for legitimacy (especially 2002–6). Thus many functions were inappropriately centralised (e.g. control of, and monitoring of, new capital developments, not least through the PFI) and others were in appropriately localised (e.g. 'commissioning', which required in many cases to be 'strategic commissioning', that is, planning, a word which New Labour—in a revelation of its thin skin and lack of intellectual confidence despite all the rhetoric—did not dare to use for fear of being thought Old Labour).

So Milburn's Damascene conversion to 'devolution' post 2001 (leaving aside the fact that it was not even decentralisation, but merely deconcentration (Rondinelli 1983), given the mode of constituting and making appointments to 'local PCTs') often undermined itself in practice—in part because of the inability of politicians to 'let go' but also because of the bias created by the hole in the middle where proper regional strategic management used to be. The Conservatives had thrown out the baby of meso-governance with the bathwater of alleged 'bureaucracy', in 1996 when Regional Health Authorities were replaced by Regional Offices, and New Labour went further in replacing eight Regional Offices with 29 'Strategic Health Authorities' in 2001/2.

How can we explain later research (OECD 2009) which implies that NHS productivity has been falling throughout the late 1990s and the 2000s, when the era of central targets—otherwise said to have produced results—was at its zenith in the early 2000s, to be followed by (allegedly) a new market by the mid-2000s. Pro-market politicians and analysts cannot have it both ways. They cannot say, 'the market produced results in the early 2000s' (even when, from 1999 to 2005, it was central control which was dominant) and yet also say, 'productivity fell because market reform had not really happened, and still hasn't.' Even less can they say the market can be used to explain marginally higher productivity in the 1990s than before and after, unless they are also willing to say that a more radical market from the mid-2000s on did *not* produce higher productivity. They might say, yes but there were other confounding factors after the mid 2000s. If so, what of the other confounding factors in the 1990s (e.g. Secretary of State's control via politically appointed Regional Chairmen i.e. command rather than market forces).

There is a confusion in some cases between 'waiting times' and productivity. Waiting times qua target waiting-time maxima fell significantly in, or just after, the heyday of central control, it seems (2000–2006). Waiting times qua average/total waiting times fell also, but later, in the years to 2010. Yet aggregate productivity has allegedly been falling in all those years, and—paradoxically—especially the latter.

We might like to recall that the NHS allegedly suffered from 'under investment' in the 1990s. While revenue budgets increased slightly, capital budgets were squeezed—a classic recipe to produce a misleading arithmetical truism of 'higher productivity' i.e. the same or increasing output/workload, 'sweating the (increasingly creaky) assets'. We saw the mirror-image of this in the 2000s: pay increases to allow NHS staff to catch up with the rest of the economy (albeit poorly handled in the case of the doctors) and new hospitals (albeit via inefficient Private Finance Initiatives)—overall, a good thing, to most people other than conventional productivity statisticians, that is, reduced productivity as an equally misleading statistical truism, owing to the same or increasing output/workload yet higher costs of labour and capital.

We can add continual reorganisations and expensive, dysfunctional, evanescent structures as a major additional cost, during the high noon of New Labour centralist tinkering (Paton 2006). But this does not increase the case for 'marketisation'. It shows, to the contrary, how much more could have been achieved *without* further marketisation, in the absence of such distractions—which increased the complexity of the purchaser/provider split, to ever-decreasing effect (and incurred other unnecessary costs, such as the mishandled paybill in the early- to mid-2000s and the large administrative costs associated with the PFI).

PROBLEM	POLICY OPTIONS	POLITICS	DECISION
No new/discernible 'problem'; underlying belief by neo-liberals and New Labour that low productivity is a problem for the NHS	Patient choice New market	New advisors at DoH/No 10; right-wing think-tanks influence Blair	Shifting the Balance, 2001 'Next Steps for Investment, Next Steps for Reform', 2002

Episode 8.5   Actual policy-making: Blairites in government, including the Health Secretary, decide to add market forces to central targets. Repeated organisational change and reorganisation follows from 2001 to 2006. Layers of policies and initiatives help contribute to 'deficit crisis' of 2005–6. In 2006, various initiatives dating back to 2002 are codified in 2006 into the so-called health reform programme.

The most obvious source of complexity here is that the 'decentralisation' represented by Shifting the Balance (2001), the creation of small PCTs and small SHAs, co-existed with the heyday of the central target regime, and yet is often assumed to be the same as, or co-terminous with, the 'new market'—which may have accompanied it in the mind of the initiating Secretary of State (Milburn) but certainly was separate in practice.

It was this confusion which allowed the English 'target achievements' of the period to be attributed to the market by Blairite policy-advisers and speech-writers (e.g. Philip Collins who became a Times columnist), albeit casually. Nevertheless this casualness produced a casualty, accuracy, and even truth—and produced also a phoney orthodoxy which persists to this day. While the 'new market' did emerge at least in some respects later (after 2006), the perception that Blairite markets had only got into full swing when they gave way in 2007/8 to Brownite drift is just that—a perception. Brown's health policy guru, Ara Darzi, had been an adviser to Health Secretary Hewitt from 2005, and his linkage of 'quality' to reconfigured delivery ('the new planning', one might call it) was not wholly a post-Blair phenomenon. Rather, it was another layer of policy overlaid on the existing, ever-thickening shag.

Yet the NHS chattering classes saw Health Secretary Burnham's surely unexceptional view that NHS providers should be the 'preferred provider' as a sea-change, as if the rarefied world of the Competition and Collaboration Commission, a pro-market quango created to invigorate market reform, was material to provision (which in most cases, it was not). As the world's largest village with the smallest breadth of punditry, the NHS has a capacity to believe its own group-think.

On a more academic note, we might suggest that the 'new market', even if it can be distinguished from the institutional decentralisation which preceded it (and which was partially reversed before it arrived), operated *either* for a short period (i.e. 2006–2007/8) which makes its 'outcomes' difficult to attribute *or* for a longer period (i.e. to 2010 and beyond) which would mean attributing the 'falling productivity' of 2007–2010 and beyond to the market.

A body of work now exists which suggests that the period was characterised by the high costs and low benefits (House of Commons 2010, 2011) of failed local commissioning. To be fair, much of this poor outcome is arguably attributable to bungled decentralisation rather than the market. So we are left no further forward than in 1997, when the first (internal) market was 'all over' (Paton et al. 1997)—not knowing whether the (at best) equivocal and (at worst) poor outcome was due to too much market or too little market, or indeed whether the market, if it were to be rendered compatible with a publicly governed NHS, was bound to be cumbersome and of poor cost-effectiveness.

The Foundation Trust (FT) policy, described above, deserves a mention. Before the Mid Staffordshire Foundation Trust scandal involving neglected patients and allegedly high excessive mortality, anecdote and more-than-anecdote (e.g. reports by independent data analyst Dr. Foster, advised by some of the most eminent epidemiologists and statisticians, up to 2010) suggested that 'finance and waiting-time targets' had taken precedence over 'quality' in much of the FT sector. We might contrast the situation in the health sector with that in education, where the FT sibling, Academies, seemed to focus more on quality. Perhaps this is simply because the 'target regime' stressed different 'must-dos' in the different sectors, at different times: the FT regime did not consist in market regulation at this times so much as in outsourced target policing, with Monitor as the outsourced performance manager.

Research into 'quality' in the first market era was limited. The internal market was not primarily about quality—in practice, whatever the (retrospective) belief that it was borne in by a consumerist tide. In practice, contracts between purchaser and provider were mostly about price and quantity, and heavily geared to restating old realities in new language (Paton et al. 1998). The most significant research about the possible effect of the internal market qua price competition upon clinical quality, in the most basic form, that is, mortality rates, suggested that, in areas of the country where competition was strongest, the weaker competitors featured worsened outcomes. This research was all the more powerful in that the lead researcher Carol Propper had advised the NHS Chief Executive on implementing the internal market, in her paper 'Local Freedoms, National Responsibilities' (DoH 1995).

Her later research was interpreted as implying that choice under a standard pricing regime was good for quality, a conclusion derived empirically for the first time in the UK (England) although US Research was more plentiful. Again, the good faith of the research and competence of the method per se is not in doubt. But doubts about the characterisations of the market in practice in these studies are similar to those noted above in Le Grand and Robinson (1994). The existence of plural providers and even of changed patient flows does not mean that patient choice (the alleged motive force of the 'new market' in the noughties) has led to reduced mortality rates (in the studied specialties—cardiac surgery and cancer care). Do we know that it is the market which has achieved these outcomes, if plural provision is not the same as a functioning market? We would need well-targeted qualitative research in the same sites, which traced behaviour and outcomes.

An alternative hypothesis, for example, is that changed patient flows result from the reconfiguration of (especially) specialised services in regional or area 'centres'. Inevitably, therefore, GP and other referrals will be increasingly to these centres, which are likely to have better outcomes. In order to set up the further research, one would have to model inter alia *how* the market was believed to have increased quality (i.e. reduced mortality, ceteris paribus). Did patients ask their GPs, or choose through 'choose and book', hospitals with better outcomes data? Was such data systematically available in the research sites at the time of the research? Did GPs alter their referral patterns in more traditional ways, for example, through 'information on the medical'grapevine? And so on.

Overall, Mays et al. (op.cit.) (2011) concluded that the market had not achieved much but had not done much damage either—but did

PROBLEM	POLICY OPTIONS	POLITICS	DECISION
NHS staff alienated by jargon and continuing turbulence of 'Health Reform Programme'	Less market ideology	Brown becomes PM, 2007	'Darzi'service reviews
	Reconfiguration of services		'Quality' reimbursement
Quality worries coming the fore, as in late 1990s	Primary and community services to obviate hospital admissions and facilitate discharge		

Episode 8.6 Actual policy-making: No new top-down reorganisations. Nevertheless, planning in-all-but-name leads to downplaying of provider competition as end in itself. Patient choice continues, but hospital reconfigurations mean it is less feasible for specialised care. Continuation of 'commissioner development' through the expensive, private consultant-driven 'world class commissioning'.

not explore the cost either of reform in general or of the transactions inherent in market relations in particular.

As in the USSR of yore, to return to the NHS Sovietology (which delights in depicting state control within the NHS as 'Stalinist') different regimes take on the character of stereotypes. Khrushchev's era was innovation; Brezhnev's 'stagnation'. So in the NHS, it is argued, where the drift of Brown allegedly followed the dynamism of Blair. Actually, Brown was simply prepossessed with other things, leaving the NHS to sort out the reforms set in train by his predecessor. If such sorting-out meant compromise, it is facile to blame Brown, just as Thatcherite believers sought to blame her successor John Major when the Thatcherite chickens came home to roost.

The research which had recently come to the notice of the Coalition government is that which suggested that the post-2006 'choice market' had improved quality (in the form of mortality ratios being reduced where choice has operated) (Cooper et al. op. cit). Again, however, much is open to doubt. The hypothesis is that there is a cut-off point, that is, the year 2006, which is used to mark when the choise policy was 'turned on', after which areas of the country characterised by 'more market choice' widened

PROBLEM	POLICY OPTIONS	POLITICS	DECISION
Growing realization of cost of continual reorganization and of 'commissioning', with dubious benefit	Nostalgia for GP purchasing Direct patient 'vouchers' and/or control	Conservative-led government after May 2010 Lansley surprises many with 'big bang'	White Paper, 'Equity and Excellence'; Health Bill
'Stafford' scandal; quality worries – especially in Foundation Trust sector; uneven quality and performance			

Episode 8.7   Actual policy-making: Major top-down reorganisation to promote 'bottom-up' commissioning of services; 'reorganisation to end all reorganisations in the future'; removal of intermediary planning/management layers; more market

their quality differential with those characterised by 'less market choice'. Yet this cut-off point, marking the 'policy off, policy on' transition, does not reflect English NHS reality. There was no country-wide adoption of choice (or changed provider behaviour) then. Indeed Peckham et al. (2012) suggest that the rhetoric of (market-based) 'choice' in England and very different rhetoric elsewhere in the UK has masked a fairly similar reality in all these countries.

Choice has varied significantly, as have different Payment by Results regimes (the ways in which patient flows are reimbursed) in different areas of the country 'on the ground (reflecting different SHA approaches), and very much so in different local health economies. English 'choice' has been 'managed choice', with the emphasis on the former to such an extent that the word 'choice' is suspect. Referral centres, which restrict choice, and different ways of running 'choose and book' (the offering of choice at the patient's point of use) were handled differently in the context of different 'market' management strategies by SHAs and different reimbursement (or non-reimbursement) policies by PCTs.

The research attempted to model market structure in different ways, to avoid confounding issues e.g. urbanisation or density of provision which may mean multiple local or regional providers but not necessarily a 'market.' But although Cooper et al seek to 'triangulate' structure, I am not sure that it is market structure which they are triangulating: the 'independent variable' (i.e. degree of market) is capable of being interpreted differently—and one would need significant qualitative research to 'unpack' this.

All the quantitative research seeking to model the effect of the market—of one sort or another—over the last 20 years is bedevilled by politics: we have not seen an internal market from 1991 to 1997; there was not a market from 1997 to 2002/6, et al. We have instead seen a complex embedding of different 'governance regimes' at different times, at national level and with different combinations of regime and timescale at meso- and local levels too (Paton 2006).

It should be noted that the financial crisis facing the NHS in 2015–16 and beyond made the 2006 'deficit crisis' look like a gentle aperitif—a self-induced problem in an era of plenty—as opposed to a major problem in a period of fiscal restraint, if not austerity, as in 2015–16. To give one graphic example: in 2006, the Staffordshire NHS economy was facing a deficit of about £40 million; in 2016, it is about £200 million. The likelihood that such ideological self-indulgences as 'pro-competitive market reform' would be allowed to dominate policy (whatever the rhetoric) was even less. Instead sweetheart contracts with providers became the order of the day.

Moreover, hospitals might follow Albert Hirschman's (1970) counter-intuitive 'example' from the Nigerian railways of being rather glad if the more demanding consumers went elsewhere.

Therefore, to the extent that Coalition policy drew on the Blairite belief that competition works, it was at best contestable and at worst 'bad science' (Pollock et al. 2012).

There has been neither intellectual consistency about, nor popular control over, health policy. What Labour decided about health policy between losing in 1992 (yet again, this time seminally, leading to the birth of 'New Labour')

PROBLEM	POLICY OPTIONS	POLITICS	DECISION
'Biggest re-organisation yet'	Reverse policy OR review policy	Tories losing new-found trust on NHS	'Pause'; Health Bill 'Mark 2' ('Mark 3', after Lords amendments)

Episode 8.8   Actual policy-making: Government uses NHS Future Forum as midwife for compromise. Unclear now as to whether market competition is to be dominant: new policy seen as fudge by neo-liberal supporters of Lansley's original Bill in both Conservative and New Labour camps (Liberal Democrat 'Orange Book' pro-market liberals are drowned out by wider Liberal Democrat fury at the reforms); House of Lords has seminal role in ironing out a few of the remaining policy's rough edges and uncertainties

and winning in 1997—very little—was less important than ad hoc decisions by Prime Ministers and/or Ministers and their small cabals, in response to (mostly media) 'events, dear boy.' What the Conservatives decided between losing in 1997 and winning in 2010—very little—was, at first, some faith-based generalities about tax-breaks for private insurance and, secondly, the reversal of that and an adoption of the New Labour approach to the market as of 2005 onwards, with a not-quite-hidden reaffirmation of GP purchasing, which later took centre stage in the White Paper of 2010 to most people's surprise. None of this had anything to do with evidence, except where it actually seemed to run counter to what extant evidence there was, as in the case of the remit for Clinical Commissioning Groups.

In general, politicians and other actors have 'learned' what they already 'knew'. Believers in the market have 'learned' that reforms tend to be compromised. They see this as reprehensible, as with the result of the 'pause', being greeted with dismay by academics such as Le Grand, Tory back-benchers of the neo-liberal variety and New Labour thrusters such as Milburn. 'Politics' is blamed, even by politicians as well as by academic economists. Yet we should distinguish between avoidable, 'negative' politics and inevitable, or desirable, 'positive' politics. Those who call for politics to be taken out of the NHS are referring to other people's politics.

Believers in a planned NHS, with or without choice, have 'learned' that the vast sums of money spent on teasing the elusive 'perfect market' into being would be better spent in more effective ways.

More specifically: Tony Blair 'learned' (Blair 2008) that he tried too little and moved too slowly, perhaps Mrs. Thatcher's view had she reflected seriously on public sector reform. His faithful but increasingly frustrated

Health Secretary, Alan Milburn, came to a similar conclusion. Labour in opposition after 2010, and especially after 2015, has retreated to its pre-2006 compromise. The Orange Book Liberal Democrats have disappeared from Parliament after 2015, with the exception of their former leader Nick Clegg. Cameron has been torn, as in policy generally, between hugging the NHS and calling for tough love, as with his infamous 'hug a hoodie' phase.

None of the above is remotely related to evidence about NHS reform, in pursuit of the market or otherwise. But more than this: the type of 'learning' which has led to the ongoing re-re-re-reform of the NHS has been, at worst, illiterate or unfounded and, at best, fragmentary and 'un-joined-up', to make Blair's neologism even uglier by inserting the negative. As an example of the former: Blair's view (Blair 2008) that he 'learned' too late that he had not done enough 'public service reform' is simply unfounded. It is a fallacy that business lives in a state of permanent revolution, a fallacy easily swallowed by those who have never worked in business but think of themselves as its proselytisers. Perhaps more tellingly, Blair's approach to NHS reform was superficial—he sought to achieve his ends without understanding the past (e.g. what sort of 'choice' already existed; what the actual result of his layers of reform might be etc.).

Regarding reform over time, we can see Plamenatz's anti-theory of progress at work:

The Tory market of the 1990s was harmful for quality and yet costly. Minor successes may have included GP pharmaceutical cost-control (although there is no serious research which addressed whether patient access to more expensive drugs was denied even when beneficial) and 'productivity', although (see above) this is almost impossible to attribute to 'the market' in the 1990s as opposed to other factors.

New Labour sought to address this partially, first by 'dampening down' the market culture and then—when it sought its own market—seeking a price-regulated market in quality. But it then sought to address problems it thought it found with its own early approach by forgetting the consequences of the reforms it had earlier sought to abolish.

Thus the 2001 policy, Shifting the Balance of Power, massively increased management costs (in fact, one should say 'administrative costs', as the costs were mostly based on fragmenting planning/purchasing/commissioning and repairing loss of strategic power 'by the back door'), arguably worse than during the 1990s market. And the problem of 'backdoor' price competition can be argued to have been opened up by the way in which purchasers/commissioners reimbursed hospitals and other providers for care beyond contracted volume.

The Coalition White Paper and the first version of the Health Bill opened up all the questions which had gradually become less controversial over the 1990s and 2000s—all was 'up for grabs' again, as the Health Select Committee (Tory) Chairman Stephen Dorrell (former Health Secretary from 1995 to 1997) put it.

This is the general overview which is spelled out in more detail in the eight periods analysed above, when policy change at each stage can be described as part-rational, part-non-rational, and part-irrational. Later change may then have failed to continue the 'rational' progress, while making 'rational' progress on another dimension (which may have consisted in undoing 'irrational' change at an earlier phase.

At one stage, 'politics' rather than (rational attempt to solve) a 'problem' may have applied in one area of policy—while rationality may have applied to the same area at a later or earlier stage. At the same time, a different area of policy may have witnessed a 'rational' approach to policy, only for 'politics' to apply later and perhaps abandon the 'rational' direction.

Note that 'politics' is not a pejorative term. For example, politicians in the 1990s (despite the market rhetoric and structures) and much more in the 2000s embraced waiting-time targets, which may have been very beneficial to patients in A and E, in outpatient clinics and in waiting times for operations or other forms of treatment. To clinicians, the perverse effects of targets often outweighed the benefits; for patients and politicians, it was often the other way around. There is no 'rational' way to gain consensus as to which is 'right' as opposed to compromise around the policy mix (i.e. moderated targets).

Different Explanations for Reform

The garbage-can theory points to how different 'streams' (politics, policy, problems) come together at 'decision points'. But since the latter are themselves occasioned by politicians or powerful interests (e.g. the media creating a 'moral panic' about an issue), it becomes a moot point how, why, and how often decision-points arise when tracing the trajectory of ongoing policy in an area such as health.

The ever-increasing circles through which health policy (in the sense of NHS governance and structure) has been twisting over the last 25 years— the accelerating increase in number and frequency of decision-points—

is explainable by the changing nature of government policy-making in England in areas where government pays the piper and pulls the levers (whatever facile rhetoric about 'decentralisation' et al it may employ and even believe). Governments seek to keep afloat in a media-sea (a phrase attributed to former Home Secretary Charles Clarke) and each street-level incident in the NHS (e.g. a confrontation with an irate patient or relative; an operation gone wrong; a much-delayed procedure causing hardship) has the capacity to escalate into a 'crisis', thence a 'moral panic', thence another initiative.

So far, so garbage-can (albeit one emptied daily even when it is almost empty). But add in the concept of hegemony. The ideological closure, in elite policy circles, around 'the market' means that solutions emphasise, re-emphasise, re-interpret, revive, re-hash, or reform 'market solutions'.

Let us now trace the overall movement from Episode 8.1, 8.2, 8.3, 8.4, 8.5, 8.6, 8.7 and 8.8—that is, the 'story' of reform over 25 years—through different 'lenses' and subsequently from a perspective which brings together these different lenses.

Lens 1 Rationality
Lens 2 Pluralist Rationality
Lens 3 Power Elite; Structural Interests; Ruling Class
Lens 4 Garbage Can
Lens 5 Ideology; 'radical' power; 'discourse'
Unifying lens: explaining 25 years

Lens 1

The NHS attracts substantial consensus around its ethical principles and its goals. Even in a neo-liberal age, neo-liberal think-tanks are not popular when they propose alternatives to the NHS. That said, their advocacy of market mechanisms to increase efficiency get more attention as the need to make state funding go further grows more pressing. As a result, the internal market was tried, then amended when its flaws became apparent. Later, alternative market versions were tried, learning from the past (e.g. replacing price competition with quality competition; then bringing GPs more squarely into the driving seat than previously as reforms such as Practice Based Commissioning were found to be too timid to achieve this.

This is the 'policy logic.' But note that this lens means one is looking though rationality-tinted glasses in the following sense: policy-makers are assumed to represent 'all good men and true' as they (1) come to rational consensus rather than political compromise; (2) to seek the best means to agreed ends, on the basis of as much salient evidence as possible; and (3) to amend policy in response to changing evidence about unchanging goals. The model is unitarist as opposed to pluralist, in that—although diversity of position in the system is recognised, perhaps—it is not thought to lead to divergence of interest.

Lens 2

The government's role under 'neo-pluralism' is to intervene with its own policy which is different from, although influenced by, the more instrumental rationality of specific interest-groups and parties. It is assumed that different specific (as opposed to 'whole population') interests (e.g. the non-health corporate sector in the economy; the medical profession; various managerial cadres created by various health reforms over time) may be 'rational' in pursuing their goals, but that these goals are incompatible, at least frequently, and that compromise is reached—both in policy-making and in implementation ('post policy')—through bargaining rather than rational consensus. The state is an actor in this process, and not merely the provider of a framework to referee the bargaining (as in classical, as opposed to 'neo', pluralism).

Note that this lens assumes rationality but 'pluralist' disagreement as opposed to 'unitarist' consensus around both goals and evidence-based policy. Policy-makers (state actors) are assumed (1) to take into account different interests which are reconciled through political compromise rather than rational consensus; (2) seek their own ends, albeit possible rationally in response to evidence about (both) system outcomes (and) or their own 'best means of achieving their interests'; and (3) to change policy in response to a balance between their own views and the relative strength of different interests (but—unlike Lens 3 below—which are spread enough in terms of power to allow the characterisation, 'pluralist', rather than 'elitist.'

The state's own interest may be considered to be either the 'public interest', whatever that is, or the special interests which a state bureaucracy, or different parts thereof, has in (e.g.) maintaining the status-quo (Allison 1971) or maximising its benefit (as in the 'rational choice' or 'institutional rational choice' (Dunleavy 1989) literature.

Lens 3

Similar to Lens 2, except that an interest is powerful enough to dominate others (elite) in the bargaining process; and/or to have a stable, structurally based position in the system to give it continuing power (structural interest); and/or to derive its power from its role as part of a ruling class based on the economic power of capital as opposed to labour.

In all such cases, policy is 'captured'—and may seem 'rational' in that opposition is weak or does not exist (in the mainstream policy elite, or the legislative process), yet this 'unitarism' is based upon power rather than rationality in the sense of Lens 1.

A power elite is not necessarily based on the power of capital (e.g. the medical profession was seen as such in many health policy literature in earlier days (Exworthy et al. 2011). A structural interest is likely to be economically based, but not necessarily as a result of ownership of private capital. A ruling class in the Marxist sense derives power from ownership of, control of or benefit from private capital.

Note that health policy need not be 'run', instrumentally, by a ruling class, but biased so that the wider interests of that class are not disadvantaged (i.e. a functionalist explanation *or* an explanation which points to the perceived or real impossibility for policy-makers of challenging this orthodoxy without economic or political ruin).

Lens 4

The garbage-can theory suggests that problems, 'policy solutions', and politics are interchangeable as primary motivations for change in policy, and that how this happens is non-rational. There may be some, or part, rationality in how evidence or experience leads to amended policy proposals ('solutions') or even adopted policy, but in the garbage-can model, this element does not have a determining or even necessarily significant role. Obviously it is an empirical matter when and where it does: the garbage-can is an approach, a framework for explanation, not a predictive theory.

To make predictions, one would need to feed empirical material into the garbage-can framework: that is, it is not 'grand theory' but a lens which seeks empirical backing of one sort or another.

How, indeed if, the garbage-can approach is compatible with explanations which rely on depiction of power, and/or ideological hegemony, is still an open question in general terms. But in England over the last

30 years, two claims can be made about policy: it is subject to short-termist change, involving persistent 're-disorganisation' of the NHS; yet also it is increasingly directed by the assumptions of neo-liberalism and market, neo-classical, economics.

Can both be true? Let us now explore this question.

Lens 5

This approach suggests that an ideology (which I define as a theory of, and proposal for, action which seeks to combine both descriptive 'realities' of, and prescriptive norms for, human behaviour and social organisation) may constrain and direct policy beyond some notion of 'ideologically neutral' evidence-base supporting how best to achieve goals. The latter notion is of course difficult, as 'goals' chosen by society/policy-makers/interests/elites may be themselves subject to ideological influence, often unperceived or unacknowledged.

Furthermore, 'evidence' as regards the effect of, or outcomes from, policy is likely to be time- and place-bound. It is ticklishly difficult to know when/if policy may be successfully transferred. Even more: to transplant systems with different values may mean changing behaviours and culture (e.g. 'the market' assumes selfish behaviour, and market models may introduce selfish behaviour where it did not exist before, or increase its role and salience—a point acknowledged by the intelligent market theorists of reform in healthcare (Le Grand 2011).

As regards English health policy over the last 25 years, the market route to reform has gradually gone from being an unusual proposal outwith orthodoxy (Enthoven 1985), through controversial policy (DoH 1989), to orthodoxy itself recently.

The instrumental ('agency') view of power is that it is exercised consciously by the powerful, or in their interests. This can be combined with a view of the system's role in promulgating 'false consciousness' on the part of the powerless (i.e. they do not know that policy is opposed to their interests) (Lukes 1974). This has sometimes been called a structural view, in the sense that there is more required to explain things than individual human agency—even though the latter is important. To this author, it would be better to call it an ideological explanation. But note that it is not a 'structuralist' view, which would suggest that 'discourse' has biases to which all who participate are subject—both powerful and powerless. This view however has problems in ascribing functionality to such power. Or, to put it another way: if such power is gradually seen to benefit someone, then consciousness of it makes its preservation a matter of agency and instrumentality after all. If on the other hand it is 'arbitrary' what sort of power comes to exist, then it is arbitrary (immaterial) whether it—or another form—exists or not. The basis for agency and social critique has been removed by the very theorists, the so-called structuralists and post-structuralists who were initially motivated by the desire to provide social critique.

As regards health policy, the ideological view would suggest that a particular discourse can become hegemonic, whether through agency initially or through something less tangible. Evidence (e.g. about the effect of market choice) may be filtered through a prescriptive lens. For example, evidence that choice 'works' to improve health outcomes may not consider the counter-factual (that it could have been achieved much more cheaply if the market route had not been the basis for the choice experiments which produced the evidence).

Now, let us consider the compatibility of the garbage-can and ideological closure around a particular approach (in this case, neo-liberal influence upon health policy). They are compatible if: market reform is the hegemonic approach, yet, the forms it takes are determined by political and other contingencies (e.g. 'solutions' adopted in response to short-term political perceptions of benefit), and the consequences produce reactions in the form of new policy which may be part-rational (e.g. replacing price competition with quality competition) yet, in timing as well as substance, arbitrary in that it is determined by political contingencies, including the availability of 'solutions' as a result of the 'marketplace' of ideas at any one time.

Unifying Lens

Considering the above lens, all may have some insight, but this weak conclusion can be strengthened by observing that the garbage-can augments the naivety of Lens 1, broadens the motivation for policy from Lens 2, allows Lens 3's insights to be complemented by the real world's messiness, and yet can also be combined with Lens 5. If this is done, the garbage-can's focus upon immediate causes can be combined with an ideological approach's focus upon underlying causes.

References

Allison, G. (1971). *Essence of decision*. Boston: Little Brown.

Blair, T. (2008). *A Journey*. London: Hutchinson.

Civitas. (2010). *The impact of the NHS market*. London: Civitas.

Cohen, M., March, J., & Olsen, J. (1972). A garbage-can theory of decision-making. *Administrative Science Quarterly, 17*(1), 1–25.

Department of Health. (1989). *Working for patients Cmnd. 55*. London: DoH.

Department of Health (DoH). (1995). *Local freedoms, national responsibilities*. London: DoH.

DoH. (2001). *Shifting the balance of power in the NHS*. London: DoH.

DoH. (2011). *NHS Future Forum. Final report*. London: DoH.

Dunleavy, P. (1989). *Democracy, bureacracy and public choice*. London: Harvester Wheatsheaf.

Duscheiko, M., Gravelle, H., & Jacobs, R. (2004). The effects of practice budgets on waiting times. *Health Economics, 13*(10), 951–958.

Enthoven, A. (1985). *Reflections on the management of the NHS*. London: Nuffield Trust.

Exworthy, M., et al. (2011). *Shaping health policy: Case studies in health policy and management*. Bristol: Policy Press.

Feachem, Richard G. A., et al. (2002, January19). The NHS versus Kaiser. *British Medical Journal*.

Hirschman, A. (1970). *Exit, voice and loyalty*. Cambridge, MA: Harvard University Press.

House of Commons. (2010). *Commissioning, fourth report of the Health Select Committee*. London: The Stationery Office (TSO).

House of Commons. (2011). *Commissioning: Further issues*. London: TSO.

Kingdon, J. (1984). *Agendas, alternatives and public policy*. Boston: Little Brown.

King's Fund. (1998). *Evaluation of total purchasing pilots*. London: King's Fund.

Le Grand, J. (2011). Comments made during questions, JLG's retirement celebration. LSE.

Le Grand, J., & Robinson, R. (Eds.). (1994). *Evaluating the NHS reforms*. London: King's Fund.

Le Grand, J., Mays, N., & Mulligan, J. (1998). *Learning from the NHS internal market*. London: King's Fund.

Lukes, S. (1974). *Power: A radical view*. London: Macmillan.

OECD. (2009). *Economic surveys: The United Kingdom*. Paris: Organisation for Economic Cooperation and Development.

Paton, C. (1992). *Competition and planning in the NHS. The danger of unplanned markets* (1st ed.). London: Chapman and Hall.

Paton, C. (2006). *New Labour's state of health: Political economy, public policy and the NHS*. Ashgate: Avebury.

Paton, C. (2012, March). Competition and integration: The NHS Future Forum's confused consensus. *British Journal of General Practice (BJGP)*, Lead Editorial.

Paton, C. (2013). Hyper-stasis as opposed to hyper-activism: The politics of health policy in the USA set against England. *International Journal of Health Planning and Management, 28*(2), 216–227 (April-June).

Paton, C., et al. (1997, August 27). Counting the costs (assessing the NHS reforms). *Health Service Journal, 106.*

Paton, C., et al. (1998). *Competition and planning in the NHS: The consequences of the reforms* (2nd ed.). Cheltenham: Stanley Thornes.

Peckham, S., et al. (2012). Devolution and patient choice: Policy rhetoric versus experience in practice. *Social Policy and Administration, 46*(2), 199–218.

Plamenatz, J. (1975). *Man and society* (Vol. 2). London: Longman.

Pollock, A., Macfarlane, A., & Greener, I. (2012, March 5). Bad science concerning NHS competition is being used to support the controversial health and social care bill. *LSE Blogs.*

Propper, C., Burgess, S., & Green, K. (2004). Does competition between hospitals improve the quality of care? Hospital death rates and the NHS internal market. *Journal of Public Economics, 88*, 1247–1272.

Rondinelli, D. (1983). *Decentralization.* Washington, DC: World Bank.

Schattschneider, E. (1960). *The semi-sovereign people.* New York: Holt, Rinehart and Winston.

CHAPTER 9

The Cost of the Market: The Price of Ideology

The most recent major reform of the NHS, during and following the Health and Social Care Act of 2012, was based on a remarkable phenomenon— not just evidence-free policy but evidence-denying policy. What research evidence there is from the only previous attempt to make GPs responsible for the whole health budget (King's Fund 1998; Mays et al. 2001) tells us that many GPs are not interested in, and therefore not very good at, commissioning comprehensive hospital services, and that should the government wish to invest in and develop such skills, this would be expensive and time-consuming in terms of management development for clinicians, a warning reinforced from recent overseas evidence (e.g. Thorlby et al. 2011). Yet the Coalition government put GPs in the hot seat of commissioning in Clinical Commissioning Groups at a time when money and time for such investment were conspicuously absent, a situation which only got worse up to and after 2015. This perverse decision resulted from market dogma: an NHS market requires both local purchasers separate from providers, and so, whatever one thinks of putting GPs in the hot seat of commissioning, to do it while deepening the purchaser/provider split prevented commissioning GPs from collaborating with (other) local health service providers.

Stretching the bounds of credulity, the Coalition government went further and argued that its market policy would actually facilitate the massive cost-saving exercise it had ordered—an amount of £20 billion which was later increased to £30billion by 2020. Yet the large opportunity cost involved in implementing and running the new market structures, added to the official estimate of the cost of these latest market reforms, put the

© The Author(s) 2016

C. Paton, *The Politics of Health Policy Reform in the UK*,

DOI 10.1057/978-1-137-47343-1_9

total cost at much more than £3 billion—suggesting that the reforms were at best a major diversion at a time when that could least be afforded and at worst a source of significant harm to the NHS.

This chapter goes on to consider the costs of continuing 'market reform' over more than 25 years, first of all recapitulating the context of costly reform in England, in contrast to the rest of the UK.

IDEOLOGY AND ADVOCACY

Health policy in England over the last 25 years has been dominated by ideologically rooted policy salesmen, based either in think-tanks funded by private interests or operating as part of 'sofa government' in health policy (Paton 2012) and this has blurred the distinction between the public interest and private interests. There has been no countervailing advocacy of equal weight in defence of the public interest (defined here as an attempt to derive the interest of the whole community or nation rather than private beneficiaries).

We may note the role of the private sector in helping to shape what I have termed the 'London consensus' in health policy—not least because it is so distinct from that in Edinburgh, Cardiff, or Belfast. The permeation of the state by private interests, while not the main cause of NHS reform, has followed such reform. The revolving door between private and public sectors has embraced high level personnel, for example New Labour's two most 'reforming' Health Secretaries, Alan Milburn (1999–2003) and Patricia Hewitt (2005–2007), taking up positions in the private sector with companies with significant past or present health sector interests (Bridgepoint, PWC, and Lloyds Pharmacy; and Boots, Cinven and BT, respectively). An example from the managerial rather than political class is the Department of Health's Director General for Commissioning and System Management Mark Britnell (2007–2009) becoming a private management consultant and allegedly drawing attention to opportunities for private involvement in provision(Observer 2011; http://www.powerbase. info 2010; HSJ 2011). Other senior managers have alternated between running NHS organisations, working for the market regulator and/or private consultancy—for example Dame Ruth Carnall, former CEO of NHS London. This is therefore not just a recent phenomenon under the latest Conservative governments. New Labour's tenure also saw, for example, an enthusiast for greater private involvement in the person of Dr. Penny Dash appointed to a senior Department of Health role as Director of Strategy.

Supposedly apolitical 'policy networks' events, such as the Cambridge Health Network, whose mission is to bring together public, private, and academic sectors, often resemble a gathering of private lobbyists.

A conventional wisdom has evolved over time in the form of group-think, embracing think-tanks (even the traditional charities such as the King's Fund and Nuffield Trust), political advisers, civil servants in the Department of Health and Ministers. These elements have reinforced in each other a belief about the inevitability and inevitable direction of 'NHS reform', proselytising seemingly perpetual 'public sector reform' which is understood to mean 'more market forces'. This is the London consensus. Furthermore, 'reform' is taken to be a *sine qua non* rather than something to be examined critically: reform as a neutral concept is superseded by reform as the norm; as a normative goal. This bias is then reinforced by powerful economic interests eyeing NHS contracts, interests given oppor-tunities by market reform, and in turn contributing to a new 'received wisdom' in policy—as they become part of the health policy and NHS pundit network and further bias in the pro-private direction is mobilised.

Yet just as significantly as the growth of private influence, health policy has been made in a short-termist and haphazard manner. The direction of travel is market, commercialisation, and privatisation, especially in delivery of care, yet there is chaos and counter-productive costliness in policy detail and implementation (Paton 2006).

DIRECT COSTS OF THE MARKET

There is much evidence that market structures in the NHS—the purchaser-provider split, commissioning or purchasing on one side and competition amongst diverse providers on the other—have cost a lot and delivered little, if indeed anything, positive—whether from 2002 to 2010 (House of Commons 2010, 2011) or from 1991 to 1997 (Paton et al. 1998).

Estimating the total costs of market reform over 25 years, let alone of the individual episodes thereof, is barely possible. No official evaluation was undertaken of the first internal market (1991–97), and the policy was applied inconsistently and in conjunction with other initiatives (Le Grand et al. 1998; Paton et al. 1998). There was an officially commissioned evaluation of New Labour's market reforms (Mays et al. op. cit., 2011) but this concluded that the costs were probably unknowable. The reasons include inter alia the changing definitions of 'management costs' over time, the difficulty in distinguishing costs directly associated with market from wider costs (e.g. investment in information systems for clinical budgeting), and indeed varying definitions of the market (e.g. the purchaser/provider split per se versus the actual operation of competitive tendering with multiple providers).

Yet the absence of a definitive figure for the total or indeed for any of the individual NHS reorganisations in pursuit of the market has helped 'pro-market' researchers to point to alleged minor benefits without reference to costs (Cooper et al. op. cit)—a strange stance for economists of all people.

It is possible however to consider the nature, scope, and scale of the costs, if not a precise quantification. Market reform has included:

1. Preparations for, and investment in, policy implementation (non-recurring costs, but likely to consist in various stages);
2. Management and leadership development through large-scale external consultancy (mainly non-recurring costs but with a recurring element);
3. Creation of market structures—new institutions, such as Self-Governing Trusts, Foundation Trusts, GP Fund-holding groups, Primary Care Trusts, Clinical Commissioning Groups, external regulators such as Monitor et al (both non-recurring and recurring, especially as a 'market NHS' requires more purchasers/commissioners and more providers than an integrated, planned NHS requires agencies);
4. The significant costs of redundancy and changing employment arrangements;
5. Pump-priming of new entrants to the market to make it 'competitive'. 'Market-making' has led to the subsidy of private providers to create competition where it does not exist, money which would arguably have been better spent on increasing and enhancing NHS provision; (mostly non-recurring);
6. Development and maintenance of information required to run a market (to be distinguished conceptually from the legitimate information requirements of a modern health service) (non-recurring and recurring);
7. The transactions costs of the 'purchaser/provider split'—advertising, negotiating, contracting, invoicing, billing, monitoring contracts and resolving disputes whether legally or bureaucratically within the NHS, and hiring and employing additional staff as well as paying for the time of senior managers who are de facto drawn into the process; and

8. The major 'opportunity cost' of the resources devoted to the market overall—what else might they have been spent on, and what might that have achieved by comparison with the 'achievements' of the market. While opportunity cost is by one way of thinking a direct cost of expenditure on the market, it is considered below in a wider context—in discussing the amalgam of benefit and harm which may have resulted from the market.

When one takes three episodes—the 1990s' internal market; New Labour's market in the 2000s; and the market further developed by the Coalition's and Social Care Act—it is clear that the non-recurring costs run cumulatively into billions, as do the recurring costs, in that the market replaces unitary health authorities with a whole range of 'self-governing' agencies embracing both 'commissioning' and provision and the relations between the two.

Taking the most recent reforms first:

The extant non-recurring cost of the current (2010–2013) reforms is likely to be nearer £3 billion than the official figure agreed by Health Secretary Andrew Lansley as early as January 2011 to be £1.4 billion (House of Commons 2011). That is because the official estimate seems to leave out much of 1, 2, and 3; possibly 5; some of 6, and all of 8.

What is more, the c.£3 billion spent on the post-2012 reforms involved less 'set up' (non-recurring) management cost than the previous two rounds of market reform, for two reasons. Firstly, top-down fiat forbade expenditure on the previous scales; and secondly, despite the rhetoric of local GP commissioning, the Clinical Commissioning Groups were created at a size which was (eventually) larger than even the post-2006 Primary Care Trusts. This was tactical, not strategic—out of necessity, in order to restrict management costs. But there was a positive strategic 'spin-off': the CCGs were at least big enough (bigger than the 2001 PCTs) to have a go, at least, at 'strategic commissioning'; that is, to work at reshaping overall service configuration.

But even so, it was the Local Area Teams, soon rechristened Area Teams as they were patently not local, which led this process. In any case, having larger CCGs which are not local organisations meant that the pretence that most local GPs would be involved in commissioning was soon exposed as as much of a pipedream as in earlier reforms. The new CCGs were PCTs in function, and only the 'statutory' GPs—the Chairman, the Principle Accountable Officer, and maybe one or two clinical leads (e.g.

on emergency care) - were fully involved (and even then, not necessarily full-time). The CCGs were, given their origin, rather a Heath Robinson creation. Even so, their clinical management costs in the sense of the 'extra time' given by GPs and other clinicians involved were not counted. These other clinicians included advisory hospital doctors, for example, from outside the area.

Quite incredibly, local hospital doctors, those who actually knew about the needs and services with which the CCGs were concerned. were debarred from this role—as involving local hospital doctors would have fallen foul of Lansley's beloved, market-ideological 'conflict-of-interest'. That is, they might have advised favouring the local hospital. 'O tempora, O mores,' as a latter-day Cicero might have said when confronted with health policy tying itself in knots to this extent. How does one cost ideology? Not in pounds, but in millions of pounds, or billions, over time.

We should therefore note with some incredulity the predictable claims by government up to 2015 that the 2012 Act reduced 'management costs'. While an arbitrary cap was placed on such costs 'allowed' to the new CCGs, the re-creation by the backdoor of the meso-level institutions (Area Teams and the like), the panoply of regulation in the latest market, and the substantial cost of compulsory tendering in the context of continuing expensive 'purchaser-provider' relationships are all continuing the high recurrent costs of the market.

To this, we might add the fact that the Clinical Commissioning Groups, whose management teams are composed of part-time GPs and a few administrators, are in no state to do 'commissioning'. As a result even the CCGs' core functions are frequently outsourced to private consultancies and other companies, making a mockery of more than 30 years of investment in leadership and management by the NHS, from the NHS Training Authority set up in 1984 to the Leadership Centre in 2001 and subsequently its successors. The leakage of talent through debilitating 'permanent revolution' has not helped, of course, and one could be forgiven for scenting a conspiracy to make private management 'necessary'. Sadly the truth is arguably even worse: it is cock-up rather than conspiracy. But the consequence is expensive private commissioning.

Additionally, in the search for 'integrated care' (see Chap. 10, Prescription), NHS agencies—hospital Trusts, mental health Trusts, community providers et al—were, by 2015 in different parts of England, being 'coordinated' by a lead provider from the private sector, which again costs a significant management overhead. Even more so in this case, one may ask why NHS 'leaders' are not up to the job of such a seminal leadership role in modern healthcare after billions of investment over decades, and, if they are, why they were not given the opportunity to lead.

It was claimed by some NHS England Regional executives in 2015 and 2016 that the 2012 Health and Social Care Act mandates that there must be a competitive tender for any services above a certain amount of value. But this ignores the fact that the new 'integrated service' (e.g. the ill-fated proposal for services for the elderly in Cambridgeshire; the cancer service in Staffordshire) need not be defined as a new service, so much as the better organisation and management of existing services delivered, after all, by the same NHS Trusts as before, only now beholden to a private 'lead provider'. In this case, conspiracy rather than cock-up may be more accurate. Define the service so that it is subject to the contentious 'obligatory tendering' clause of the 2012 Act, and private entry is facilitated. This does not mean 'billions of pounds of privatisation', as some have claimed, as the actual services remain in most cases in NHS Trust hands. But it is a sleight-of-hand at best.

Turning to the previous market reforms under New Labour: the non-recurring costs of the 2001–2008 reforms have been estimated at c.£3 billion (Channel 4 2007; *Sunday Telegraph* 2007)—with a major part of the cost incurred by the following elements:

1. Shifting the Balance (2001): the replacement of 100 Health Authorities (HA) with more than 350 Primary Care Trusts (PCT); Board/senior management replication, with the new PCT officers receiving similar remuneration to those at the previous HAs—arguably £1 billion of direct waste, given (4) below
2. Transfer of community Trusts to PCTs—employment/redundancy costs;
3. Market-making: the two tenders for Independent Sector Treatment Centres being prominent; also investment in outsourced commissioning and support to commissioning;
4. Commissioning a Patient-Led NHS (2005): the merging of 353 PCTs into 150 PCTs—major redundancy and transitional costs;
5. The development of commissioning from 2001 to 2008, culminating in major consultancy expenses allocated to 'World Class Commissioning', with the 'revolving door' between the Department of Health and the private sector again in evidence;

6. The divestment by PCTs of their 'provider functions', prefigured in (4) above but only implemented in 2008—reversing (2) above and creating 'community Trusts' all over again—on the grounds that a 'market' required health agencies to be solely purchaser or solely provider.

Regarding the earliest (1991) market reforms, the scale and scope of the main initiatives only is indicated below:

1. Replacement of unitary health authorities with separate purchasers and providers; triplication (at least) of senior management tiers and Boards, as unitary Health Authorities are replaced by purchasing Health Authorities, self-governing hospital 'Trusts' and self-governing community and mental health 'Trusts';
2. Preparation for and development of Self-Governing Trusts—major management consultancy exercise;
3. Preparation for and development of GP Fund-holding and purchasing alternatives such as 'Total Purchasing';
4. Redundancy and other transitory employment costs.

The Nuffield Trust-funded research into the 1990s internal market (Paton et al. 1997, 1998) suggested that while cost had been considerable, outcomes defined in terms of three variables—degree of functioning market; more sensitive 'purchasing' to replace previous 'planning'; and changed priorities on the part of health authorities—had been negligible. Propper et al. (2004) found that where the market had operated in the form of price competition, surgical outcomes of certain types had worsened and quality had suffered. While it could be argued that a better-designed market would produce better outcomes, later systematic review of both the 1990s internal market (with price competition) and New Labour's market (in which prices were fixed) suggested that costs were much higher than any putative benefits (Civitas 2010).

Arriving at a figure for the 'recurrent' costs of market reforms over time is equally difficult. There has been persistent instability and variation of market structure within and between the three eras of market reform since 1989; the research was not done on a large enough scale, if at all; the 'counter-factual' (i.e. a non-market NHS) is difficult to define, for example, what managerial infrastructure would it require even in the absence of a market. Yet the extra cost required to run a market is likely to be billions. The management costs (conservatively defined) of the English

NHS in 2010 were approximately 12% of £100 billion by comparison with 4% of a lower total in both numerical and real terms in the 1980s. Even if one-half of these costs are attributed to 'necessary' non-market infrastructure costs, then we can guess at recurring costs of the market being around £4 billion.

Market or Multiple Reorganisation as Source of Direct Cost?

It could of course be argued that the story of market reform in the NHS over 25 years from late 1988 to date overestimates the 'necessary' costs of the market. It is important to be fair and acknowledge—indeed draw attention to—the fact that much cost has been incurred by the fact that the English NHS has not been travelling in a straight line towards 'more market' over time. It has been a combination of zig-zags and loops, with the form of the market changed as governments have changed, and indeed within the terms of governments. The 1990s saw the Conservative government blow hot and then cold about the market (Paton et al. 1998). The New Labour government dismantled GP Fund-holding while retaining the purchaser/provider split; then instigated a radical decentralisation of purchasing/commissioning (DOH 2001) as the prelude to its own 'new market'(DOH 2002), which itself went through various mutations unconnected to the needs of the NHS. The Coalition changed the nature of its own market reforms even before they had been legislated (Timmins 2012; d'Ancona 2013).

Additionally, markets incur transactions costs (Coase 1937; Williamson 1997) between contractors yet integrated or planned services may incur high internal bureaucratic costs. It is an empirical matter as to which are larger, and which form of organisation is more appropriate, in different circumstances. It is important to enumerate, as well as 'waste' in panned systems as well as market systems, the necessary costs of a non-market NHS in terms of required managerial infrastructure. That is, it is important not to compare an imperfectly designed market with an 'ideal type' of planning or vice versa.

Yet there is much theory and evidence that markets are inappropriate for health-care (Hunter 2013) especially where equity is valued. Even were we to subtract a major portion of the 'non-recurring costs' wasted over the years in setting up and dismantling short-lived market policies (as one structure gave way to another), there would still be high non-recurring costs remaining and recurring costs on a large scale. It is also important to recognise that the political reasons for such organisational inefficiency are not going to disappear overnight. The market cannot be implemented in a vacuum, with a total absence of political noise, by a dictatorship of neo-classical boffins, and that is probably just as well. That is, what neo-classical economists may consider tampering with the market, politicians and citizens may well consider acting in the public interest. As a result, market reform is likely to involve stop-start, reversals and renewed effort. The costs of such cannot be assumed away as unnecessary if they are part of the legitimate functioning of the real world.

WIDER, INDIRECT COSTS OF THE MARKET

The direct cost of the market in terms of management and managerial transaction is one thing. And perhaps we should talk of administrative, not managerial, cost. For the cost has been not strategic but operational as it has consisted in servicing cumbersome duplication across 'purchasers' and 'providers' as a result of both the essence and frequent re-iterations of the 'purchaser/provider split', as we have moved from health authorities through the variants of GP Fund-holding, 'Total Purchasing', Primary Care Groups, Primary Care Trusts Mark 1 (small), Primary Care Trusts Mark 2 (merged), Practice-Based Commissioners, and now Clinical Commissioning Groups.

But even more significant are the 'opportunity cost' of the market and the wider costs of harm to the healthcare system, respectively. The two are linked. Opportunity cost refers here to what might have been achieved if the resources consumed by the direct costs of the market. For example, what could have been achieved had the significant time given to devising and implementing the NHS market by policy-makers, senior managers and clinicians instead been devoted to other purposes?

Major substantive problems in health-care which have essentially been unsolved for decades, could have been addressed, such as: the appropriate mix between specialist 'super hospitals', local hospitals and community services; the pursuit of clinical safety and quality on a consistent basis; and the diminution of inequalities in health.

This notion of opportunity cost (opportunities foregone) shades into harm to the system if and when the consequences of creating market structures and a market culture actually retard the solution of, or indeed worsen, major substantive problems. Some of the key leitmotifs of market reform, present in all three key phases of the market, are:

- Disintegration of both local and regional health communities into constituent parts without leadership of the whole, leading to dysfunctional and uncoordinated 'local health economies';
- Failure to consider at first how specialised services will be planned ('commissioned strategically') if planning is abolished and 'commissioning' devolved to local purchasers/commissioners: service concentrations and clinical networks have had to swim against the market tide;
- Reliance upon external regulation of individual market agents rather than internal (intra-NHS) strategic planning and whole-system performance management. Regulation and/or management of the market which has posed a dilemma: is its aim to damp down market forces where they threaten equity or go beyond the bounds of political acceptability, or the reverse—to seek to create competitive markets where, otherwise, 'market making' would simply turn a public service into a private monopoly? Policy here has been Janus-faced in all three phases of the English NHS market, primarily because clinical quality and economy require specialisation, concentration, and complementarity whereas competitive markets require excess capacity.

Let us consider merely the first of these three issues:

In the first market, 1991–1997, it came to be recognised that, in reality, purchasers had the money whereas providers had the services, leaving an imbalance which led both to play games with each other rather than cooperate sensibly. At the outset of the second market, and especially in 2005–6, this led to beggar-my-neighbour responses to financial crises. My own study of the North Staffordshire health economy (Paton, in Exworthy et al. 2011) provided a case-study of beggar-my-neighbour policy par excellence. Individual 'marketised' health agencies—NHS Trust and Foundation Trust providers; Primary Care Trust (PCT) purchasers—all sought to break-even, or avoid worse deficits, at each other's expense. Primary Care Trusts in particular sought to 'dump' costs at the hospital door, and the GPs within the PCTs' boundaries referred patients to hospitals in large numbers effectively transferring costs of treatment away from GP budgets and onto PCT budgets. Hospital cuts were made by providers on the assumption that community services would be commissioned to replace them; meanwhile, cuts made by purchasers (PCTs) reduced community services.

From 2013 through to 2015, we saw yet another crisis in emergency care, as Accident and Emergency departments all over England have been pushed to breaking-point. Clinical Commissioning Groups are powerless to prevent this, as they have both to pay Foundation Trust hospitals legally for care which leaves them unable to invest in the alternatives. If they avoid paying hospitals for the workload which ends up at hospital doors, then they simply push the hospital into financial crisis. This is a consequence of the market in that separate purchasers and providers seek to 'dump' patients, costs, and problems on each other. Yet ironically the whole point of the 'purchaser/provider split', especially in the eyes of those of its advocates who did not come from a hard pro-market stance, had been to allow purchasers to prioritise care in the community, in order to obviate hospital admissions where possible and to reduce lengths-of-stay where admission had occurred. 'Beggar my neighbour' behaviour in the marketplace can be expected to be even worse in the context of the resourcing crisis facing the NHS up to 2018.

MARKET OUTCOMES: BENEFIT OR HARM?

It is important to consider the 'other side of the coin' from the cost of the market—the outcomes which result. These would normally be classed as the benefits, although it is important to hold out the possibility that, instead of benefit, harm results (which would be a 'lose-lose' situation— high cost, negative benefit).

If the market in England creates a higher risk of quality lapses (as in Mid Staffordshire from 2005/6), then such should be part of any comparison—and indeed arguably part of the cost (lives lost unnecessarily) attributed to the market. Admittedly this is contentious territory, and one should admit that pre-market quality lapses came from a different cause, and equally that there have been 'scandals' in non-market UK NHSs, as in Wales. But these difficult questions should be posed, not least as the Mid Staffordshire story is increasingly revealed as one of a kind rather than the exception which proves the rule. The jury is out as to whether 'central targets' buttressed by top-down politicisation of the service and 'Stalinist' command by central managers, on the one hand, or the market, on the other hand—or both—have underlain contemporary horror stories and less prominent quality lapses. But if the market is implicated, then the empirical research which correlates the fixed-price market with improved mortality ratios (see below) would have to be revisited, broadened, and made more plausible, or else the dark side of the market might be suspected to outweigh any beneficial side.

In terms of benefit, there was no evidence-base for the NHS market-let alone cost-benefit. There was not even policy-based evidence, defined as acceptance and implementation of the policy followed by attempts to make it successful through limited evidence available from limited experimentation within the politically permissible contours of the policy. Instead there was only post-implementation modelling, following the NHS market. Enthusiasts 'modelled' the perfect market (Le Grand et al. op. cit.), seemed to assume that market reform had been implemented and attributed to competition some improvement in outcome (Cooper et al. 2011) or in process efficiency (Cooper et al. 2012). To be fair, these later empirical studies do not stand or fall on the basis of whether or not earlier NHS reforms created a 'perfect market.' But methodologically (see below), they do assume much more coherence in policy, and especially precision in the planning and timing of implementation, than occurred

Yet when the cost of 'market reform' is taken into account, the benefit-cost ratio of market reform is likely to be very low at best, and at worst a 'double negative', that is, lots of cost incurred in doing harm rather than creating benefit. One might argue: who knows whether an alternative to the market would have been any better? But the counter-factual is not necessarily some unknown policy with unknown costs and benefits. One might instead consider the concept of cost-effectiveness and hypothesise that, instead of the non-recurring (one-off) and also annually recurring costs of the various reforms over 25 years, the NHS in pre-1989 form had seen the same money applied directly to patient care through existing (or incrementally improved) mechanisms. One might alternatively estimate how much money would have been needed to bring about the same 'improvement' by direct allocation. It is unlikely to have been anything like as much as the cost of market reform.

As well as outcome in terms of (clinical) benefit, there is of course process efficiency. There is some fairly equivocal evidence that the efficiency of the NHS as gauged by a limited measure of productivity, defined in terms of manpower/cost as input and the crude measure of medical activity known as 'Finished Consultant Episodes' as output, was increased in the 1990s (Le Grand et al. 1998). There is also some limited statistical evidence of increased efficiency during a part of New Labour's market (Cooper et al. 2012).

But a real concern is that the 'inputs' in these studies do not capture the full costs either non-recurring or recurring of the market. They consider only the direct costs of manpower et al at provider level, and not the wider system costs of the policy.

Most evaluation of New Labour's market with one exception concerns process rather than outcome, and is summarised well in Civitas (2010). The exception is the positivist research of Cooper et al. (2011), which came to the notice of the Coalition government. This concluded that the post-2006 'choice' policy based on hospital competition improved quality (in the form of mortality ratios being reduced where choice has operated).

Yet much is open to doubt. The results of the study may show an association rather than a causality. Reasons for doubting the causality are multiple. The hypothesis is that there is a cut-off point—2006 which is used to mark when the policy was 'turned on', after which areas of the country characterised by 'more market choice' widened their quality differential with those characterised by 'less market choice.' Yet this cut-off point, marking the 'policy off, policy on' transition, does not reflect English NHS reality. There was no country-wide adoption of choice (or changed provider behaviour) then. Indeed Peckham et al. (2012) suggest that (on my interpretation, in my words), the rhetoric of (market-based) 'choice' in England and very different rhetoric elsewhere in the UK has masked a fairly similar reality in all these countries.

Choice has varied significantly, as have different Payment by Results regimes in different areas of the country 'on the ground reflecting different SHA approaches), and very much so in different local health economies. In the latter, for example, English 'choice' may have been 'managed choice', with the emphasis on the former to such an extent that the word 'choice' is suspect. Referral centres, different ways of running 'choose and book' et al have been handled differently in the context of different 'market' management strategies by SHAs, different reimbursement (or non-reimbursement) policies by PCTs et al. Additionally, post-2006, in response to the 'deficit crisis' of 2005/6, the NHS Chief Executive ran a centralist regime, with local commissioning freedoms subservient to the financial agenda.

It is important to put the Cooper et al. (2010) study in perspective. It argues that mortality from acute myocardial infarction (AMI), in emergency care, fell 0.3% faster per year post-2006 in areas characterised by the authors as hosting more 'competition' rather than less. The degree of difference between more and less competitive areas is not large:

therefore the question is begged as to the cost per life saved. Was this the most efficient way to achieve these results?

Cooper et al. (2011) seek to 'triangulate' different measures of competition between hospitals yet changed referrals of patients by GPs in those locations which they characterise as more competitive may or may not have been caused by 'patient choice'. But perhaps the most serious problem is that Cooper et al assume implicitly that the hospital is unitary. They assume that quality improvement in Acute Myocardial Infarction (AMI) cases—their strange choice for a study of choice, being part of the one area (emergency care) where patient choice unequivocally does not apply—results from the whole hospital's quality being improved through the operation of competition in elective care. This is simply not how the service works, not how a hospital works. If competition increases quality, then one should seek a correlation between choice and outcomes in elective procedures. Only by a bold qualitative hypothesis should one then investigate a mechanism or behavioural link whereby this effect spread to other specialties and departments of the hospital. Yet hospitals are notorious for their uneven performance, of which the phenomenon of 'good departments in bad hospitals and bad departments in good hospitals' is an example. Even within electives, there is little correlation between quality in different specialities within hospitals. Heart-based death rate is in fact not a good indicator for quality of a hospital. Mortality from heart disease, even within the 30-day cut-off point following AMI, depends greatly on social and environmental factors, particularly smoking (Holland 2010).

Pro-competition academics and advocates tend to proselytise studies such as Cooper's. Prime Minister Cameron for example seized upon the Cooper study to claim, just as the NHS Future Forum was re-launching Health Secretary Lansley's reforms in June 2011 after the infamous 'pause' (Timmins 2012), that 'LSE research' had shown that competition in a market worked. Yet there is a failure to look at wider contrary evidence. For example, one may compare changes in a measure of health status, Infant Mortality Rate (IMR) between three UK countries with differing NHS governance—England via competition and Scotland and Wales via collaboration and co-ordination. Examining IMR in these countries over an 80-year period, since 1930, produces the conclusion that, whereas England was previously better than the other two countries, these two have overtaken England in the ten years to 2008 dominated by the market in England (Holland 2010).

It may be the case that informed patient choice is demonstrated over time to help to produce improved outcomes. Cooper et al.'s (2011) work, if it is the harbinger of similar results to come, essentially is about choice rather than markets per se, and choice within the NHS to boot. Thus to conflate patient choice with hospital competition may be wrong, if by the latter one means a market operating through market incentives and the behavioural characteristics of market actors. Both professional and altruistic desires to do better may be the motivation, and hospitals may not be 'competing' except in terms of reputation and pride. Indeed a valuable conclusion from Cooper et al.'s (2012) work on hospital competition and efficiency is that they find no added value from private sector competitors, indeed quite the reverse. All the putative benefits of competition are realised through improvement in NHS hospitals.

There is a warning here for those who seek to 'market make' by encouraging or pump-priming private sector competitors such as the Independent Sector Treatment Centres (ISTCs) promoted by the Blair government. It is perfectly possible to enable choice of NHS provider without market paraphernalia. All that is required is to restore GPs to their core role as provider of primary care and (non-budget-holding) referrer when necessary—in line with patient wishes. This removes the GP's conflict-of-interest created by the Health and Social Care Act of 2012, which makes them custodians of a limited purchasing budget as well as patient advocate. Choices and the consequent flows of patients can then be modelled by regional authorities in planning and funding hospitals and other supra-primary providers, which should be part of an integrated NHS, cooperating with each other. We can call this a market if we must. But to do so is tortuous, and a relic of the rusty neo-liberal hegemony which throws defenders of the public onto the defensive. It would be more valid to call it a publicly planned NHS delivered in line with expressed patient wishes.

CONCLUSION

Consider the major cost of achieving, at best, minor positive outcomes (choice leading to raised standards; some process efficiencies at the micro level) from time to time and indeed negative outcomes as well (worse quality in the 1990s internal market; worse quality in key locations in the New Labour market, as in the Mid Staffs scandal, facilitated by an obsession with job cuts to enable lean Foundation Trusts to emerge in the name of competition even where they are not viable unless built upon inadequate clinical staffing levels). The officially funded evaluation of New Labour's market reforms suggested that 'the absence of harm' was the most that could unequivocally be said (Mays et al. 2012).

Given the huge costs, this is surely an indictment. And the 'absence of harm' is looking precarious, post-Mid Staffordshire and as analogous worries about quality come out of the woodwork in its aftermath. Already, corner-cutting by private providers who have won large contracts following the implementation of the Health and Social Care Act from April 1st, 2013, have been noted (BBC Radio 4 2014).To conclude from the fact that market reform has disappointed so far that the answer is more market reform suggests a mobilisation of ideological bias on a spectacular scale.

This is especially true when one reflects that the 'pro-market' evidence is in fact pro-choice evidence—not the same thing. It is perfectly possible to have choice of NHS provider without the recent approaches to creating market structures which are so costly. Just as markets may not involve choice, choice does not require markets except in the basic sense that plural provision exists. Choice existed from 1948 to 1991, after which the market restricted it. The challenge in the 1980s was to improve the resource allocation formula through regional strategy: then the mechanisms to reconcile choice with effective service reconfiguration would have existed. But this agenda seemed dull to the 1980s Thatcherites who wished to marketise the NHS for ideological reasons. And this prosaic truth has been lost over 25 years of market hegemony.

The final chapter sketches the political outlook for the English NHS if it remains on the current path, and makes suggestions as to how it can be stabilised both politically and in terms of sustainable health policy.

References

BBC Radio 4. (2014, November 12). File on 4, 8pm

Channel 4. (2007, February 26). The NHS: Where did all the money go? *Dispatches.*

Civitas. (2010). *The impact of the NHS market.* London: Civitas.

Coase, R. (1937). The nature of the firm. *Economica, New Series, 4*(16), 386–405.

Cooper, Z., et al. (2011). Does hospital competition save lives? Evidence from the English NHS patient choice reforms. *The Economic Journal, 121*(August), 228–260.

Cooper, Z., et al. (2012). *Does competition improve public hospitals' efficiency? Evidence from a Quasi-experiment in the English National Health Service.* London School of Economics, Centre for Economic Performance, Discussion paper no. 988: Extension of 2010 version.

d'Ancona, M. (2013). *In it together: The inside story of the coalition government.* London: Penguin.

DoH. (2001). *Shifting the balance of power in the NHS.* London: DoH.

DoH. (2002). *Implementing the NHS plan: Next steps for investment, next steps for reform.* London: DoH.

DoH. (2005). *Commissioning a patient-led NHS.* London: DoH.

Exworthy, M., et al. (2011). *Shaping health policy: Case studies in health policy and management.* Bristol: Policy Press.

Holland, W. W. (2010). Competition or collaboration?: A comparison of health services in the UK. *Clinical Medicine, 10*(5), 1–3.

House of Commons. (2010). *Commissioning, fourth report of the Health Select Committee.* London: The Stationery Office (TSO).

House of Commons. (2011). *Commissioning: Further issues.* London: TSO.

HSJ. (2011, May 17). Exclusive: Britnell responds to privatisation storm. London: Health Service Journal. And see also http://www.powerbase.info/images/f/fe/Apax_Healthcare_conference_2010.pdf. Contribution by Mark Britnell: Quotations: In future, The NHS will be a state insurance provider not a state deliverer; The NHS will be shown no mercy and the best time to take advantage of this will be in the next couple of years.

Hunter, D. (2013). *To market, to market!* CHPI. http://www.chpi.org.uk

King's Fund. (1998). *Evaluation of total purchasing pilots.* London: King's Fund.

Le Grand, J., Mays, N., & Mulligan, J. (1998). *Learning from the NHS internal market.* London: King's Fund.

Mays, N., et al. (2001). *The purchasing of health care by primary care organizations.* Buckingham: Open University Press.

Observer. (2011, May 15). David Cameron's adviser says health reform is a chance to make big profits. (posted online May 14, 20.34).

Paton, C. (2006). *New labour's state of health: Political economy, public policy and the NHS.* Ashgate: Avebury.

Paton, C. (2012, March). Competition and integration: The NHS Future Forum's confused consensus. *British Journal of General Practice (BJGP),* Lead Editorial.

Paton, C., et al. (1997, August 27). Counting the costs (assessing the NHS reforms). *Health Service Journal, 106.*

Paton, C., et al. (1998). *Competition and planning in the NHS: The consequences of the reforms* (2nd ed.). Cheltenham: Stanley Thornes.

Peckham, S., et al. (2012). Devolution and patient choice: Policy rhetoric versus experience in practice. *Social Policy and Administration, 46*(2), 199–218.

Propper, C., Burgess, S., & Green, K. (2004). Does competition between hospitals improve the quality of care? Hospital death rates and the NHS internal market. *Journal of Public Economics, 88*, 1247–1272.

Sunday Telegraph. (2007, February 25). Going round in circles.

Thorlby, R., et al. (2011). *GP commissioning; Insights from medical groups in the United States.* London: Nuffield Trust.

Timmins, N. (2012). *Never again.* London: King's Fund and Institute for Government.

Williamson, O. (1997). Hierarchies, markets and power in the economy: An economic perspective. In C. Menard (Ed.), *Transaction cost economics: Recent developments.* Cheltenham: Edward Elgar.

CHAPTER 10

Diagnosis, Prognosis, and Prescription: Will England Join the UK?

The role of the modern philosopher is neither to construct grand metaphysical schemes nor to seek some abstruse truth which is inaccessible to mere mortals. Instead it is to debunk nonsense and expose error when it is proposed and where it is to be found. This is a significantly less romantic role but a vital one nonetheless: the hollow laugh is arguably more important than herd-like adherence to theoretical fad. During the Enlightenment, it was religion which was undermined and exposed as nonsense on stilts, and its persistence today does not alter its theoretical untenability. Today, it is the self-indulgent exaggerations of modern metaphysics—the post-modernisms and post-structuralisms which the Anglo-American academe has cravenly adopted from its precious Parisian origins over more than 40 years—which philosophy ought to be demolishing.

As a public policy academic specialising in health policy who has a background in politics, philosophy, and economics, it seems to me that there is a parallel, albeit moving from the philosophical sublime to the policy ridiculous. The challenge for health policy analysis—which actually should mean the analysis of healthcare politics, an inconvenient truth which is itself often ignored—is often more to demolish fashionable, faddish, and foolish 'new orthodoxy' (if one can accept the oxymoron) than to propose some new policy 'solution'. The problem is that 'solutions' are sexier, and also form the basis for an industry which sustains not only management consultants and private profiteers but also academics, think-tankers, and political advisers who combine punditry with policy proposals, to the delight of politicians who are seeking their very own monument in the form of a 'reform'.

© The Author(s) 2016
C. Paton, *The Politics of Health Policy Reform in the UK*,
DOI 10.1057/978-1-137-47343-1_10

DIAGNOSIS

The unromantic fact, when comparing the health services of England, Scotland, Wales, and Northern Ireland, is that the achievements and problems are by and large the same; the policy 'solutions' adopted in England through nearly 30 years of restless 're-form' have been largely irrelevant to solving those problems, but they have also been very costly. So far, so banal. This book has been concerned with explaining politically why irrelevant solutions have been 'the story' in England, as regards health policy. So, at one level, the response could be, 'So what? Yes, a lot of money has been wasted; now, let's move on.' This of course is the politician's response. Labour politicians, the more perceptive of whom are aware of how the Labour government squandered a significant proportion of the financial boom for the NHS between 2000 and 2008 in circular re-disorganisation, swept that fact under the carpet and concentrated on attacking Tory 'privatisation'. The Conservatives did not dwell on Lansley's hostage-to-fortune, but quietly dropped what his Cabinet colleagues privately called the 'policy wonk'-ish language underpinning his embarrassing monument and moved on, and Jeremy Hunt sought to reframe the debate in terms of 'patient safety', a 24/7 NHS and the need for new ways of working given the financial challenge. No mention of how Conservative reforms in the 1990s and after 2010 were irrelevant, and very likely damaging to those prospects—although ironically Hunt's mishandling of his chosen issues have not helped the Conservatives live down Lansley's damage to their reputation regarding the NHS.

The reason that Scotland, Wales, and Northern Ireland have featured in this book only as 'not England' is because this book's topic has been policy reform in the sense of political initiatives to 'marketise' the NHS, and the rest of the UK has presented accurately as exactly that—not England. As noted above, Scotland and Wales rowed back from the 1990s UK internal market in legislative stages, but all stages were—by and large—in the same, intended direction. One may call their policy rational, therefore, in the basic procedural sense, that is, identifying an 'end' (goal, aim, or merely objective) and moving towards it through 'means' which are judged to fit that end.

Of course there are degrees of rationality. Scotland's 1999 and 2003 restructurings could in theory have been accomplished in one go. Nor was the 1999 restructuring—rationalising services so that each Health Board area had one acute hospital Trust and one community and mental health trust—overtly planned as a forerunner to the 2003 follow-up, which abolished Trusts altogether and reintegrated provider services into the Health Board, albeit managed as separate units (as in all the UK from 1983 to 1991 after the Griffiths Report of 1983 but before the internal market). Things evolved rather than being planned wholly rationally but in an intended direction, and with less knee-jerk panic than underlay many of the English reforms.

In Wales, to be fair, one could wryly point out that the internal market was abolished three times, after devolution, with only the third reorganisation 'reintegrating' the NHS is the sense of abolishing the purchaser (commissioner)/provider split. It would be naive and romantic to pretend that the UK Celtic fringe is rational whereas England is not. It is however a matter of degree.

By rejecting England albeit primarily for political reasons rather than for specialist policy reasons, the rest of the UK has avoided a blind alley by good luck rather than by genius. And one should not always believe the rhetoric emanating from the Celtic fringe. For example, Wales has laid claim to making 'community health', and perhaps a wider public health, its priority, rather than England's alleged fixation with productivity in the hospital sector. But as Simon Stevens, appointed NHS England's Chief Executive in 2014, used to imply ten years earlier when he had recently been Prime Minister Blair's health policy adviser, this was arguably a fig-leaf for failure to achieve the sort of productivity improvements which (at that time) were most prominent in England. Such is not to decry the Welsh Assembly Government's ambitions, but to temper them with reality.

Nevertheless, Wales when compared to Scotland has had less resource per capita when weighted with the needs of its population, and so it would be unfair to single it out as regards NHS problems. The Cameron government in the UK has sought to do this, playing naked partisan politics and attempting to contrast the Labour-run Welsh NHS with Conservative-run England. The main bone of contention here has been 'scandal' in individual hospitals, as in Cardiff. But England is on thin ice here, as the home of many 'scandals', from the Mid Staffordshire NHS Foundation Trust (as was) to many others both in the acute sector and in the mental health and mental handicap/learning disability field—and including many of the supposedly 'flagship' Foundation Trusts.

Both Scotland and Wales have toyed with different versions of 'locality planning', that is, involving GPs and others in advising Health Boards in Scotland and local commissioners in Wales (in earlier versions of post-devolution restructurings there) on the basis of the needs of localities. One could therefore superficially conclude that this was England in Celtic drag. But that would be misleading. In Scotland this has been an evolutionary initiative based on planning requirements rather than the fixation with GP commissioning, and its role in market reform, as in England. In Wales, it was part of the attempt to make local commissioning serve the needs of wider health and not just 'illness'—whatever the results or lack of them.

This is not to say that English trends and 'fads' have not had resonance in the rest of the UK. Admittedly being 'not England' has been attractive in an age of devolution—so an English initiative is by no means guaranteed a hearing and indeed might be damned before being examined fully. But there has also been a nervous 'looking over the shoulder' to England. In the dark night of the devolved soul, the fear that England's market initiatives and 'efficiency' drives might produce fruit has also had its influence—a bit like the protagonist in Larkin's poem, Vers de Societe, who rejects company at the beginning but then feels forced to accept it for bleak reasons in the end. So some 'English' policy has been adopted—but usually that which slots easily into prevailing structures.

After all, there is nothing radical or exciting about advice to English strategic commissioners or Scottish Health Boards from locality-based GPs and others. And indeed there is not much evidence to suggest it is worth the time of the GPs: it is more a feel-good or motherhood-and-apple-pie policy. To oppose it is rather like opposing 'patient and public participation' even although many of us know that the latter is often a tick-box exercise in political correctness.

There is nothing exciting about NHS restructurings and (lack of) 'reform' in the rest of the UK. All systems have their shortcomings. Integrated public organisation in an NHS does not guarantee integrated culture or practice. Nor was the English/UK NHS before 'the market' organised, in fact, such that the full benefits of integration could be achieved. So improvement is not only possible but necessary.

But to point to English reform and say, 'well, if you reject that, what will you put in its place?' is to make the mistake that the debunking philosopher must point out. If something is unnecessary or harmful (at least in the sense of wasting money and possibly more), then to argue that, if one rejects it, one must propose an alternative, is just silly. It is like shooting oneself in the foot, and saying, 'well, if I don't do that to the other foot, I am going to have to do something else instead.'

This is where neglecting politics and concentrating solely upon 'policy' is harmful as well as incoherent. Policy always has politics embedded in it, even although it is sensible to distinguish the two, as we do in English (In French, 'la politique' serves as the word for both). The main thing the UK's non-English NHSs have, warts and all, is political stability. There is not the now-almost-annual 'moral panic' which we see in England about whether the NHS is sustainable, affordable, practical, efficient, effective, or whatever alarm-bell-ringing word is chosen at the time of panic.

Indeed the English moral panics are rather like the 'reform' which they often occasion: on closer examination, they are illusory, but a lot of time and effort has to be spent undoing the damage they cause. As regards England's 'permanent revolution' in NHS change, the moral might be, to quote Labour Party leader Clement Attlee in 1945 when he rebuked his excitable party chairman Professor Harold Laski, 'a period of silence on your part would now be welcome.'

Prognosis

The political result of persistent English NHS upheaval is to weaken the legitimacy of the English NHS. The public, by a slow osmotic drip, comes to think that there must be something intrinsically wrong if the NHS is always being reformed, and if politicians, their advisers, and the media are persistently hand-wringing about it. As argued above, once an ill-thought-out reform is set in motion and not 'nipped in the bud', it takes on a logic of its own. Reform begets reform—in part to repair mistaken initiatives from the previous round, and in part to make new initiatives, in the belief common to both 'managerialism' and 'market ideology' that there is a better alternative out there.

This is not an argument against any reform at any time: it is an argument for more rationality in reform. Yet, it may plausibly be argued, I have presented a compelling case as to why such rationality has been absent from the trajectory of English health policy reform. That is true. There is no magic solution—and certainly not in merely a 'structural' reform to 'depoliticise' the NHS. Taking politics out of the NHS would be to take politics out of politics. The answer is unspectacular and by no means a 'silver bullet' to solve the problem: the answer lies in a cultural change in terms of how politics, and in particular so-called public service reform, is viewed and practised.

The prognosis for England's NHS is currently bleak, mostly as a result of the financial squeeze. There are also new policy tensions emerging. More use is being made of block contracts, which makes nonsense of the pretence that providers are paid 'by results' in line with actual workload. Despite the government's cumbersome and expensive policy of mandatory tendering for services, geared to involving the private sector, commissioners have not been rushing to use private providers, unless leaned upon politically—and where they have, they have found many problems.

But the financial squeeze has become the main story. Given the increasing scale of financial deficit for hospitals, the savings targets look like a dead duck: £22 billion savings to render the NHS self-sufficient for the future look like pie in the sky. And the growing deficits are not the result of 'inefficiency' but of the growing gap between demand and need, on the one hand, and money available for front-line services, on the other hand. Even if self-care and prevention tackle some costs—a brave assumption—new demands on the service will more than absorb these. Yet politically driven policy drives the NHS. For example, the policy of 'NHS Health Checks' probably costs the NHS far more than could be saved, but it was felt to be politically beneficial. One may also point to the fixation with a '24/7 NHS'—against all sense of cost containment and indeed at best equivocal need or demand for it (with the exception of emergency care and emergency-related specialties). De facto, political fads—including persistent reforms—shrink the budget for core care, which politicians then demand is rescued by increasingly untenable 'efficiency savings'.

The financial squeeze—irrespective of the £8 billion granted by the Conservative government up to 2020, with £3.6 million 'frontloaded for 2016–17—ironically can give grist to the reform mill which suggests that 'there is a better way of financing healthcare.' But bluntly there is not a better way—if the aim is to maintain the core ethical principle of a health service free at the point of use, for hospital and specialist care at least, with equal opportunity for access to care for those with equal needs (what economists call 'horizontal equity').

Moving to 'insurance' would immediately beg the question: do we mean private or public insurance? If we mean the latter, then we are not talking of commercial insurance with premiums related to risk but simply a means of generating revenue, which may more accurately be called a 'health tax,' that is, a hypothecated (earmarked) tax rather than general taxation to fund the NHS—as in Canada, for example. If we are using the word 'insurance' in this sense, then we may stretch it further and describe the NHS's current financing system as the ultimate in social insurance, that is, the public insuring itself against healthcare need.

If we mean private insurance, then we are either talking about abandoning the weakening the core ethical principle of the NHS or ensuring that all are equitably covered for private insurance. That would make the system much more expensive, not cheaper. The USA could be invoked (and even after the Obama reforms, there is nothing resembling equity in access), but so can the Netherlands, where 'managed competition' by private insurers, with all citizens covered through what is effectively a 'health tax' although it is called social insurance, has been accompanied by a rise not a fall in healthcare costs—a rise which other explanations (the incorporation of elderly care into the system) can only partially explain.

So if the debate about alternative means of financing healthcare continues, then not only will the current 'supply side' reform process continue to prove expensive but the pressure to abolish the NHS as a system of financing (i.e. even if one is prepared to define the NHS in minimalist terms as a financing system only) will be ratcheted up.

There is another criticism of the NHS model which is aired regularly by its critics in England, which is based upon a critique of central economic planning, which affects both NHS financing and provision—both demand and supply. It is argued that central planning in the economy generally can only meet demand if the planners have information about the relative marginal utilities of different goods, and that to obtain such—while not theoretically impossible as the Austrian neo-liberals had argued in the early part of the twentieth century—makes state planning more cumbersome and inefficient than the market.

Yet this objection neglects the difference between demand—for goods which are not needed to remove a negative phenomenon (pain, illness, or absence of well-being)—and need in the latter sense. One can quibble at the philosophical level about the overlap between the two, but to most people the distinction is real and meaningful. In the case of health services, such needs are registered by people consulting a clinician. Many needs are not 'demanded' in the market place for different reasons (e.g. inability to pay and unawareness of the need being capable of being met). In any case, just as the state may have difficulty in measuring needs or demands and trading them off in order to mandate production, the market may manipulate tastes, preferences, and basic awareness in order to create its production schedule. The reality of the advertising-dominated market is a far cry from neo-classical theory's 'autonomous consumer' with fixed tastes.

In healthcare systems such as the NHS, these caveats aside, there is a ready-made means of gauging needs—the patient/primary care clinician consultation, and/or presentation at hospital. It is then of course a matter for 'the system' to prioritise these needs, even in a state of relative plenty in which they can all be met at some stage. But this is not a criticism of the system so much as a demonstration that a means other than economic demand of providing healthcare 'goods' is sought, in the interests of equity and either social preference or 'expert decision'.

The sceptic regarding planning may then point to the distinction between scarcity and shortage, as Weale (2015) has recently done. His argument is worth considering, as it is made by an intelligent commentator who does not see individual purchase in the market as opposed to collective purchase through the NHS as a panacea. Scarcity is the human condition, except in an imagined utopia, whereas shortage is allegedly the consequence of either central planning or central administrative decisions such as price controls or budgetary limits for providers. Weale gives the example of the Treasury's recent demand for 'efficiency savings' on a large scale, translated into the 'Nicholson challenge' in the NHS (somewhat archly named after the former Chief Executive's demand, on behalf of Ministers, for first £20 billion and then later £30 billion savings by 2020). He argues that the 'suppressed inflation' inherent in price (wage) controls et al leads to shortages as staff shortages result, and services are restricted. This is a powerful point in terms of a portrait of how an arbitrary demand for savings may translate through the implementation process into rigid plans at local levels.

But this problem is not insuperable. The unmet need can be registered— indeed is likely to be registered through waiting-lists et al.—and measured, and alternative means of spending the budget decided. It is a question of how national financing and local decision-making are combined. Weale argues that local revenue-raising and budget-setting can be combined with national priorities in a different way, without spelling this out. In reality, such choices are political, not economic. If people are willing to pay more to ensure hospital treatment, either this can be done privately or through local collective purchase as a result of local decision as to how much, or how much extra, revenue to raise (i.e. abandoning the national formula which allocates resources to different localities in the name of equity of access). At the end of the day, allowing local revenue enhancement may be considered preferable *if* the alternative is flight to the private sector by enough people to undermine the legitimacy for funding the NHS as a national universal (for everyone) and comprehensive (covering major needs) service. Alternatively, an adequate budget may be sought nationally, along the lines of the proposal made below.

Turning to a different issue, there is also a mistaken emphasis upon the corporate organisation as the focus of reform—for example, making Trusts compete, and assuming that corporate loyalty will be adequate to get staff to 'buy into' the market system. But the truth is that the medical, clinical, and other staff see the corporate organisation as a remote entity. Indeed the reason why Cooper's (op. cit.) research is so implausible (see above) is for this reason. Their loyalties are to particular services, professions, employee organisations, and regional and national networks, with a mixture of professionalism and altruism dominating their 'ethos'. There is no doubt that self-interest exists. Remuneration is important, and so are terms and conditions. But to motivate staff to 'accept' national, regional, and local priorities is best achieved through terms and conditions for staff groups, not expensive reform which makes the corporate Trust the 'unit' to be incentivised. There is no sign that this lesson has been learnt.

PRESCRIPTION

So what might we prescribe for the NHS of the future, not least drawing upon lessons and warnings from the story told in the pages above? It is not strictly necessary to do this here, as my primary aim has been to tell a story, structured through the lens of politics, about what has happened in England. Yet for those readers who are interested in policy-making, sceptical of the 'anti-market' case or simply asking 'so what would you do?' as a natural response to the above, the following is a brief account of an alternative which would be much less costly, and which could liberate about five billion pounds of wasted 'market' overhead—without even factoring in the huge cost of the Private Finance Initiative by comparison with a properly measured public alternative.

A salient advantage of an NHS funded from general taxation at the national level is that both equity in access to services across the whole population, on the one hand, and economy in running the system, through single-payer funding with the revenue parsimoniously collected, on the other hand, can be combined more effectively than in any alternative.

In England as well as in the rest of the UK, we have hitherto retained this system, created by the 1946 Act. Leading up to this Act, there was debate about whether funding should be national or local, and the Labour cabinet was split between Aneurin Bevan, the Health Minister, who saw the argument for local funding but chose national, and Herbert Morrison, the Home Secretary, who championed local funding. One reason for the ultimate choice of national funding was that the medical profession, to which Bevan knew he had to make the new NHS as appealing as possible, feared that local government control of the new NHS would lead to political jerrymandering of service provision by local politicians. Knowing what we do about the frequent parochialism of local government, this was a reasonable fear even if some other fears about the service on the part of the more conservative medical politicos were far-fetched.

Of course it can be argued that, in the era of the split between the purchaser (commissioner) and the provider, local government funding does not mean local government control of provision. But this is naive, as the split is never likely to be as complete as market advocates imply. Moreover, retaining it means retaining the excessive administrative and managerial costs described in the previous chapter. Although England has retained the most economical funding system, it has squandered some of this dividend by implementing the increasingly expensive 'purchaser-provider split.' So, if England moves away from the market theology in the future and closes this schism, then the objection to local government control would be reinstated. It is best to retain national funding and nationally accountable governance of the service generally. The more this principle is vitiated, what is more, then the more equity is threatened.

It can be argued of course that the more difficult it is to raise taxes, then the more problematic adequate funding of the NHS is to secure. Related to this is the need for stability of funding as well as adequacy. The less progressive (i.e. taxing the better-off proportionately more) taxation becomes, then the more unacceptable high taxes become to the less well-off, who have to pay a greater share of the burden. So, ironically, those who need the NHS more may become less enamoured with the taxation required to make the NHS both healthy and stable, that is, sustainable.

But this is a wider political challenge, beyond the structure of the healthcare system, and there is in any case no magic solution available through changing the funding system if taxation becomes problematic. Moving to public/social 'insurance', for example, in effect means putting a payroll tax on wages to fund the service, with the government still needing to pay for the unemployed and unwaged. This is a more regressive system still, in almost all cases, and securing the required funding from it is no easier, indeed probably much more difficult. It is failure to see this which informs much of the 'moral panic' around NHS funding.

A STABLE FOOTHOLD FOR NHS FUNDING

Regarding stability in funding, a useful rule might be: allow the growth in the NHS budget (in real terms) to mirror the growth in economy-wide GDP. It might be possible to get that unusual phenomenon—party political consensus—around this principle, as NHS funding is a bugbear to all governments in that increases are fast forgotten yet restraint attracts opprobrium. Indeed, given that a growing GDP means that the economy as a whole is growing and that there is greater 'real' income in private hands, it could be agreed that, in a growing economy, the NHS attracts 'the GDP growth percentage plus 1 %'. In unusual times of zero or negative growth, the rule could be, maintain the NHS funding in real terms. From 2008 for the years when growth was zero or less, the Coalition government promised to do this, and technically did, but cuts to social care impacted severely on the NHS and made the promise a deceit. Moreover when growth was reinstated, the NHS did not grow along with the economy.

CARE VERSUS PREVENTION AND HOSPITALS VERSUS THE COMMUNITY ARE A FALSE ANTITHESIS

Another useful decision would be to abandon the politically correct orthodoxy that the NHS should be a society-wide health-promotion service rather than an 'illness service'. This sounds like motherhood and apple-pie. But it leads to the NHS carrying the can for cure, care, prevention, and promotion without the resources to be such a multi-agency magician. Better that the NHS handles cure and care, and prevention where that is clinically led, but that the wider social and environmental causes of ill-health, or failure to achieve good health, are tackled elsewhere. As regards personal behaviour which leads to illness, tackling that raises issues of libertarianism versus the public purse (one may only be free to choose ill-health if others do not have to pay) which may affect the NHS budget. But since these factors are correlated with social factors, then both the NHS budget and other budgets may be affected in dealing with the problem (wider social budgets) or failing to deal with it (the NHS budget). Having distinct budgets still makes sense. And if individuals persist in unhealthy lifestyles, then there may be case for NHS charges funded through mandatory supplementary insurance.

Ironically, then, 'joined up' government in the everyday, politically correct sense of the term, might be worth abandoning: better that different government Departments do their own job and do *not* join together. A whiff of this may have come in one less-noticed part of the 2012 Health and Social Care Act, which gave the function of public health back to local government (with the exception of some national programmes). Admittedly and predictably this has led in some cases to local politicians seeking to mould the budget for public health according to their pet likes and dislikes. Moreover, territorial equity is not best achieved through local government funding, where public health and indeed most budgets can be raided for other purposes. This is a problem even if the national formula to subsidise local government's expenditure in poorer areas with greater social need works well—which it does not, mostly due to national jerrymandering of the formula. So local government control may not be the best place for public health. But separating the challenge of public health in the widest sense of the term—that is, covering health and well-being as affected by factors well outside the control of the NHS—makes sense.

The 'focus on health as opposed to illness' lobby cannot have it both ways. If the causes of much ill-health are way outside the scope of the NHS (as many are, embedded in inequality, poor housing conditions, poor diet, dangerous environments et al.), then it does not make sense to suggest that the NHS itself alone ought to tackle these rather than other social policies and institutions. Add to this mental healthcare—the bulk of which should stay within the NHS (as mental illness, mental health problems more generally, and disability are most certainly the stuff of healthcare) but with an additional and wholly separate funding stream, which also recognises that mental health needs are embedded in other institutions such as prisons. The poverty of mental health services has not been reduced by the 1980s emphasis upon 'community care', and recent 'initiatives' by politicians to recognise the problem are inadequate.

In a nutshell and in all of the UK, expecting the NHS to 'do everything' can sound progressive and indeed has become politically correct, even with a feminist flavour ('health is about more than male-dominated hospitals' is a refrain still heard on the Left), but woolly quasi-Left thinking can aid the Right in cutting hospital budgets. One recalls Health Secretary Patricia Hewitt sending in what were notoriously 'macho' (and male) hit squads to enforce hospital budget cuts in 2006 while at the same time advocating personal trainers paid for by the NHS. Ridicule for such a stance is not only the preserve of the tabloids. At the risk of indulging in pop psychology, one suspects that such posturing—subjectively progressive but objectively reactionary—is a surrogate for the socialist planning which its practitioners have abandoned.

Whatever the truth of such speculation, the link of such sentiments to the NHS reforms which have created the 'purchaser-provider split' is quite strong. Advocates of the split, including those on the Left who decided to adopt—and attempt to coopt—the Conservative reforms as their own, have argued that separating the purchasing (commissioning) and provision of healthcare will enable the purchasers (commissioners) to challenge hospitals' 'greedy' demands for funds and make decisions as to spending priorities without also having to run (and therefore support) hospitals. But however well-intentioned, they could not have been more wrong.

As for those who argued at the end of the 1980s and the early 1990s that the internal market should be accepted as a means of heading off actual privatisation, that is, as a tactical retreat, this may have been plausible at the time. But it depended upon the next Labour government rejecting the market road. Since the Blair market, each 'market' initiative seems to hasten the move away from a public NHS rather than preserve it pragmatically.

Abandon Local Commissioning and the Local Purchaser/Provider Split

Firstly, the 'purchaser-provider split' has been a myth, albeit an expensive one, as government has mandated purchasers to follow political priorities. Secondly, and perhaps even more importantly in an imputed long run when government may hypothetically be less 'hands-on', the split exposes the underfunding of hospitals and the fact that England has a shortage of hospital beds by any humane standard as to what bed occupancy and efficiency might be (the former about 82%; the latter about where the NHS is now), yet at the same time brushes this exposure under the carpet and leaves it to ill-equipped local 'commissioners' to sort out the mess. This is, again, against orthodoxy: it is against the Right-wing orthodoxy that the NHS is inefficient (just as democracy is a terrible system which just happens to be better than all alternatives, the NHS is no doubt inefficient but just happens to be more efficient than any alternatives), and the Left-wing orthodoxy that the NHS should deemphasise hospitals and emphasise 'the community'—which sounds good but in fact creates a false antithesis (Black 1984) between the two.

Thirdly, the argument that the split forces greater efficiency in the hospital sector and therefore allows more expenditure on other 'neglected priorities'—or simply allows purchaser/commissioners to spend on these priorities, whatever hospital efficiency—has been refuted, in the case of

England at least, by the facts, as discussed in previous chapters. Purchasers have been good at hand-wringing about 'priorities' but powerless to achieve much, given the false premise upon which they start—that the hospital service is overfunded.

BE SANGUINE ABOUT ABROAD

An important lesson when considering healthcare systems and health policy reform elsewhere in the world is that, while *de*scriptive or analytical 'path-dependency' may be a trivial tautology or else simply false, *pre*scriptive adherence to a path may make sense in certain circumstances. For example: given both the existence of the NHS and continuing adherence to the value of equality of opportunity of access to healthcare for those with equal need irrespective of ability to pay, maintaining the 'comparative advantage' of the NHS makes sense.

Elsewhere in the world, it may make sense to build on existing policy and therefore existing healthcare institutions *if* social values and choices are attainable effectively and efficiently within such. Thus, for example, there is no sense in saying that Canada ought to replace its system with an NHS; or that Medicare in the USA ought to stop regulating doctors' fees and replace such contracts with a salaried service. Such decisions are contingent rather than intrinsic. Paths matter in terms of decisions for the future (as they may signal the extent of costly upheaval required to transplant a different model) even if path-dependency is overrated as an explanation of change or lack of it.

As for England and the UK, the headline lessons from abroad, concerning 'market reform', are that what sound like similar reforms on paper (e.g. 'introducing internal markets'; 'the purchaser-provider split'; 'managed competition') may be very different in practice. Politics matters. Even in the global era, national politics matter. And what we can tell from evaluation of other national market reforms in the few countries where they have been pursued over decades is that the market may not always do harm but it rarely solves the sort of problems which characterise public healthcare systems based on the search for either equity or its less ambitious cousin, 'solidarity.'

In the Netherlands, 'managed competition' has been a false dawn, both costly and more geared to Germany, competitive pressures may have helped temporarily where the system was both private and 'bloated'—and the same was arguably true in a Beveridge (NHS) context in Sweden in the early

1990s. But these were temporary contributions in systems where greater efficiency was required and where there was no tradition or initiative of national control or 'general management' to solve the problems more directly—either because the system was private and diffuse, as in Germany, or because there was no such tradition for cultural reasons, as in Sweden.

This means ensuring that policy reform does not remove the NHS's economical administration (or management, or leadership, or whatever language adherents to the fad of the moment like to use) while also ensuring that health policy embraces the pressing healthcare needs of the country. The frustrating, indeed almost tragic, story of English 'reform' is that the former has been abandoned in pursuit of a rhetoric which emphasises the latter but signally fails to achieve it. Thirty years on, the public and media debate about the NHS—and indeed its core problems—remain unchanged. That is an indictment of a very expensive tissue of reforms, which might be described as much ado about nothing were they not so expensive. And a fascination with 'lessons' from abroad has not helped. Again, this view is unfashionable but should not be mistaken for a blindness to good advice, so much as a rejection of facile, 'sexy' solutions.

THE FUTURE ENGLISH NHS IN A UK CONTEXT

This is not the place to analyse the substantive needs of the future NHS, but it is worth mentioning them briefly if only in order to suggest how signally irrelevant the 'reform agenda' in England has been to addressing them. The key challenges, the main priorities for attention, are: ensuring that patients' needs are met throughout their illness or episode of healthcare, irrespective of where their care is being provided at any particular stage of that illness or episode; ensuring both that there are enough hospital beds but also ensuring that length-of-stay in hospital is not prolonged beyond what is required for high-quality care; and ensuring that services in the community are adequate to obviate 'unnecessary' hospital admissions and also to provide timely care after hospital so that patients can be discharged as early from hospital as makes clinical sense (Few people want to stay in hospital unnecessarily, but the main problem for many today is overly early discharge in the context of non-existent or inappropriate community services). 'Priorities' other than hospital services have been addressed, pound for pound, in the rest of the UK without the 'reforms' which England has justified (beyond the confines of neo-liberal dogma) on the grounds of exactly those priorities.

The above challenges also require that the NHS and what in the UK is called 'social care' (i.e. care services which do not require clinical treatment but which are associated with ill-health or which are required to prevent physical or mental degeneration and/or hospital stays) are seen as contributors to 'integrated care' in the original sense of the term before the reform industry made it a buzz-word, that is, care of the patient across different locations of care and addressing different needs associated with his condition viewed overall.

In the UK, social care is means-tested—except up to a point in Scotland for nursing care at home and in nursing and residential homes, but even in Scotland the main cost (residential costs) are means-tested. This means that one cannot simply unify the NHS and social care in a 'National Health and Care Service' (let us call it the 'NHCS') without breaching the principle that the NHS/NHCS is free at the point-of-use for institutional care (i.e. in hospital or any other institution). In the 'devolved' countries, the aspiration is to reduce or abolish charges where they still exist (e.g. Scotland has abolished prescription charges for drugs in the GP services), not increase them or institutionalise them. Nevertheless, it might make sense to unify the NHS and social care and allow means-testing for clearly demarcated non-clinical services within the new unified service.

Then local health services could be organised around the patient's continuing needs without complicated (and often counter-productive) 'collaborative agency work' and/or inter-agency contracting which—as the English reforms have taught us—tends to become the story rather than a means to an end. Health service executives end up concentrating more on trading skills than caring skills, and not necessarily very effectively. In the memorable if somewhat lofty and disdainful, not to say politically incorrect, words of a leader of the British Medical Association at the beginning of the 1990s' internal market, 'giving the market to NHS managers is like giving whisky to Red Indians.'

There is no guarantee that organisational integration produces properly integrated services. But bluntly it is more likely to give a head start than the *dis*-integrated agencies swarming and competing for turf in the English NHS. The irony of today's integration debate is that many of those now calling for 'integrated care' are the same pundits who supported the disintegration of care through the panoply of market reforms analysed in this book. The market model might require approval if it were demonstrated that it produced either more effective or more efficient services (without diminishing quality or equity) or both. It has however done no such thing.

Additionally, to argue that providers (and market advocates generally fail to distinguish between the whole provider organisation and the diverse types of staff working within) will only respond effectively and efficiently to market incentives because they are 'knaves' is to state the case, not make it. There is no evidence that this is the case in the UK NHS, and some evidence that 'contractualising' a relationship of trust loses a significant surplus of contribution which was based on goodwill. 'The market', if it is a tool of compliance in the way that top-down state control through targets is, will of course produce short-term compliance in the way that all 'command and control' does (The market in the NHS has not been an alternative to command-and-control but a variant of it). But the more rewarding challenge is to harness professionalism, altruism (a different thing to professionalism, although the two are by no means mutually exclusive), and meaningful targets to steer well-meaning staff, not control them on the assumption that they are 'knaves.' Assuming the latter is a self-fulfilling prophecy, not a scientific judgement.

What can be done to re-integrate the NHS without excessive reorganisation (ironically the challenge Labour set for itself in 1997, long since betrayed): that is, to avoid all the costs of more root-and-branch reorganisation, not least further staff demoralisation? It is important to recognise that the English NHS has moved far from the pre-market model based on unified Districts. Additionally, the need to integrate the NHS with social care makes the pre-1991 District less central or suitable as the unit around which reintegration should be based. And reintegration should involve as little disruption as possible—while not, on the other hand, being fudged purely in the name of avoiding any reorganisation at all.

It is important here to avoid political correctness. There has been a tendency in the story of reform recounted in these pages to see the 'big bad hospital' as the problem and 'commissioning' as the solution. This should be turned on its head. Given that one of the pragmatic reactions 'on the ground' (i.e. by local health economies/communities in different parts of the country, where the hospital Chief Executive and Board attempt to make sense of the prevailing mess) to the current fragmentation in the English NHS has involved the hospital 'taking over' some primary care services (i.e. employing GPs) and even preventative services, and in some cases also the community services which have hitherto been separate Trusts, it would make sense to have the hospital as the budget-holder for integrated care. This goes directly against the orthodoxy of the day, but makes serious sense.

One of the problems inherent in all the market reforms instituted since 1990 has been the conflict between the commissioner and the provider over budgets. What has sounded like market logic in theory has been a messy battle over funds at 'year end' in practice. By giving the hospital the budget for care for all patients referred to hospital by the GP, one actor can plan the patient's care. If for example the patient is ready to leave hospital, then the community services required will be part of the same organisation. Even social care may be provided in house in the public sector, where the hospital considers this a sensible investment, or in some cases inevitably contracts will have to be made with the private sector—but by the actor (the hospital) in whose clinical and financial interests it is to ensure that the patient is not retained inappropriately in hospital. This makes the hospital more than a hospital, of course. But what's in a name? Whether it is called an NHS Trust or the '_____(substitute geographical or hospital name) NHS' does not matter.

Already one can anticipate the howls of objection from the managerial and 'insider' policy communities. So what might some of the objections be? The first can be put simply: whither commissioning (or 'purchasing', as it used to be called)? A straightforward question requires a straightforward answer: it should be abolished. It has been the dog that has not barked for 25 years, and that is not primarily because it needs 'more investment' or 'better people doing it', although the latter would have helped (One of the indictments of Alan Milburn's 2001 reform is that it created myriads of small commissioners without there being anything like enough managerial talent to fill the jobs). It is because 'commissioning' has been squeezed, marginalised in the middle, between opposite forces—the valid desire and requirement that the NHS is national (i.e. where one lives should not determine what services are available—no 'postcode lottery'); the tendency of national government to override local choices by commissioners when they are politically unacceptable or embarrassing or both; and the local reality that 'need' is best expressed through the door of the GP, that is, closely aligned with demand, and that where need is submerged, the GP practice is the best location to probe this.

So does this not mean GP commissioning, as in the current system? No. It does not mean giving GPs the budgets—it means GPs referring those patients who require care beyond the GP surgery to the most appropriate integrated provider in the region. Recent reforms have congenitally confused the roles of patient referral and whole-service commissioning. GPs are mostly good at the former and mostly bad at the latter. Nor does this approach abolish GP-mediated patient choice—except to the private sector (where even pro-market research has shown that the latter has not contributed to better greater efficiency in the round).

The planner of regional services (no longer called the commissioner unless that name still appeals; again, what's in a name?) will take on the role of 'commissioning'. What is the point of having local commissioners if 'local choices' go against the grain of a nationally available menu of services? Instead, significant savings can be made by modelling patient flows (i.e. patient and GP choices) and, over time, ensuring that hospital expansions and contractions reflect these. The region can also ensure that specialist services are appropriately sited and funded. This may be seen as the rebirth of the regional health authority. If so, about time too: its functions are carried out by necessity in any case, but currently by the back door, without transparency, through regional offices and area teams of NHS England. Market rhetoric has cast the region of old as the face of bureaucracy in the pejorative sense. But if patient choice and referrals are made at local level, it is nothing of the sort.

A major advantage of hospital-based integrated provision is that the hospital's finances would improve the more patients were discharged to community provision. But since market competition would not be the main dynamic of the system, there would be less risk of inappropriately early discharge. To those who argue that the market is needed to motivate, the response is that it does not motivate clinicians in any case, and that managers and indeed staff generally can be motivated through the pay-and-reward system. The market (setting corporate 'profit' against clinical priorities) has actually retarded clinician-manager cooperation. Moreover clinicians are more likely to take on management roles—where appropriate, as opposed to as a kind of politically correct expectation, as now—if such roles are more about arranging appropriate clinical care rather than managing finances.

One question which arises is the organisation of community services to care for patients discharged from hospitals (which they have chosen, and/or which are the most appropriate for their treatment) which are not close to their home. That is they need community or home after-care from a different organisation (local to the patient) from the one in which they have received their hospital care. Actually that is no different from now—community Trusts are separate organisations in any case. It is just that the discharging hospital, rather than the now-non-existent local commissioner (CCG, previously PCT) would be responsible for organising this. This is one area where cross-charging (call it a market if you will; what's in a name, once again) would make sense. In Sweden, county councils run the hospitals and local municipalities run community and social care: the latter have to pay the former if they cannot arrange community care and therefore the hospital incurs the cost of delayed discharge. In England, if the hospital provider holds the budget, it could work the other around: the hospital itself incurs the cost (automatically) if it does not organise discharge into its own community services or by paying another organisation's community services (most likely the organisation closer to the patient's home).

This arrangement would clean up a lingering mess in the organisation of community services in the NHS, recounted above. Since the internal market, community services have been separate Trusts (created between 1991 and 1993 and lasting until 2001); then absorbed into the new PCTs (commissioners which also managed non-hospital provision, creating a major tension and conflict-of-interest in the marketplace, giving PCTs an incentive to starve hospitals of funds yet feather-bed their own community services); then once again 'floated off', firstly as separately managed 'provider arms' of the PCTs then as separate NHS Trusts altogether once again, after the failure to interest the trendy 'Third Sector' of charities and non-profit organisations in taking over the role, to nobody's surprise save politicians and 'free thinky' think-tankers. Along the way, mergers, dissolutions, and re-mergers saw the size of such organisations, what is more, constantly changing.

A Blueprint

So how would the current 'market' NHS map onto such a tidied-up English NHS?

Current	Proposal
'Commissioning' CCGs	Abolished
Community NHS Trusts	Absorbed into hospital Trusts on a geographical basis
Hospital Trusts (NHS or Foundation)	Become integrated providers on a geographical basis Could be named geographically or by historical hospital name eg 'NHS Staffordshire' or 'Bart's NHS' Currently 'NHS Staffordshire' refers only to commissioning, leaving hospitals and other providers apparently outside the NHS. This is an illegitimate means of redefining the NHS as a financing system only, in line with market reform and neo-liberal ideology. The integrated providers would also include **mental health** The absence of an emergency mental healthcare portal other than general 'A and E' is a disaster. One answer is to create a specialist mental health division within A and E, just as GP care care can be sited there to allow triage between general/primary problems and more specialized needs. The public will always use the hospital in a self-perceived emergency, and it is futile to pretend otherwise
Mental Health Trusts	They become part of the integrated provider but with their own division and management team
GPs as both individual referrers and members of CCGs commissioning all non-specialist services	GPs as individual referrers only (allowed to refer to any integrated provider)
Regional offices (four) of NHS England; Area Teams within these	Regional Health Authorities (ten) which now plan services across the region to which GPs refer
Care Quality Commission and MONITOR, now NHS I, (in its role as whole-system regulator)	Merged into one authority responsible for quality assurance and governance, including financial governance. Could be called simply NHS Governance
NHS England	NHS England as now, only responsible for the whole NHS and not just the purchasing/commissioning function plus or two other functions (eg management of the GP contract, which CCGs were not allowed to handle on account of a conflict-of-interest, as discussed above). Thus NHS England would be responsible, through the Regional Health Authorities, for the newly-enlarged NHS integrated providers, and for regulating and performance-managing GP services (including for example their development into larger polyclinics)

Current	Proposal
Monitor and the NHS Trust Development Authority (the non-Foundation Trust performance manager) (now merged as NHS Improvement)	Both abolished. Separate provider regulation is no longer necessary. If one must think in terms of a 'commissioner-provider split', the Region is the 'commissioner'—actually, the service planner. The GP is the referrer, and planning and patient choice/referrals are mutually embedded Integrated providers are funded by the Region in line with their workload, which in turn is determined by referral involving as much patient choice as patients want. GP-mediated patient choice therefore becomes intrinsic, as applied in theory from 1948 to 1991

The above design would end local commissioning, and put an end to the dichotomy between the NHS as a national service with a menu of services common to all irrespective, on the one hand, and the undemocratic system of local rationing by appointed managers rather than elected authorities on the other. The latter aspiration—so-called local variation in priorities—would be ended.

Sitting planning (commissioning's replacement) at Regional level would save significant sums of money, as instead of about 150 local commissioners (350 in its heyday) there would be about ten regions. Attempts to paint this as centralism and state bureaucracy would be predictable but actually nonsense. Referral decisions would be more local before, as the conflict between the referring GP and the local commissioner—a key bugbear from 1991 to date—would be ended. In reality patient choice has fallen victim in England to commissioning's rationing, on the one hand, and contracts with specific providers, on the other hand—and, as noted above, has no more applied in any meaningful way in England than in the rest of the UK where the purchaser-provider split has long since been abolished.

Importantly, such a mode of clarifying and rationalising the English NHS would take account of recent history, in order to minimise the disruption of restructuring. And yet simply looking at the above table and reading its components make it clear that significant savings would ensue in management costs. Existing institutions and pragmatic trends—hospital Trusts; hospitals taking over other services; regional planning and management brought into the open rather than done covertly; GPs free to refer within the bounds of available services in the public sector—would be built upon, yet the system would be transformed.

The savings indeed would go *beyond* those significant savings from the overt structural simplification, including the expensive split between local purchasers/commissioners and providers. For a major overhead cost in the English NHS has been incurred by making all referrals and individual patient transactions subject to costing and pricing so that providers can be paid according to workload. It is often assumed that this is the necessary cost of the desirable aim of ensuring that providers are paid according to quantity and complexity of workload (and that *is* desirable, as it ensures that providers are able to survive financially even if the incentive to 'maximise income' or make a surplus is somewhat overrated in importance). But it is perfectly possible to allow choices and referrals to be locally determined (i.e. by the patient and the doctor) yet the financial flows which result to be handled at a higher level, that is, the regional level, in my model.

This is not to deny that a modern health service will incur the costs of providing appropriate information about hospitals and other providers, and GP practices, to enable patients to be intelligent users of health services, including choice. Innovation in IT et al in fact is something which has been almost a disaster story in the era of the market: there is no suggestion that the market is the cause, but it is not self-evidently the solution. And it is the extra costs of the market which are at issue here, and which feature in the estimated costs in the previous chapter.

Ensuring that hospitals are funded according to workload does not require US-style or European social insurance style individual patient billing. It can mean giving hospitals and all other providers an indicative budget based on specialty and departmental costing, and adjusting that budget to reflect the marginal cost of increased workload. Block grants (a dirty word following the Thatcher reforms), rechristened 'block contracts' in the market era, have their place, if they are calculated appropriately as a starting point. Amending them through cost and volume adjustments can then be made by the regional planner. Such planning can actually be described as a simulated market, as the financial flows are based on the many individual local patient/doctor decisions made. But a simulated market is not an actual market in the sense of local purchasing with money, and the resulting myriads of transactions costs.

Handling financial flows at the regional level also reduces, indeed minimises, financial risk based on year-on-year statistical variation in medical need in smaller populations. This has been a major problem for the former Primary Care Trusts and, now, the Clinical Commissioning Groups. And it allows the perverse incentives which existed before the era of the market as well as during the era of the market (as explored in this book) to be tackled. Before the market, allocating funds to smaller Districts meant a discrepancy between the money nominally available for local, intra-District patients and patients treated in-District from outside its boundaries. And additionally, such 'nominally available' money—that is, target allocations for Districts under the prevailing formula for allocation, and reimbursement by national average 'specialty cost' for patients travelling across District (or even Regional) boundaries for care—was not always available in practice, to add to the discrepancy between the two. This was because 'robbing Peter to pay Paul' (i.e. removing money from an 'over-target' District to allow an 'underfunded' District to reach its target) could not always be done quickly—for primarily political reasons (i.e. less money for 'losing' populations) but also logistical reasons (i.e. threatening the viability of providers whose financial balance depended upon money from 'losing' Districts). Also, as regards reimbursing Districts for patients from outside the District (at national average specialty cost for that patient's condition), the payment went into the District's target allocation rather than actual in-year money. So it might not come as quickly as needed.

But handling flows at a regional level means that allocations can be made in-year for workload. This would only not be so if the workload in the NHS was not affordable, that is, if 'available services' across all the medical specialties could not be paid for at the required volumes and/ or if inefficiency in provision was a problem. The former is a political issue—what can be afforded under the allocated NHS budget, nationally and within Regions—and it is currently fudged by pretending that it is a local decision when in fact local budgets are given from on high. The latter is a managerial issue—and performance management rather than a competitive market based on closing or downsizing 'inefficient' providers is a perfectly acceptable way of handling things.

In many ways, the story of the last 25 years is one of a threat to good-quality services, had the policy of 'leaving the market to decide' been pursued to its conclusion, and in any case, politicians rarely do that, as the story of Lewisham hospital tells us recently and the wider story of planning London's future NHS provision has shown us both during the 'internal market' of the 1990s (when the Conservative government commissioned the Tomlinson review to bypass the market) and the New Labour market, when NHS London (a region) planned the future configuration of hospitals.

When Andrew Lansley came into office in 2010 after Labour's defeat, he suspended all this work (which led to a leakage of disillusioned talent out of the London NHS management community), as a result of opportunistic promises made during the 2010 election campaign, only for it to be reinstated some time later. We saw a similar rash promise made by Jeremy Hunt, Lansley's successor as Health Secretary, during the 2015 campaign regarding Stafford Hospital (to seek to reopen its A and E full time) which equally was shelved after the election victory. Across England, not just in London, market rhetoric has yielded, when strictly necessary, to managerial decision and last-ditch political compliance or even diktat, which is just as well. The face-saving use of market language (as with the 'special administrator' being appointed when a 'failing' hospital is 'going bankrupt', on the advice of the economic regulator) should fool no one. This is playing at markets, not creating real markets.

One should also distinguish between the sort of simulated market proposed above (i.e. not a market but deriving the advantages of a market in terms of choice) and the so-called quasi-market which NHS market reform has created. The latter involves local purchasing with money, however managed from above it may be. The former does not.

The NHS would therefore be redefined unequivocally as a *public* service. Where private involvement was desirable, it would be a matter of local choice by integrated Trusts for particular components of a patient's treatment—say, for mental health services in particular circumstances; and probably more so for social care. But the NHS would benefit from long-term investment in its own infrastructure and services, rather than suffering leakages to the often 'here today, gone tomorrow' private provider. This would in the medium- and long-term be a much more economical of expanding NHS infrastructure than the cripplingly expensive Private Finance Initiative.

More generally, the private sector has found itself usually unable and unwilling to compete at NHS prices, in any case, once the loss-leaders and sweeteners of the early 2000s have disappeared and it has to compete on a level playing field. The trend has been repeatedly since the 1990s: herald a brave new world of private involvement; discover in practice that only one or two headline initiatives take-off; herald these as 'the first example of private management'; then later see them quietly abandoned. One thinks of the private management of Sutton Coldfield's Good Hope Hospital, heralded and then abandoned; the rise and fall of Circle's aspirations; and other private contracts whose holders fail to re-tender as they cannot derive profit at NHS prices.

Overall, savings in management costs—the costs of the market and the costs of fragmented, over-small agencies and providers—would be augmented on the 'benefit' side by the chance for strategic planning to concentrate on the key issues facing the NHS—quality; service redesign to accommodate changing technology and the required mix of specialised super-hospitals and local services; and of course medium- and long-term affordability rather than merely short-term financial balance.

Another major advantage of ending the purchaser/commissioner-provider split is the removal of NHS services, and indeed financing, from the ambit of both EU competition law, including the EU's agreement with the USA known as the Transatlantic Trade and Investment Partnership (TTIP), and wider global economic regulation through the World Trade Organization. Even if outside the EU, a market NHS is up for grabs through global trade agreements. Attempts to assure the public that these do not apply in the English NHS are both unconvincing and subject to change. Otherwise, the NHS could de facto be replaced gradually by a Dutch-type system of competing private insurers and private providers—as a result of decisions by unelected 'judge bureaucrats'.

A FINAL WORD: INTEGRATED CARE

The aim of the above proposal is not just more economical management and governance, but a better chance of achieving care which is planned to suit the patient's needs in the most appropriate location at different stages of illness or need. One organisation which holds the responsibility for care is more likely to design 'care pathways' with the correct incentives to staff along that pathway. That is the lesson even from the USA, where the most cost-effective Health Maintenance Organizations have done this.

That is the true meaning of integrated care, which sadly has become the latest buzz-phrase embodying motherhood and apple-pie in the English NHS. What is more, the reform industry, including health policy academics, has in some cases spent more than 25 years proposing and advising on reforms which 'dis-integrate' the NHS only to come late to the table of integration.

The alternative means of seeking integrated care is to create a specification for a new 'integrated service', which then has to be put out to tender under the 'mandatory tendering' clause of the 2012 Health and Social Care Act, as briefly discussed above in Chap. 9. This means preserving separate organisations but subjecting them to the diktat of, or overt economic incentives created by, the lead (private) provider. There is no evidence that this is the best way to proceed, and indeed a few straws in the wind by the end of 2015 suggested that it was anything but, as in Cambridgeshire. But squaring the ideological circle between 'private good, public bad', on the one hand, and integration, on the other hand, makes this an attractive option to latter-day 'public service reformers', whether Conservative or Blairite Labour.

The main reason that handing over billion-pound-sized chunks of NHS services for client groups or specialties (such as 'the elderly' or 'cancer') is a risky approach at best is that private consortia tend to see 'the downsizing of the hospital' as the easy pickings when it comes to savings and both living within the cost of their tender and making a profit. Yet simply assuming that avoiding hospital admissions and discharging patients earlier form hospital can be achieved this way, with the provision of a community alternative, is what has brought the NHS low, at least financially, in many parts of the country. The task is much more complex, and necessitates double-funding in short and even medium terms, so that appropriate new services can be operational before certain hospital services are rendered obsolete—if indeed that is possible at all, given the drastic underfunding of the hospital sector by 2016.

Postscript: Whither the Politics of Health Policy?

The idea of taking politics out of the NHS has been shown to be a vain pursuit: every committee of the great and the good, and every report by an external 'worthy', proposing such comes to nought. One thinks of numerous reports from the King's Fund and publications by the Nuffield Trust, as well as recommendations by eminent businessmen asked by governments to 'investigate' the NHS. The one government-accepted recommendation advocating a non-political Management Board for the NHS (from the Griffiths report in 1983) was nullified and then reversed in practice. Making the NHS 'non-political' is probably undesirable in any case.

So what of the possibility of consensual politics, if removing politics is not on—that is, an inter-party agreement on the contours of NHS policy, of the sort called for in January 2016 by former Liberal Democrat Health Minister Norman Lamb and supported by former Conservative and Labour Health Secretaries Stephen Dorrell and Alan Milburn? Never say never: it is just conceivable that the major parties might decide that striking out alone on NHS policy is no longer worth the candle. But it is unlikely. For a more left-leaning Labour party, as established after the 2010 election loss to a small extent and to a much greater extent after the leadership victory of Jeremy Corbyn in 2015, is not likely to endorse the sort of 'centrist' position which would emerge from such an agreement. We may note for example that Alan Milburn is now viewed, and views himself, as far to the Right of the post-2015 Labour approach. Moreover, in England, a 'centrist' position would be likely to retain the market, and even more likely the commissioner-provider split, and this ironically is a source of high cost without much benefit as the more perceptive analysts on the Right see as well as those on the Left who disapprove in their gut reaction.

What is required to establish a health reform, or 'anti-reform', along the lines proposed above is something very different. It requires a consensus that health policy and the NHS do not benefit from market initiatives and 'public service reform' as a code for the market, whatever may be the case in the wider economy. In other words, one can be a believer in free markets and free trade, yet draw a line when it comes to health and some other public services, such as railways, which are either 'natural monopolies' or have other special characteristics. In the headlong neo-liberal rush hastened by the collapse of communism and the opening up of closed economies more generally after 1990, much of positive economics which makes these distinctions has been ignored not only by policy-makers but also by many economists. Interestingly, in the 2015 election, the UK Independence Party took the stance that playing at markets within the NHS was expensive, as in the case of the PFI. If the Conservative Party followed suit, it would be easier for even the Right of the Labour Party to do likewise, for their belief in market reform to the NHS was always substantially about not appearing Left to the floating-voter section of the electorate. This is highly ironical, as it is the one area where the electorate would not object to an anti-market stance.

Thus to change the current lazy orthodoxy in English health policy would require a reconfiguration of policy stances more widely, which could then enable health policy to be 'freed up' from being a symbol for something else. This is not surprising, although difficult to engineer, for health policy at root is the application of politics to the field of health. In the absence of such a reconfiguration, the Labour Party may of course take a hard anti-market stance under its post-2015 leadership. But the chances of it being elected are slim in the extreme, as a result of its stances on taxation, welfare, and foreign affairs. And so the Conservative-led marketisation could continue apace, even after the post-2015 back-peddling of market rhetoric, that is, when the next 'moral panic' sets in and there are calls for 'public service reform' without it being pointed out that such 'reform' has hastened, if not caused, the financial difficulties of the NHS.

Another word is in order on any 'consensus' on the NHS, such as that proposed by Lamb, Dorrell, and Milburn, in the absence of a wider policy reconfiguration. Such consensus would tend to involve warm words about prevention and promotion—which take no account of the fact that people are not going to live more healthily on a large enough scale any time soon. Public health initiatives are important. They should be vigorously pursued. But one should be sanguine about the extent of their success. The ability of the NHS to make £22 billion savings, to add to the extra £8 billion forthcoming from the public purse, relies on optimistic projections about self-health promotion, as did the scenario of the Wanless Report in 2002 which assumed that the population would be 'fully engaged' in prevention and promotion, upon which later projections have seemingly built. Just as environmental protection takes a back seat at times of economic hardship, so does any radical tackling of the food and drink industry, for example, the 'hard sell' and domination of the supermarket shelves of which lies behind the biggest cause of preventable, 'personal' ill-health, obesity.

If the NHS budget (with or without the waste incurred through ill-targeted reform) cannot cope as a result, then a better alternative should be found to the arbitrary and cruel 'rationing' by some local 'commissioners' which we have seen, for example, no operations funded for those with a Body Mass Index of more than 30. We may have to consider supplementary public insurance—that is, a personal health tax—for 'repeat offenders' whose healthcare needs are increased by (e.g.) preventable obesity, a failure to stop smoking or drink-related ill-health and NHS use. Dangerous expensive sports are another possible target for supplementary insurance, to avoid the sense that is an attack upon the poorer and so-called working-classes. More importantly, social care will require to be funded through means-tested mandatory public insurance if the erosion of the core NHS by the growing crisis in both funding and provision of social care is to be reversed.

Finally, we should of course be sanguine about any redirection of health policy along the above lines. The problems facing the NHS go well beyond such an approach. The 'audit society' has grown in the public sector, covering healthcare, school education, universities et al, such that process-observance and 'box-ticking' often chokes the altruism of staff and obstructs services and learning. The causes of this are political. To the ideological Right, the public sector cannot be trusted and must be audited comprehensively where it is not actually privatised. To the bossy, increasingly politically correct Left, audit is a means of the control which is no longer available in the wider economy. There is no magic solution. But awareness of the problem, of this unholy coalition, is a start.

REFERENCES

Black, D. (1984). *An anthology of false antitheses*. London: Nuffield Trust.
Weale, A. (2015, October). *Address on the occasion of the 10th anniversary of the journal, Health Economics, Policy and Law*. London: LSE.

Erratum to: The Politics of Health Policy Reform in the UK: England's Permanent Revolution

Calum Paton

Erratum to: Acknowledgments
DOI 10.1057/978-1-137-47343-1

The original version of this article was inadvertently published without the Acknowledgments section, which has been included now.

The updated original online version for this book can be found at
DOI 10.1057/978-1-137-47343-1

Calum Paton
Keele University
United Kingdom

INDEX

© The Author(s) 2016   207
C. Paton, *The Politics of Health Policy Reform in the UK*,
DOI 10.1057/978-1-137-47343-1

Printed by Books on Demand, Germany